SOUTHEY

ROBERT SOUTHEY

*From an undated miniature, attributed to Edward Nash,
in the possession of Mrs. F. F. Boult*

SOUTHEY

by

JACK SIMMONS

Collins

14 ST. JAMES'S PLACE LONDON

1945

TO
JOHN O'BRIEN
IN FRIENDSHIP
AND COMMON AFFECTION
FOR THE ENGLISH LAKES

COPYRIGHT
PRINTED IN GREAT BRITAIN
COLLINS CLEAR-TYPE PRESS : LONDON AND GLASGOW
1945

PREFACE

IN the course of the last fifty years there has been a great development in our knowledge and understanding of Words-worth and Coleridge, through the work of such scholars as Professor de Selincourt, Professor Harper, Mr. E. H. Coleridge and Mr. Dykes Campbell. No corresponding attention has, however, been paid to their fellow "Lake Poet", Southey: he has been the subject of only one modern work of importance— Professor Haller's study of his early life and poetry, published in 1919. Yet a great deal of new material has become available for his biography in recent years: his immense manuscript corres-pondence with his friends Grosvenor Bedford and Henry Taylor, now in the Bodleian, for example, and that with C. W. W. Wynn, now in the National Library of Wales. I cannot claim to have examined every one of his extant letters: war-time conditions have denied me access to certain sets of secondary importance. But in this book I have tried to present a fuller, and on some points a more accurate, account of his life than has hitherto been written.

It is with his biography that I have been primarily concerned. I hope I have made it clear that I regard him as an important and admirable writer, whose work is seriously undervalued to-day: I have given my grounds for this estimate in the concluding chapter. But my main attention has been fixed on his personal life and his relations with his great contemporaries—especially with his brother-in-law Coleridge; while his political ideas have here received more respectful attention than has usually been accorded to them.

The notes will be found grouped together at the end, numbered in one continuous series. General references are as a rule given in the first note to each chapter. As to spelling and punctuation: in the case of extracts from printed books, corrected by the author himself, I have followed the original; but with letters—often written in haste, with abbreviations and light pointing—I have made whatever changes seemed to me necessary to render the sense clear, and in general I have modernised the spelling.

I am greatly indebted to various members of the Southey family, to owners of unpublished material, and to other friends who have helped me in the preparation of this book. First of all to Mrs. F. F. Boult, Southey's great-granddaughter, for making available to me, at the cost of considerable inconvenience in war-

5

time, her valuable collection of Southey manuscripts and relics, as well as for much other kindness. For permission to examine and in some cases to publish extracts from documents in their hands I am similarly obliged to Mrs. H. D. Rawnsley, Miss Lydia S. Awdry, the Rev. Professor R. H. Lightfoot, Mr. James Ross, City Librarian of Bristol, the Vicars of Bedminster and Long Ashton, Somerset, Messrs. Henry Sotheran and Mr. Raphael King. Mrs. Boult, Mrs. Rawnsley, Miss H. Read of Grasmere, Mr. H. W. Howe, Mr. Nicholas Coleridge, and the Trustees of the National Portrait Gallery have courteously allowed me to reproduce illustrations of which they hold the originals.

I have been very generously supplied by Captain R. G. Southey with information as to the history of the whole Southey family, which he has studied in great detail. Senhor J. de Sousa-Leão, Counsellor-Minister of the Brazilian Embassy in London, has kindly assisted me on some points relating to Southey's connexion with his country and with Portugal. Mr. Lawrence E. Tanner gave me the benefit of his great knowledge of the history of Westminster School. Together with all those who took part in the Southey centenary celebrations at Keswick last year, I remember the hospitality of Mr. and Mrs. H. W. Howe on that occasion with gratitude and pleasure; while Mr. Howe has frequently helped me, particularly in dealing with Greta Hall, of which he is the historian. Mr. Wallace B. Nichols has been good enough to read the proofs of the last chapter, making some valuable suggestions on it. Canon M. H. FitzGerald, who has for many years been the leading authority on Southey's works, has read the whole book in proof, and it has benefited greatly throughout from his constant assistance and most kindly criticism. I ought to add that neither Mr. Nichols nor Canon FitzGerald wholly agrees with my estimate of Southey's poetry.

My last and heaviest debt is to Mr. A. L. Rowse, who first urged me to write this book and who has taken a close interest in it from the beginning. I am deeply grateful to him for his invaluable advice and encouragement.

OXFORD,
17th November, 1944.

CONTENTS

ILLUSTRATIONS

NOTE

*The silhouette portrait of Southey on the jacket is reproduced from a
contemporary original in the possession of Mr. Nicholas Coleridge.*

I

CHILDHOOD

(*1774-1788*)

AT THE FOOT of the Blackdown Hills in Somerset, looking
across the rich Vale of Taunton Dean to the Quantocks,
stands the little town of Wellington. It is a quiet place,
distinguished by its lofty red sandstone church and given up for
six hundred years now to the manufacture of woollens. In this
industry a leading part was once played by the family of Southey.*
Their name is to be met with in Wellington from the fourteenth
century onwards. In the reign of Elizabeth, Thomas Southey of
Woodford was one of the great clothiers of the district. He died
about the year 1601, and was remembered in his family: there
was a tradition that he " had eleven sons who peopled that part of
the country with Southeys". However that may be, it is certain
that among his great-grandsons were two named John and
Robert. John in due course inherited the Woodford property,
became a thriving Taunton attorney and married Mary Cannon,
co-heiress of Fitzhead Court near Milverton. Robert's wife came
of a poorer, though not less interesting, family: she was the niece
or the first cousin once removed of John Locke. Thomas, their
eldest son, moved out of Wellington to become a farmer in the
delicious upland parish of Lydiard St. Lawrence; and here, about
the year 1745, his third child, Robert, was born.[1]

The boy was brought up on the farm and developed an early
taste for field sports and all country pursuits. He might have
made a good farmer; but unhappily he was put into trade instead.
After a year's apprenticeship to a grocer in London, he was placed
with a draper in Wine Street, Bristol. Here he remained for over
ten years, until in April, 1772, he and his brother Thomas set up
a draper's shop of their own three doors away. With a wistful

---

* There should be no doubt as to the proper pronunciation of the name: "Sowthey".
The poet himself complained that people in the North would call him "Mr. Suthy".
Byron showed that he knew better (*Don Juan*, Canto I, Stanza 205):

> Thou shall believe in Milton, Dryden, Pope;
> Thou shalt not set up Wordsworth, Coleridge, Southey,
> Because the first is crazed beyond all hope,
> The second drunk, the third so quaint and mouthy.

glance at the beloved sports of his youth, he took a hare for his sign. Later in the same year, on 25th September, he married Margaret Hill in Bedminster church, just outside Bristol.[2]

On her father's side she too came of long-established Somerset stock. Her mother, a Herefordshire woman, was twice married: first to a man of her own county named Tyler, to whom she bore four children; secondly to Edward Hill of Long Ashton, Somerset (the seventh successive holder of that name). Margaret was the youngest child of the family, and she was brought up at her father's house in Bedminster. At the time of her wedding she was aged twenty.

The Southeys' first child, a boy christened John Cannon, appeared within a year of their marriage and died before he was three months old.[3] Their second child, the future poet, was born on 12th August, 1774, and received the family name of Robert.

He has vividly described his childhood in his fascinating fragment of autobiography.[4] When he was two years old his mother's half-sister, Miss Tyler, bore him off to live with her at Bath. That imperious woman dominated Margaret Southey by the force of her personality and Margaret's husband by the power of her purse. Not that she was rich, or generous by temperament: she lived ostentatiously, well beyond her income, and her ruling passions were pride and snobbery. But the Southeys' financial position was even less secure than her own, and, from whatever motive, she did assist them from time to time. When Robert came to live with her she was aged thirty-seven and "remarkably beautiful, as far as any face can be called beautiful in which the indications of a violent temper are strongly marked". She had lived for many years with her uncle the Rev. Herbert Bradford, curate of Shobdon in Herefordshire: after his wife's death she had kept house for him and busied herself over the affairs of the parish. (She bears a strong resemblance to Mrs. Norris in *Mansfield Park*.) Here, too, she became a friend of Lady Bateman, the wife of a local magnate, with whom she passed much of her time—"enough", says her nephew severely, "to acquire the manners of high life, and too many of its habits and notions". When Mr. Bradford died, he left nearly all his property to her, on the strength of which "she began to live at large, and to frequent watering places". In 1774 she took a trip to Portugal, where she established her half-brother Herbert Hill as chaplain to the British factory at Oporto: on her return she decided to settle at Bath and took a substantial house in the parish of Walcot, on the northern outskirts of the city, looking over to Claverton

Hill. This she furnished suitably: the parlour contained a French writing-table, a cherry-wood armchair in which she always sat, and two Angelica Kauffmann prints; while on the green-papered walls of the drawing-room hung her portrait by Gainsborough "with a curtain to preserve the frame from flies and the colours from the sun".

Here the boy spent the greater part of his time from 1776 to 1780. It was not a comfortable household for a child, and looking back to these years in later life Southey remarked that his aunt's treatment of him was "thoroughly injudicious". He slept in her bed: when he awoke in the morning, about six, he had to lie quite still, for fear of disturbing her, until she chose to get up, at nine, ten, or even eleven o'clock. He beguiled the time, he says, by playing with his fingers, and fancying pictures in the green squares of the check curtains, and "wondering at the motes in the slant sunbeam, and watching the light from the crevices of the window-shutters, till it served me at last by its progressive motion to measure the lapse of time". And when at last he was allowed to get up, the hours passed slowly. "I had no playmates. . . . If my aunt was writing letters, I was to sit silent. There was a garden, but in playing there my clothes might be soiled."[5] That was Miss Tyler's peculiar horror, for she worshipped cleanliness, and her ideas of its opposite were " almost as irrational and inconvenient as those of the Hindoos". His early upbringing had a clear influence on Southey's character. It made him dislike foolish eccentricity; it taught him some of his patience, his cheerful endurance of drudgery and boredom, and his self-sufficiency; it must also have contributed to form his generally sensible attitude to children: but at the time it was certainly a dreary and lonely experience.

There were, however, some compensations. One of his aunt's friends had married the son of John Newbery, the publisher of *Goody Two-shoes* and the rest of those delightful eighteenth-century children's books—"radiant with gold and rich with bad pictures", as Leigh Hunt called them; and in due course the boy was presented with them all. (As we should expect, he read early.) Then there was the theatre, to which Miss Tyler was passionately devoted—the more so, no doubt, because she was able to obtain free admission to it through her friendship with the owner's family. The standard of acting at Bath was then unusually high, for Mrs. Siddons headed the cast. Robert saw his first play, Fielding's comedy *The Fathers*, at the age of four; and from that time onwards his attendance at the theatre was frequent. "There

was no subject of which I heard so much from my earliest childhood", he records. The theatre dominated his imagination and
his vocabulary: he once brought down wrath upon himself by
remarking, most innocently, to his family, as they all returned
from church one Sunday morning, "that it had been a very *full
house*". Better even than the play, there were occasional walks
into the country, sometimes (best of all) involving the use of one
of the ferries to cross the Avon, towards the Sham Castle or
Beechen Cliff, those unattainable goals nearly two miles away.

From time to time he paid visits to Bristol and Bedminster.
Once when he had been ill his father came to see him and found
him looking so pale and thin that he angrily ordered him to be
brought home.[6] Here he had some one to play with, his sister
Eliza, who was born in 1776 and died in 1779, and even though
Wine Street was in the middle of the city there were still the
country walks he loved, to Kingsdown, Brandon Hill, and Sea
Banks.

His greatest treat was to go to his grandmother's at Bedminster, for that was really in the country and there he might
play in the garden and get dirty: "the very paradise of my childhood", he called it sixty years later.[7] The house was Georgian,
built by his grandfather about 1740. Its porch was covered with
jessamine inside and out; it had a flagged hall, giving access to
the parlour on the right and the "best kitchen", in which the
family lived, on the left. This was " a cheerful room, with an air
of country comfort about it", stone-floored, wainscoted, furnished
with cherry-wood chairs and table, its walls hung with old maps
and mirrors in white frames. Over the parlour was the green
room, occupied by Edward Tyler; over the best kitchen was the
yellow room, for visitors; and above the other kitchen was the
blue room, belonging to the old lady herself. On the back of the
house was a fruitful vine. Beyond it lay the barton, with an
outhouse containing dairy, laundry, and stables, almost completely
covered with clipped yew. Here too there was an orchard, and one
of those charming kitchen gardens where flowers and vegetables
grow together, bounded by a wall on which cherries and peaches
and nectarines climbed.

It mattered little that Bedminster was a squalid village, or that
the house had no interesting view. "The little world within was
our own. And to me it was quite a different world from that in
which I lived at other times. . . . Here I had all wholesome liberty
. . . and the delight which I there learnt to take in rural sights
and sounds has grown up with me and continues unabated to

this day." Plants and insects now enthralled him, and he passed
many happy hours in searching for new kinds of grasses and
watching the habits of ants. He always looked back to Bedminster
with nostalgic affection, and the smell of syringa or the everlasting sweet pea or the evening primrose—his favourite flower,
which his grandmother used to call "mortality"—never failed to
bring it back to his mind.

He was a very sensitive child, and he was made more nervous
by his foolish family. "They used to amuse themselves", he says,
"by making me cry at sad songs and dismal stories. I remember
' Death and the Lady', ' Billy Pringle's Pig', ' The Children Sliding
on the Ice all on a Summer's Day', and Witherington fighting on
his stumps at Chevy Chase. This was at two years old, when my
recollection begins—prior identity I have none; they tell me I
used to beg them not to proceed."

Before he was three he was sent to a dame's school. "Ma'am
Powell", who kept it, "had as forbidding a face (I well remember
it) as can easily be imagined: and it was remarkable for having
no eyelashes, a peculiarity which I instantly perceived. When the
old woman, therefore, led me to a seat on the form, I rebelled
as manfully as a boy in his third year could do, crying out, ' Take
me to Pat [his nurse]! I don't like ye! You've got ugly eyes!
Take me to Pat, I say!'" He remained at this school for three years.
All that he tells us of them is that he wore "a fantastic costume
of nankeen for highdays and holydays, trimmed with green
fringe; it was called a *jam*"; that he planned to migrate to an
island with two of his schoolfellows; and that he displayed a
penchant for soldiering. At six years old (he was tall for his age)
he exchanged his "jam" for a green suit, Miss Tyler's house for
his father's, and Ma'am Powell's school for a very different one.

This was at the top of St. Michael's Hill in Bristol, and it was
kept by William Foot, a Baptist minister, old, inefficient, and
brutal. The boy was too terrified of him to learn anything.
"Lessons in the grammar, which I did not comprehend, and yet
could have learnt well enough by rote under gentle discipline and
a good-natured teacher, were frightened out of my head, and then
I was shut up during play-time in a closet at the top of the stairs,
where there was just light enough through some bars to see my
lesson by." Bullying was rampant in the school: as he was a
day-boy, the young Southey escaped the worst of it; but—perhaps
it was in consequence—his pugnacity developed, and though he
was one of the smallest boys there, he "used to fight a dozen
battles a day and of course get a dozen thrashings".[8]

After he had been there a year Foot died, and the boy was removed to a school at Corston, nine miles from Bristol and three from Bath. Thomas Flower, his new headmaster, was interested only in abstruse mathematics and astronomy: he left the teaching almost entirely in the hands of his son Charley, who was quite unequal to the work. From Charley the boys were supposed to learn writing and arithmetic. Twice a week they received Latin lessons from an amiable Frenchman named Duplanier; but Southey did not learn so much of the language from his master as from being obliged by the Flowers to teach it to boys who were bigger and less intelligent than himself: "a tax levied upon me by the law of the strongest", he called it, while admitting that "the effect was, that I made as much progress as if my lessons had been daily".

Not only was the teaching neglected: the boys' health and cleanliness received even less attention than was usual at eighteenth-century schools; Mrs. Flower drank; the food was disgusting. At the same time, Southey's judgment on it in 1821 —"there could not be a worse school in all respects"—is, on his own showing, too severe. The discipline, though it was strict, was by no means savage: "I never saw so little punishment in any school", he remarks. The situation of the house was attractive, surrounded as it was with orchards, standing in its own grounds, through which a stream ran.[9] The boys were allotted their own gardens, in which they grew radishes, lettuces, mustard and cress. All this is pleasant enough: it is clear that the lives they led there were not unhappy. They played "conkers" with snail-shells, shot arrows and flew kites. Once they had a glimpse of a great man. In the autumn of 1782 they were taken down to the inn at Newton on the main road to see Rodney, home from the Battle of the Saints, as he drove by on his way to dine with the Corporation at Bristol: he responded kindly to their cheers.

That Southey was by no means miserable at Corston appears too from a poem he wrote at Oxford in 1794 and published the following year. "The Retrospect" in its original form is a mildly melancholy affair of nearly 300 lines: it describes a visit he paid to the house in 1793, after it had ceased to be a school. This is how he sums up his reflections:

> Silent and sad the scene: I heard no more
> Mirth's honest cry, and childhood's cheerful roar,
> No longer echo'd round the shout of glee—

It seem'd as tho' the world had chang'd, like me! . . .
I too have felt the hand of fate severe—
In those calm days I never knew to fear;
No future views alarm'd my gloomy breast,
No anxious pangs my sickening soul possest;
No grief consum'd me, for I did not know
Increase of reason was increase of woe.[10]

His recollections of Corston were certainly not all gloomy.

After a year there he was removed and sent, as a day-boy once
more, to a school at "The Fort" in Bristol, above St. Michael's
church. Here he remained a little more than four years, "which,"
he says, "if not profitably, were at least not unhappily spent".
He speaks of its master, a Welshman named William Williams,
with tempered approval. "He pretended to very little, and what
he professed to teach he taught well. . . . The pleasantest of my
school years were those which I passed at Williams's. . . . Of all
my schoolmasters [he] is the one whom I remember with the
kindliest feelings." Williams was quick-tempered—like the
formidable Boyer of Christ's Hospital he wore an old wig when
he was in a bad humour and a new one when he found life more
pleasant; immovable stupidity angered him beyond endurance:
but he was not a harsh man, and he treated Southey with kindness.
His school was at this time on the down grade: its numbers had
fallen from a hundred to forty. It catered mainly for the sons of
wealthy tradesmen and merchants of Bristol and the West Indies
(there were a number of Creoles there), and the greatest emphasis
was placed in the curriculum on writing and arithmetic, particularly the former. Though Southey spent untold hours at his
copybook over "pupil" and "tulip" and such words, his handwriting never satisfied Williams; but, what is more important,
in his later life it became clear and graceful, a perfect instrument
for a prolific author. He had now some daily instruction in
Latin, and apparently learnt a little French: these, with some
lessons in dancing—for which he displayed an "unconquerable
incapacity"—were the limits of the instruction the school
afforded.

The boys' time there was enlivened by the visits of some of
Williams's old cronies. There was crazy Dr. Jones, who thought
himself a poet and who showed "a positive happiness in his
insanity; it was like a perpetual drunkenness". And there was a
breeches-maker named Pullen, "a glorious fellow", whom Southey
sketches brilliantly. He is a figure straight from Hogarth. "His

eyes were of the hue and lustre of scalded gooseberries, or oysters in sauce. His complexion was the deepest extract of the grape; he owed it to the Methuen treaty. . . . He would laugh at his own jests with a voice like Stentor, supposing Stentor to have been hoarse; and then he would clap old Williams on the back with a hand like a shoulder of mutton for breadth and weight. You may imagine how great a man we thought him."

During his first two years at Williams's school, the boy lived at home in term-time and with Miss Tyler in the holidays. She had now left her Walcot house and was living with friends, or in lodgings, still at Bath. In the summer of 1783 she took her nephew to Weymouth, where he had his first sight of the sea. They went over to Portland, they were astonished at the Chesil Beach, they saw the swans at Abbotsbury; and the visit was one that he always remembered with pleasure.[11] Early in 1785, "when Miss Tyler had lived about among her friends as long as it was convenient for them to entertain her, and longer in lodgings than was convenient for herself", she came to live in Bristol, taking the lease of a small house in Terril Street: as it was a good deal closer to the school than the Southeys' home, the boy now returned to live with his aunt.

He continued under Williams for another two years, until it was decided to send him to a public school. Westminster was proposed by his uncle Herbert Hill, who wished his nephew to become a King's Scholar there and so get elected to Christ Church, of which he had himself been a Student. This advice was taken— it could hardly have been rejected, since Mr. Hill was to pay the entire expenses of the boy's education at Westminster and Oxford. To prepare him for the much higher standard of work that would be required of him at his new school, he was sent for four hours a day to a tutor, Mr. Lewis, who lived in the Redcliffe Parade. Lewis did not teach him much (with one important exception, to be mentioned later). He had been an under-master at the Bristol Grammar School, but he made a poor coach; and even if he had been a good one, he would have found it almost impossible to remedy the faulty grounding the boy had received at the numerous inferior schools to which he had been sent. However, under Lewis he began Greek, and in Latin advanced as far as the Odes of Horace. His fellow-pupils were uncongenial to him. One of them he dubbed Caliban, "for he might have played that character without a mask, supposing he could have learnt the part. . . . He had a sister whom I shall not libel when I call her Sycorax."

In the meantime he was reading extensively on his own. His visits to the theatre with Miss Tyler had given him an early taste for plays. "Shakespeare", he says, "was in my hands as soon as I could read. . . . I went through Beaumont and Fletcher also, before I was eight years old." This led him to try his hand at composition, and at a very tender age he achieved an act and a half of a drama on the continence of Scipio. Although his father read nothing but *Felix Farley's Bristol Journal*, there were nevertheless a few books in the Wine Street house, mostly old plays and magazines, including the inevitable set of *The Spectator*. Among them he found with delight Mrs. Rowe's English version of certain episodes in the *Gerusalemme Liberata*. Soon after he came back from Weymouth he was given a copy of Hoole's complete translation of the poem, and from this he passed on, enchanted, to the *Orlando Furioso*. These two books opened out a whole new world to him. "It was for the sake of their stories", he remarks, "that I perused and reperused these poems with ever new delight; and by bringing them thus within my reach in boyhood, the translator rendered me a service which, when I look back upon my intellectual life, I cannot estimate too highly."[12] Hoole's notes introduced him to Spenser, for whom he came to feel the same passionate devotion as Wordsworth and Keats and most of the great Romantic poets. He then went on to Mickle's translation of the *Lusiad*, to Pope's *Homer*, the *Arcadia*, Josephus, and *The Arabian Nights*. In this school his reading began, and he was never to abandon or grow tired of it: the composition, translation, and reviewing of epics and romances was to fill a large part of his life. "No one", he wrote in 1823, "had ever a more decided turn for music or for numbers, than I had for romance."

The step from reading epics to writing them was a short one, and it was quickly taken. At the age of nine he began a continuation of the *Orlando*, written in heroic couplets; but a reading of the first volume of Bysshe's *Art of Poetry* convinced him of the superiority of blank verse. Before he went to Westminster he had tackled Brutus the Trojan, the death of Richard III, and the story of Egbert; translated from the Latin; written heroic epistles and "a satirical description of English manners, as delivered by Omai, the Taheitean, to his countrymen on his return". This is interesting as a primitive ancestor of *Espriella's Letters* and as his first recorded prose work.

To Southey's poetry his official education contributed very little; to his prose something. Williams began it by setting him to write a letter as a school exercise. After great initial difficulties, anxiety, and despair, he suddenly began a description of Stonehenge (remembered from an account in a guide-book), with which he filled his slate and delighted his master. He took his next step in prose composition under Lewis, who made him write "themes" on set subjects: in this way he learnt, as he characteristically puts it, "that it was not more difficult to write in prose than in verse".

He remained a little more than a year with his tutor. Of this period he remarked in 1824: "I do not remember in any part of my life to have been so conscious of intellectual improvement as I was during the year and a half before I was placed at Westminster". He did not consider that this advance was due to Lewis's teaching, but to the "development of mind" produced by his own poetical efforts.

He was now considered fit for his public school. Miss Tyler, scenting an opportunity for a visit to London at some one else's expense, volunteered to escort him up; and in February, 1788, they set off in a carriage hired by her friend Miss Palmer (sister of the famous Comptroller of the Post Office), who accompanied them. They broke their journey at Salt Hill, in order to meet Miss Palmer's nephews from Eton and to see Windsor Castle, and on the fourth day they reached the grand lodgings Miss Tyler had taken in Pall Mall. Six weeks then passed in a round of visits, gossip and playgoing. It was a paradise for the two ladies up from the country, but the boy was less happy: he took an instant dislike to London, which in later life he never overcame; he was bored with the parties to which his aunt dragged him; and, no doubt, he was nervous at the prospect of a public school—such a contrast to the easy-going, inefficient rule of Williams and Lewis. At the beginning of April Mr. Palmer took him off to the school. He was presented to the Head Master, his name was entered in the books, and he was placed in Ottley's boarding house.[13]

II

WESTMINSTER

(1788-1792)

THE WESTMINSTER SCHOOL that Southey entered in 1788 differed in many respects from that of to-day—in its appearance, in the kind of education it provided, and in the position it held among other schools.[14]

Of the Dean's Yard he knew, only the east side now remains unaltered: the west and north sides are occupied by modern buildings; while to the south the handsome Georgian terrace has recently been pulled down to make way for Sir Herbert Baker's Church House. There was then no railed-in "Green", only a small enclosure planted with trees, into which a row of buildings projected from the west.

Immediately before Southey's arrival at the school and during his time there, Little Dean's Yard underwent great changes. In earlier years the boys had known only a narrow cobbled pathway running east and west, bordered by posts and chains and the high garden-walls of the houses. But about 1785 the walls were demolished, and in 1789-90 three fine houses were built on the south side of the open Yard, of which two remain to-day. At that time none of the buildings on the north side of the Yard belonged to the school. The archway and the flight of steps to the east are unchanged, but "School", the great hall to which they lead, has been much altered. In Southey's day the whole school (some 260 boys) was taught in this room: it was divided into two parts, the Upper and the Under Schools, by a curtain; there were benches round its walls for the boys; the masters sat on chairs facing them; it was entirely unheated.

The King's Scholars, then as now, lived in College, Burlington's great building overlooking the garden. Of the rest of the school—the "Town Boys"—some lived at home, but the majority boarded in houses round about, in Little Dean's Yard, Dean's Yard, College Street, Abingdon Street, Sanctuary. Each house was run by a dame, assisted by an usher who was supposed to maintain discipline: if he was inefficient, this system was open to considerable abuses.

In Southey's day the school provided a severely classical education: the curriculum was still governed by the great shade of Busby. Latin and Greek were not merely the chief subjects taught; they were almost the only ones (though the composition of English verse was encouraged, and it seems to have been at this time that arithmetic was first admitted—by the smallest of back doors, as an extra subject taught by the writing-master on half-holidays). Latin was the language of instruction in the Upper School; there were Latin "themes" to be written; there was the "Horace Lesson", which consisted in turning one of the Odes into a different metre from the original; it was Southey's inability to make Latin verses that automatically put him into a low form, the Under Fourth, at his entrance. The tradition was elegant and charming—the Latin poems of Vinny Bourne, beloved of Lamb, are its fine flower. It had fostered the genius of poets (Dryden, Prior, Churchill, and Cowper had all been educated at Westminster); it had formed the basis of the very real culture of such men of the world as Carteret and Mansfield: but by the end of the eighteenth century it was beginning to lose vitality and value, to run down like an unwound clock.

This was symptomatic of a decline in the school's position, soon to become painfully clear, which Southey was often to comment on regretfully. In the long competition between Eton and Westminster for the first place among public schools, Eton was just at this time beginning to draw ahead. It was partly a matter of politics: Westminster was a strongly Whig school, and the Whig party was then entering on a period of eclipse; for this reason it lost the patronage of the Court, and George III transferred his interest to Eton. The early years of the nineteenth century were to see Westminster's numbers fall (until in 1841 they stood at 67), its importance decrease; and when it revived under new methods and with new ideals it took a place beside the great new schools of the Arnold pattern, one among many, no longer at the head of all. It is necessary to remember that when Southey was at Westminster it still held the pre-eminence among English schools, disputed only with Eton; and that the education he received there, however inadequate or inefficient it may appear to us to-day, was the best he could possibly have had.

The Head Master when Southey entered the school was Samuel Smith. He was mild and easy-going, "very dull and good-natured" according to the younger Colman—though when Francis Burdett led a rebellion against him he knocked the boy down with a stout stick. Before the end of 1788 he retired and was succeeded by William Vincent, a man of heavier calibre. Vincent was a considerable scholar: his special field was ancient geography, in which he did very valuable work. The whole of his life from the age of nine, with the exception of his four years at Cambridge, was spent at Westminster, as Town Boy, King's Scholar, Usher, Under Master, Head Master, and finally Dean. He had been reputed a harsh Under Master: Colman calls him "plaguily severe", adding that "he lost his temper, and struck and pinched the boys, in sudden bursts of anger". When he became Head Master his discipline relaxed. His boys were allowed to shoot paper darts at him with impunity, and he would "go down school with his wig full of them": twice there were rebellions against him, with which he dealt far too mildly. Like Smith, he had a strong spice of indolence. He was of a conventional academic type: his opinions were strictly conservative, and as long as they were not affronted he never made trouble for himself; but when they were attacked, he behaved with instant severity.

His assistants call for less notice. Southey was taught "sensibly and kindly" by his first form-master, Edward Smedley. Although the usher of his house, Samuel Hayes, was nicknamed "Botch" on account of the "the manner in which he mended his pupil's verses", he was a facile and skilful versifier and had been seven times winner of the Seatonian Prize at Cambridge. That was his one talent: for the rest, he drank heavily and could keep no order. When Vincent became Head Master, Hayes expected to succeed him in the Under-Mastership; but John Wingfield (who according to Southey had "no talents whatever") was promoted to it over his head, and he left in dudgeon. Towards the end of his school career, Southey expressed his opinion of all these masters in pert couplets:

> . . . Wingfield sitting in the ill-gained chair
> Lifts up his finger with the learned stare.
> Unknown to cringe or worthless lords to praise,
> Merit retires from Westminster with Hayes.
> Vincent extends his arbitrary laws,
> And Smedley cuts good jokes and grins applause.[15]

Hayes's slack discipline is reflected in Southey's early experiences at the school. Lord Amherst (the future Governor-General of India) was head of Ottley's, but though he was universally liked he did not take much part in its affairs: having a room to himself, he saw little of what went on. The boys were under the dominion of various tyrants. One of them, whose expression "was rather that of a savage than of a civilised being", would pour water in Southey's ears when he was asleep and throw his porter-pot or his poker at him; and "he once attempted to hold me by the leg out of the window; it was the first floor, and over a stone area: had I not struggled in time, and clung to the frame with both hands, my life would probably have been sacrificed to this freak of temporary madness". Eventually Southey summoned up the courage to complain of him to Hayes, and his troubles in this quarter ceased.

Southey never forgot the miseries he endured from his various tormentors at Westminster. Later in life he came to disapprove strongly of the boarding-school system because of the scope it offered for such tyranny, and he frequently denounced it.[16]

It was the custom at Westminster (it is still) to assign each new boy, for his first week or two, to the care of a boy slightly senior to himself, who was responsible for initiating him into the ways of the school, and who bore the penalty for any offence against the rules committed by his ward. The tutor was called the "substance", his pupil the "shadow". Southey's "substance" was George Strachey, who quickly became a close friend and remained one throughout the time they were at school together. He used to ask Southey to his home in Queen Anne Street, a pleasant invitation to a boy who did not live in London. After Southey went up to Oxford they drifted away from each other—partly owing to a youthful quarrel, more because Strachey went on to Cambridge and then to India, where he eventually rose to be Chief Secretary to Government. But Southey always spoke of him with affection: in 1812 he described him as "one of the best-hearted men I ever knew".[17]

He was not long in making other friends. Very soon after he arrived he got to know Charles Watkin Williams Wynn, who had entered the school in 1784 (though he was a year younger than Southey) and also boarded "up Ottley's". When in due course Wynn became head of the house, Southey shared a room with him.[18] After he left to go up to Christ Church their friendship continued unbroken: it ended only with Southey's death. Of all his friends Wynn had the greatest influence on his career; and in spite of certain incompatibilities, in politics and in temperament, no serious misunderstanding ever came between them. Wynn was the complete type of old-fashioned Whig: immensely proud of his birth (his father was the baronet of Wynnstay, the un-crowned king of North Wales; his mother a Grenville); stiff,

high-minded, upright, exceedingly generous. He entered the
House of Commons as Member for Old Sarum at twenty-one and
became in due time, almost as a matter of course, a Cabinet
Minister: it is said that he declined the Governor-Generalship of
India three times. He was inefficient in business and showed little
real understanding of political problems; but this was offset by
the instinctive capacity for governing that his birth and tradition
gave him.

The other lifelong intimacy formed by Southey at school was
of a different kind. Charles Bedford, the deputy who performed
Horace Walpole's duties as Usher of the Exchequer, sent his two
sons, Grosvenor Charles and Horace Walpole (the Usher's godson),
to Westminster. Southey knew and liked them both: later on,
he gradually lost touch with Horace, but Grosvenor became his
closest friend. They corresponded continually. "Excepting
Wynn", Southey told him in 1814, "you are the oldest friend I
have, and with no one has my communication been so unin-
terruptedly frequent. For many, very many years there has never
occurred a day in which some circumstance or other has not
brought you to my mind." Again, discussing an article on
Wellington for the *Quarterly* a year later: "I tell you of it for
sundry reasons; one of which is, that I tell you everything"—
and Southey did not say such things lightly.[19] Bedford grew into
a cautious, unexciting, utterly reliable civil servant; as typically
bourgeois as Wynn was typically an aristocrat. Therein lay his
value to Southey: they were on a level socially, and consequently
understood one another well; Bedford's discretion made him a
perfect confidant, his common sense enabled him to give good
advice or a sound opinion whenever either was wanted; and
beneath the crustiness of his exterior, which became more pronounced with deafness in old age, he had a deep affection and
admiration for Southey. Besides, they shared an interest in the
macabre and the lower reaches of the fantastic, and a passion
for cats.

Southey made many other friends at school, though none so
close as Wynn and Bedford. Among them was Peter Elmsley,
who became a distinguished classical scholar, not unworthy to be
mentioned with Porson, and died Camden Professor of Ancient
History at Oxford. It is unfortunate that his correspondence with
Southey has not been preserved; but we know that they kept in
touch, and that on one occasion Elmsley rendered his friend a
generous and most timely service.[20] Southey never lost interest
in the careers of his school contemporaries; and he recognised

that the friends he made at Westminster, still more the habit of friendship he formed there (which proved a valuable brake on his egotism in later years), were the most important things the school gave him. "Scarcely a week passes", he wrote in 1818, "in which I do not dream of Westminster, so strong a hold have those years upon the mind"; and when he thought of Westminster, it was above all of his friends that he thought.[21]

He did not always go home for the holidays. He often stayed at Cheshunt with the Misses Delamare, "excellent women", friends of his aunt's. Their widowed sister, Mrs. Dolignon, seems to have acted as his guardian for the time he was in London. "She had known me at Bath", he says, "in my earliest childhood; I had the good fortune then to obtain a place in her affections, and that place I retained, even when she thought it necessary to estrange me from her family." She had been with him and Miss Tyler on the famous holiday at Weymouth; she it was who had given him his treasured copy of the *Gerusalemme Liberata*: he always remembered her "with the utmost reverence and affection".[22]

His career at school, apart from its spectacular ending, was not eventful. In 1789, following the lines laid down for him by his uncle, he tried for a King's Scholarship, taking the gruelling viva voce examination known as the "Challenge": as he was unsuccessful, he remained "up Ottley's", the headship of which he took over from Wynn in 1791. Of his school work he tells us little. In old age he still remembered the dullness of the grammars from which he was taught Latin and Greek, and in a note to his biography of Cowper he entered a sly protest against them: "Cowper even liked the school well enough to admire the worst things belonging to it—its grammars. . . . As for their being compendious and perspicuous, I should not be more surprised at hearing them called entertaining." He distinguished himself in the composition of English verse, for which he was several times awarded pieces of "maundy money", the only prizes then existing at Westminster. Nor were his activities confined to verse: in the Bodleian reposes the manuscript of *Harold*, a prose romance begun on 13th July, 1791, and finished on the 6th of the following month.[23]

Out of school hours he read widely, often in directions that authority would not have approved. He was made free of the library at the Bedfords' house in New Palace Yard: there, looking out across the Thames, he spent many blissful hours over Picart's *Religious Ceremonies*, with its incomparable illustrations. His acquaintance with Picart proved as important to him as his first reading of Hoole's *Tasso* had been : "The book impressed my imagination strongly", he wrote long afterwards; "and before I left school I had formed the intention of exhibiting all the more prominent and poetical forms of mythology which have at any time obtained among mankind, by making each the groundwork of an heroic poem." In fact, he laid the foundations of *The Curse of Kehama* in his teens. Along with Picart he read other books at this time, which more directly undermined his orthodoxy— *The Sorrows of Werther* (published in the year of his birth), the works of Voltaire, Rousseau, and Gibbon. His reading also included Malory and *Evelina*.[24]

He took little interest in games, and he showed early signs of unruliness. He joined in a raid on a private school close to St. Margaret's churchyard and was nearly recognised afterwards as one of the perpetrators by his curly head. It seems almost certain that he took part in the rebellion (or, as the *Public Advertiser* called it, the "terrible fracas") of November, 1791. On that occasion the whole school decamped to "Green" in Dean's Yard to see a fight between two of the boys, Deacon Morrell and Joseph Phillimore, over a bit of ribbon; they refused to return until the battle was over, even when personally summoned by the Head Master; and when he announced that he was going to flog the head boy (John D'Oyly, who afterwards had a distinguished career in Ceylon) for disobeying orders, "the sentence was demurred to by the whole school, the consequence of which was a general desertion for the present". Eventually, "by the persuasion of Lord Stormont and some distinguished characters", D'Oyly graciously agreed to perform an imposition set him by Vincent and to make a public confession of his error. More than ten years later Southey retained a piece of the ribbon which was the *casus belli*, and he admitted in 1818 that he had had his share in rebellion at school: it is hard to resist the conclusion that he was actively concerned in this one.[25]

The hint that it might have been he who mutilated Major André's statue in the Abbey by cutting off its nose has been enshrined in the *Letter of Elia to Robert Southey*. There is no proof at all that he was the culprit—though it is noticeable that he never specifically denied responsibility; but he must certainly have sympathised with the deed, for he was by now a vehement republican.[26]

The French Revolution had begun a little more than a year after he entered Westminster. To him, as to most of his intelligent and generous-minded contemporaries, it seemed to offer the promise of a new world, and he welcomed it with characteristic youthful fervour. "Few persons but those who have lived in it", he wrote in 1824, "can conceive or comprehend what the memory of the French Revolution was, nor what a visionary world seemed to open upon those who were just entering it. Old things seemed passing away, and nothing was dreamt of it but the regeneration of the human race."[27] It is not difficult to realise what he felt as he saw the most powerful despotic government in Europe bow before the determined attack of its subjects (Louis accepted the new constitution in September, 1791). It does Southey an injustice to minimise the strength of his revolutionary feelings, from a desire to make his life appear consistent with itself: we shall see that it has a consistency of its own, even though he passed in the course of it from extreme republican opinions into high Toryism.

At school, fortified by his unorthodox reading, he soon began to proclaim his radical ideas. Perhaps, as Professor Haller has suggested, they became more conspicuous and violent through arguing with Bedford and Wynn, who held more conventional views: at least we know for certain that Vincent gave him back his theme one day "with a long row for abusing Burke in it".[28] More serious trouble lay ahead.

Five years earlier a group of Etonians centring on the young Canning had founded a paper called *The Microcosm*, in which they discoursed with playful satire on the world they saw around them: it is generally held to be the most brilliant feat in the history of public-school journalism. Inevitably, Westminster must compete with it, and in 1788 *The Trifler* was set on foot as a rival. It too was well above the average level of such magazines, though far less sparkling than *The Microcosm*, with which it carried on a desultory and puerile warfare. Southey made an attempt to contribute to it, sending in a poem on the death of an infant sister, but this was rejected. In 1792 he and his friends determined to start another Westminster paper, to emulate *The Trifler*. They called it *The Flagellant*, and the first number appeared on 1st March, published by a leading London bookseller, Egerton. Though he was one of the founders of the magazine, Southey was not at first a contributor. But the fifth issue (29th March) included a paper of his, over the pseudonym "Gualbertus". This was a frontal attack on corporal punishment, on these lines:

It is utterly inconsistent with the character of a school master, particularly with the ministers of the Church of England as most School Masters are, thus by making use of so beastly, so idolatrous a custom to follow the abominations of the children of Moab, of the Hittites and the Shittites and the Gergusites and other idolaters whose names alone remain an awful instance of divine justice. . . . Flogging was esteemed by Heathens as an act of piety and the Deity of all Pagan nations was the Devil. . . .

Whosoever will be saved, above all things it is necessary that he should hold the Catholic Faith. Now, the Catholic Faith is this, there be three Gods and yet but one God. Whoever denies this cannot be orthodox, consequently cannot be fit to instruct youth. Now, since there is but one God, whosoever floggeth, that is, performeth the will of Satan, committeth an abomination: to him therefore [and] to all the consumers of birch as to priests of Lucifer,

Anathema, Anathema,

Gualbertus.[29]

When he read this manifesto, Vincent was extremely angry. Rebellions—even when "distinguished characters" intervened in them—were domestic affairs, not to be taken too seriously. But this was an impudent attack on the established order of things, issued by a London publisher for every one to read: it advertised to the world that the forces of anarchy and irreligion had secured a foothold in his school.

He took immediate action, in the most effective way possible. Learning by discreet inquiry that the effusion was attributed to Southey, he wrote off to Mrs. Dolignon in his most portentous style:

Madam,

Southey is supposed to be the author of a Publication reflecting very indecently upon public education, and the characters of those who conduct it. As I have commenced a prosecution against the publisher, I should wish that you would keep Southey under your protection, till I see the effect of the steps I have taken. If he is not the author, I will receive him with pleasure and do him the most ample justice: if he is, I know not any reparation he can make for his offence. I wish to have a line from you, and remain

Your humble servant,

W. Vincent.

Dean's Yard,
Ap. 9, 1792.

To this Mrs. Dolignon returned a formal acknowledgment, undertaking that the boy should remain with her sisters at Cheshunt until the result of the investigation was known. At the same time, Vincent threatened to prosecute the publisher for libel and demanded from him the name of the author. Isaac Reed, the editor of Shakespeare, attempted to shame him into refusing to disclose it; but he "would act like a rascal", says Reed, "in spite of all I could do"; and he revealed that the essay had been written by Southey.[30]

This must have been welcome news to Vincent. We have seen that he had already reproved Southey for his unorthodox attitude to Burke: there must certainly have been other occasions of friction between them, and no doubt he was glad of a chance to show himself severe with little trouble, after cutting such a poor figure in the disturbances of the previous November. He expelled Southey instantly.

It was now the boy's turn to be angry. He was thunderstruck at the severity of the blow, and beneath the flood of indignation that he poured out in his letters to Grosvenor Bedford we can easily sense his alarm, his fear of what he had brought on himself by his *jeu d'esprit*. Not that he was a coward. That was never true at any time of his life: he was immovable in the defence of his opinions, he endured endless abuse rather than concede an inch to popular clamour. His courage may not have been of the aggressive masculine pattern, but it was firmly embedded in the triple rock of his obstinacy, his conscious rectitude, and his pride. It is true that he weakened for a moment now: he was induced, perhaps by the kind folk at Cheshunt, to write and apologise to Vincent. But this was the only occasion on which he ever yielded anything in controversies of this sort; and he immediately repented of his lapse, fell into an agony of self-contempt, and confessed to Bedford what he had done. "I deserve to be despised," he wrote with genuine, if ludicrous, solemnity, "I deserve to be shunned. . . . I am despicable in my own eyes and criminal in those of my friends."[31] Whatever he conceded in his letter of apology (which seems now to have disappeared), it was insufficient to appease Vincent, who not only declined to receive him back but took the further step of warning Cyril Jackson against admitting the dangerous young revolutionary to Christ Church, where his name had already been entered.

Southey did not know of this move as yet, though he suspected something of the kind. His letters to Bedford at this time are full of abuse of the authorities, above all of Vincent his arch-enemy,

alternating with a self-pity that borders occasionally on persecution mania. Thus on 16th April he writes: "My resolution is
fixed and perhaps before this Vincent has the letter to announce
my departure. I will never submit. . . . Should I be rejected at
Oxford the grave is always open—there at least I shall not be
molested." Next day his mood changes: "I live in the *charitable*
hope of one day dosing Vincent till I kill him. . . . Expulsion is
a bitter pill . . . but for every pill I swallow Vincent shall have
a bolus."[32]

After visiting various friends, he went home in the middle of
June. His fears of a hostile reception from his family were soon
allayed: "Not one reproach have I heard concerning Westminster.
It does not hurt me, for I have not acted improperly." In the
same letter he shows the direction his mind was taking at this
time: "If I could get an appointment to the East Indies I should
like it. The church is a hypocritical line of life, the law a dishonest
one." Amid such speculations he sat down to write a new
romance, entitled (very properly) *An Improbable Tale*.[33]

A few weeks later his life was disturbed by a domestic crisis
of the first order. Robert Southey *père* had not made a good
linendraper: it is easy to see that he was incompetent at the work,
that his temperament was unsuitably generous and confiding, and
that he had set up with too small a capital—not more than £500.
Moreover, his heart had never been in shopkeeping: he was
always thinking of the country and its sports. Under these
conditions it is not surprising that his affairs should have fallen
gradually into ruin, which was accelerated by "the treachery of
his relations and the injustice of his friends".

The young Southey now made himself useful. "Since my
last", he wrote to Bedford on 21st October, "I have been continually journeying backwards and forwards upon business." One
of his trips was to Taunton, to see if he could induce his uncle John,
who was a prosperous lawyer, to help his father. Here he was
unsuccessful. It was apparently at this moment that the elder
Southey was actually arrested—"not for his own debts," adds his
son, "but for a bill endorsed for a deceitful friend. I saw him . . .
in prison". Miss Tyler now came to the rescue (how horrified
she must have been to see one of her relatives in gaol!), and the
immediate financial pressure was relieved. The Southey family
had by this time left Wine Street, migrating to No. 9, Duke Street,
Bath, where Mrs. Southey started a lodging-house.[34]

Robert had originally intended to go up to Oxford in time
for the Michaelmas term of 1792; but this had to be postponed,

partly owing to the family crisis and partly because he now learnt that Christ Church would not receive him. On 29th September he wrote to Bedford: "Dr. Vincent's arts . . . have shut me out from Christ Church. . . . I fancy I shall enter at Balliol, Oxford." Balliol proved more liberal, or more rash, than Christ Church, and he matriculated from there on 3rd November.

On his way up to Oxford he stopped at Bath to see his father, who, he says, "had been long declining. Evident though this was I still deceived myself. . . . I stayed at my father's and saw him in his bed. He pressed my hand with affection and for the only time in his life blessed me." He never rallied from the shock of his failure in business, and early in December he died. Southey attended his funeral on the 17th: a month later he went into residence at Balliol.[35]

III

OXFORD

(*1793-1794*)

DURING the memorable autumn of 1792 Southey continued
to follow the progress of the Revolution in France with
close sympathy. Neither the imprisonment of the royal
family in August nor the slaughter of the Swiss Guards nor the
September Massacres drew any protest from him: the battle of
Valmy on 20th September and the proclamation of the republic
the following day must have seemed to him to crown the great
work. Yet it was at this point that he gave the first, very faint,
signs of wavering. Like many sentimental English romantics,
he was in two minds as to the treatment of the King. "I can pity
Louis *the last*," he wrote on 21st October, "as one who is unfortunate. The man deserves not pity, the King less; the abject
prisoner certainly claims it. Perhaps they may canonise him *à la*
mode Charles I. I hope not. I think not."[36] But here he was
wrong. On 21st January, 1793, as he was settling in at Balliol,
Louis XVI was guillotined. Eleven days later Britain and France
were at war.

Whatever he may have thought of the execution of the King
(and he does not seem to have regarded it as a great crime), his
sympathies were not doubtful now: they were wholly with
France. "My brother is on board the *Venus* frigate," he wrote in
March. ". . . He is going to fight for England. I wish I could
wish him success."[37] Now and for some time to come, Southey
earnestly desired a French victory. His feelings, and those of the
many other English revolutionaries who agreed with him, have
been summed up by Wordsworth:

> I rejoiced,
> Yea, afterwards—truth most painful to record!—
> Exulted, in the triumph of my soul,
> When Englishmen by thousands were o'erthrown,
> Left without glory on the field, or driven,
> Brave hearts! to shameful flight. It was a grief,—
> Grief call it not, 'twas anything but that,—

31

A conflict of sensations without name,
Of which *he* only, who may love the sight
Of a village steeple, as I do, can judge,
When, in the congregation bending all
To their great Father, prayers were offered up,
Or praises for our country's victories;
And, 'mid the simple worshippers, perchance
I only, like an uninvited guest
Whom no one owned sate silent, shall I add,
Fed on the day of vengeance yet to come.[38]

These were Southey's views exactly; and when we consider his
worry over the war, his impatience and contempt of discipline,
and his preoccupation with his own writing, it becomes evident
that his university career had little chance of success from the
start.

It proved in many respects a repetition of his career at school.
Both at Westminster and at Balliol he was ill taught, the curriculum was old-fashioned and discipline slack; at both of them his
mind was dominated by revolutionary ideas; and at both he
formed valuable friendships. The institutions themselves were
similar, too: both were inefficiently conducted at this date. But
there was this difference: that Westminster was entering on a
period of decline, gently falling asleep, while Balliol was just
beginning to wake up. John Parsons, to whom the revival of the
college was primarily due, had been elected to a fellowship in
1785. His influence had not yet become considerable: the Master,
Dr. Davey, was an orthodox Tory of the old school, and Parsons
did not get his chance until he succeeded him in 1798. But the
more scandalous features of eighteenth-century Balliol disappeared with its Jacobitism, and in Southey's day it was already
showing a few signs of reformation.[39]

His first reaction to the college and its discipline was one of
lordly contempt—an attitude he maintained ever afterwards to
its official institutions. "Would you think it possible", he wrote
to Bedford, "that the wise founders of an English university
should forbid us to wear boots? What matters it whether I study
in shoes or boots? To me it is a matter of indifference, but folly
so ridiculous puts me out of conceit with the whole. When the
foundation is bad the fabric must be weak."

He had determined, like other good revolutionaries, to leave
his hair unpowdered, out of protest against Pitt's powder-tax,
imposed in 1786. This was a considerable mark of independence,

COLERIDGE IN 1795
*From a painting by Peter Vandyke in the National
Portrait Gallery*

for it was held *de rigueur* to wear powdered hair: a barber was occupied for two hours before dinner every day in dressing the heads of the undergraduates and fellows. But Southey's first appearance with his hair in its natural state went by quietly: "I came off very well as our hall is repairing, and in the room appropriated for eating Liberty and Equality are prevalent." Next door, at Trinity, Walter Savage Landor, who had come up at the same time as Southey, was taking the same method of showing his opinions. In later life they were to be friends, but at Oxford they never met.[40] Southey knew Landor by repute, however, as a "mad Jacobin", and he heard of the shooting affair in Trinity for which he was sent down in June, 1794.

Southey passed much of his time with his Westminster friends Wynn and Elmsley, who were now at Christ Church; but the closest new friendships he formed were made in his own college. Before he had been up a fortnight he had fallen in with Edmund Seward, a man three years older than himself, who had matriculated in 1789. Seward came from Lower Sapey, on the borders of Worcestershire and Herefordshire, where his family owned some property.[41] It would be easy to dismiss him, on the basis of what Southey tells us, as nothing but a young prig. Priggish he certainly was, but he must also have had charm and a good heart, for Southey always referred to him with particular affection. His virtues are indeed somewhat forbidding, and his conversation reads rather like the dialogue in *Sandford and Merton*: "At the age of fourteen he began learning, and the really useful knowledge he possesses must be imputed to a mind really desirous of improvement. ' Do you not find your attention flag? ' I said to him as he was studying Hutchinson's Moral Philosophy in Latin. ' If our tutors would but make our studies interesting we should pursue them with pleasure.' ' Certainly we should,' he replied; ' but I feel a pleasure in studying them because I know it is my duty.'" It is clear that he curbed the more dangerous excesses of Southey's revolutionary romanticism, and that it was he who converted Southey to the "Christian Stoicism" that he professed, and found comfort in, for the rest of his life. As an undergraduate Southey read Epictetus—"I carried Epictetus in my pocket," he remarked afterwards, "till my heart was ingrained with it": he considered this a landmark in his intellectual and moral development, and it may certainly be put down to Seward's influence.[42]

He formed another friendship at Balliol, which was to be lifelong, with Nicholas Lightfoot, a Devonian two years senior in standing to himself. "We literally lived together at College",

S.   C

Southey told Caroline Bowles thirty years later; "for we break-fasted together every morning, read together, and passed every evening together."[43] They saw little of each other in after years, as Lightfoot returned to Devon, where he became master of the grammar school at Crediton and finally, in 1831, rector of Stock-leigh Pomeroy: but they kept up a steady correspondence at infrequent intervals, and in old age they met once or twice.

Of Southey's other friends at this time, two more must be mentioned—George Burnett and Robert Allen. Burnett was the son of a Somerset farmer: at Balliol he became an ardent revolutionary and showed great intellectual promise, which his pathetic career disappointed. Allen, now a sizar at University College, was that handsome boy from Christ's Hospital of whom Lamb and Leigh Hunt tell a delicious story. His friendship with Southey did not prove permanent, but it had one momentous consequence.

With this circle of friends, and many more casual acquaintances, Southey disputed and gossiped. But his days did not pass entirely in talk. He found time to learn to row and swim (later in life he used to say, a little ungraciously, that those were the only two things Oxford taught him), he ran through a large number of books, and he wrote many thousand lines of verse.

His reading was wide but quite unsystematic, ranging from Homer and Tacitus to *Leonidas* and *The Man of Feeling*. Here he was carrying on the studies he had pursued in the Bedfords' library at Westminster: at school and at the university he acquired a considerable knowledge of classical and English literature, which was to be displayed in the *Specimens of the Later English Poets*, in the twelfth chapter of his *Life of Cowper*, in *The Doctor*, and in the notes to many of his poems.[44]

Verse continued to pour forth from him in an incessant stream: most of it he wisely destroyed. Writing to H. W. Bedford on 22nd December, 1793, he estimated that up to that date he had written 35,000 lines (excluding those in his letters, which would swell this total considerably), of which he thought 10,000 had some merit. In this calculation he must have included the earliest draft of his first epic, *Joan of Arc*. He conceived the idea of this poem, so he tells us in the preface, in July, 1793. He seems to have discussed it with Grosvenor Bedford, who came down to Oxford to see the installation of the Duke of Portland as Chancellor at the beginning of that month, and on the 14th he reported: "Joan of Arc continues to occupy my thoughts."[45] She was to go on occupying them for the next two years. The only other important poem he wrote in this period was "The Retrospect", already mentioned.

He spent his first vacation, a short one of three weeks, in a walking-tour with Seward. They went across the Cotswolds to Evesham and Worcester, where they stayed three days. Thence they made a short excursion to Kidderminster, returning by way of Bewdley. Ribbesford House, which belonged to the Herbert family, sent Southey into a reverie of the past: "an old mansion . . . now mouldering away, in so romantic a situation, that I soon lost myself in dreams of days of yore—the tapestried room, the listed fight, the vassal filled hall, the hospitable fire, the old baron and his young daughter; these formed a most delightful day-dream". (It might be a sketch for the setting of *Christabel* or a poem of Scott's.) They then pushed on westwards to Ledbury to visit Seward's brothers, and after staying there a day or two returned to Oxford.

The first part of the long vacation he dutifully spent at home, though, as he wrote to Bedford, it was "far from being to me the comfortable retreat you enjoy. . . . The idea of it when it comes across happier scenes clouds them. Keen as my relish is for the pleasures of domestic life, I have experienced them but little." At his mother's lodging-house at Bath he was "compelled to associate with fools and to know they think it condescension".[46] The alternative to his own home was Miss Tyler's—no unmitigated delight either.

Towards the end of July he rode off to Herefordshire to see his uncle Mr. Hill, who was home on a visit from Portugal. He then went on to stay with the Bedfords at Brixton. On 13th August he resumed *Joan of Arc*, and working every morning in a summer-house in the Bedfords' garden he finished the first version of the poem in six weeks.

For some reason he did not keep the Michaelmas term at Oxford, but spent the rest of the autumn at Bristol with Miss Tyler. In December he went up to stay with the Sewards at Sapey. There he fell in love with a girl named Augusta Roberts; but it turned out that Edmund Seward's brother John had a prior claim to her, and Southey at once resigned her to him with a gesture of magnanimity. He consoled himself by writing an account of the affair to H. W. Bedford: the same letter contains a reference to the Fricker family, in which he was to find more permanent happiness.[47]

During this autumn he was going through a second crisis. It was not this time a question of finance, but of his future career. His uncle, who was paying his expenses at Oxford, had always wished him to take Orders, and he had previously accepted this destiny, though with some misgiving. But he now began to have serious doubts as to whether he could in conscience become a clergyman. "What is to become of me at ordination, heaven only knows!" he writes in December. "After keeping the straight path so long, the Test Act will be a stumbling-block to honesty." And again, later in the same month: "When I look forward to taking Orders, a thousand dreadful ideas crowd at once upon my mind."

Such evidence of unorthodoxy was naturally distressing to his son, who compiled his *Life and Correspondence* nearly sixty years later, for he was himself a parson, and thought of his father as a champion of Protestant Christianity against both Roman Catholics and infidels. It is to his credit that he suppressed very little of the evidence for his father's religious doubts at this period; and he makes an honest, and on the whole satisfactory, attempt to account for them. Southey's upbringing and education, he says, had not been religious, for Miss Tyler paid no more than lip-service to the Church (perhaps not even that) and he often spoke of the irreligion which prevailed in the schools of his day; the Church of the late eighteenth century could offer little inspiration to a young idealist; the doctrines of the French Revolution, which he took up with an enthusiasm that might in other times have been given to religion, ran directly counter to orthodox ideas of Christianity, as of politics. Southey makes no statement, even at this time, of out-and-out infidelity: his attack is directed instead against the established Church as an institution. He disapproved of it, in fact, on political rather than doctrinal grounds; and even in his high Tory old age he never wholly abandoned his opposition to its wealth and pomp.

But at this moment it was useless for him merely to refuse to take orders: he must choose an alternative profession. He had, after all, three younger brothers; his mother was a widow of exiguous means; and he could look for nothing, as he soon found, from his father's family. Accordingly, he decided to study medicine, and he went up to Balliol in January, 1794, determined "to come out Æsculapius Secundus". This resolution did not last long: he found he had an invincible repugnance to the study of anatomy, and he could think of nothing but literature.

He now took a step in quite another direction. His father had been approached three years before, at the time of his bankruptcy, with an offer to purchase his reversion in an estate belonging to his brother John, the rich Taunton lawyer. "The offer was made at such a time", adds Southey, "and in such a manner as to rouse his feelings (naturally strong), and he turned the man out of the house. I have since regretted my absence at the moment, as it might have procured me much information on the subject."[48] He made up his mind to try and sell his reversion, and to this end he asked Bedford to make some inquiries about it at Doctors' Commons. But they proved fruitless, and his visions of "a sufficiency in independence" faded away.

In spite of this failure, his determination not to take orders remained unshakable. His dislike of the idea only increased as time went on, and to those who advocated it he reinforced his counter-arguments by pointing out that if he did become a parson his chances of securing a competent income were slight. "Upon every religious system", he told Bedford, "I deny the necessity of an established faith, and of a religious establishment. Upon my own principles I doubt (to say the least) the system my friends destine me to support, and the hope of content in life would induce me to avoid a prospect which leads to starving in creditable celibacy upon £40 a year."[49]

His next thought was of the civil service. Could not Bedford get him into his own office, the Exchequer? There he might earn his bread and butter, and have enough leisure to write as well. Anything was better than the Church: "is six hours' misery to be preferred to wretchedness of the whole 24?". In spite of a discouraging response from Bedford, he persisted in the idea, until it was borne in upon him that for this purpose he would have to supply testimonials from Oxford, which would be certain to refer to his revolutionary sympathies—a fatal bar to employment in a government office.[50] He was by now definitely known as a "Jacobin": that label carried with it the same stigma in the eyes of authority as the label "Communist" has carried in more recent times, and for much the same reasons.

In these circumstances—obliged to earn his living, barred from the profession he wished to enter, urged to adopt one he detested—Southey turned seriously to a project that had hitherto been nothing more than a delightful fantasy. Why not emigrate, with some friends if possible, and begin a new life in conditions of primitive simplicity, far from Pitt and the relatives he found so unsympathetic? The idea had been germinating in his mind for some time. Only three weeks after he arrived at Balliol, he had written: "I could form the most delightful theory of an island peopled by men who should be Christians, not Philosophers, and where Vice only should be contemptible, Virtue only honourable; where all should be convenient without luxury, all satisfied without profusion. . . . If the *Bounty* mutineers had not behaved so cruelly to their officers, I should have been the last to condemn them. Otaheite [Tahiti] independent of its women had many inducements not only for the sailor but the philosopher."[51] The following November he referred to Cowley's idea of retiring to lead a hermit's life in America, and added: "My asylum there would be sought for different reasons (and no prospect in life gives me half the pleasure this visionary one affords); I should be pleased to reside in a country where men's abilities would ensure respect; where society was upon a proper footing, and man was considered as more valuable than money; and where I could till the earth, and provide by honest industry the meat which my wife would dress with pleasing care." So now, under the pressure of his accumulated difficulties, he wrote: "Either in six months I fix myself in some honest way of living, or I quit my country, my friends, and every fondest hope I indulge, for ever." Just at this moment, as the plan was taking shape, it received vigorous support from a more powerful mind than his own.

In the second week of June, 1794, Samuel Taylor Coleridge set out from Cambridge with a friend, Joseph Hucks, on a walking-tour to North Wales. Their route lay through Oxford, where they stopped to enable Coleridge to see Robert Allen, who had been a contemporary of his at Christ's Hospital. Allen realised that Southey and Coleridge had a great deal in common, and he lost little time in introducing them to each other. At once, on 12th June, Southey wrote off to Bedford: "Allen is with us daily, and his friend from Cambridge, Coleridge. He is of most uncommon merit—of the strongest genius, the clearest judgment, the best heart. My friend he already is, and must hereafter be yours."[52]

Coleridge was nearly two years older than Southey and, at a superficial glance, very similar to him in character and opinions.[53] He was a Jacobin, an enthusiast, a prolific writer of verse, a rebel, an escapist from a world in which he felt himself a misfit. His youth had been stormy: it had recently been crowned by the fantastic episode of his enlistment as a trooper in the Dragoons under the name Silas Titus Comberbacke—a scrape from which his family had rescued him and for which, after some demur, he had been forgiven by the authorities of Jesus College. But this resemblance was more apparent than real. Even now it could be discerned that Southey's was the stronger will and the shallower mind, and that beneath all his absurd excesses of optimism and despondence there lay a common sense, a native caution, that Coleridge never knew. This was soon to be demonstrated very clearly.

Coleridge stayed at Oxford three weeks.[54] During that time he was constantly in the company of Southey and his friends Seward and Burnett: together they hatched a scheme which gave substance to Southey's dreams of emigration.

There has been some discussion as to who invented the plan: in old age Southey attributed its origin entirely to Coleridge and his friends.[55] The question is of little importance, and it cannot be answered with certainty; but the story is clear enough in outline. For nearly eighteen months, as we have seen, Southey had been thinking of leaving England and starting a new life in some remote part of the world. It was not merely a passing idea: he returned to it again and again, and at the time of his meeting with Coleridge it was prominent in his thoughts. He had certainly been influenced, too, by Godwin's *Political Justice*, published in the previous year (especially by Book VIII, "Of Property"), which he had read and Coleridge had not. From what we know of him it is safe to assume that he quickly communicated the whole project to his new friend; and from what we know of Coleridge, and the fertilising power of his mind, the rest follows. There can be no doubt that it was he who gave the scheme its name—Pantisocracy, translated by Southey as "the equal government of all"—or that its more visionary and romantic features were due to him.

It is impossible to tell how far the plan advanced during Coleridge's visit to Oxford, since no full account of it, written at this early stage, appears to have survived.[56] But its main lines were simple. A party of young men—their number was later limited to twelve—was to found an agricultural community in America; their possessions, the land and its produce, were to be held in common; they were all to be married and to take their wives with them. The original participants were Southey, Coleridge, Burnett, Allen, Seward, and Robert Lovell, a friend Southey had made at Bath in the previous December.

Rapt in visions of Pantisocracy, Coleridge left Oxford with Hucks at the beginning of July. His meeting with Southey was an important turning-point in his life, as he generously acknowledged many years later in the *Biographia Literaria*: "I dwell with unabated pleasure on the strong and sudden, yet I trust not fleeting, influence, which my normal [?moral] being underwent on my acquaintance with him at Oxford, whither I had gone at

the commencement of our Cambridge vacation on a visit to an
old school-fellow. Not indeed on my moral or religious principles,
for *they* had never been contaminated; but in awakening the
sense of the duty and dignity of making my actions accord with
those principles, both in word and deed. The irregularities only
not universal among the young men of my standing, which I
always *knew* to be *wrong*, I then learned to feel as *degrading*; learnt
to know that an opposite conduct, which was at that time considered by us as the easy virtue of cold and selfish prudence, might
originate in the noblest emotions, in views the most disinterested
and imaginative. It is not however from grateful recollections
only, that I have been impelled thus to leave these my deliberate
sentiments on record; but in some sense as a debt of justice to
the man, whose name has been so often connected with mine for
evil to which he is a stranger."[57]

Southey's mind was not so malleable as Coleridge's. The
effects of Coleridge's influence upon it were slower to appear,
less direct, and perhaps less important. Between them there was
never the reciprocal penetration of intellect that there was to be
between Coleridge and Wordsworth: their period of intimacy
was too short, and their minds too differently constituted, for that.
But no one could be long in Coleridge's company without coming
under his spell, whether consciously or not; and Southey, for all
his independence and self-sufficiency, was no exception to this
rule.

The immediate effect of Coleridge's visit and of Pantisocracy
upon him was to unsettle his mind further and to make him still
more dissatisfied with Balliol. It was now the end of the summer
term, and he made up his mind to leave Oxford for ever without
taking a degree. Seward and Lightfoot had already gone down,
Allen was about to do so: the prospect of another two years
without their congenial company was unattractive. He had never
liked the university or benefited much from it. And, in any case,
was he not soon to leave the country for America?

His resolution was a wise one, even if the motives for it seem
to us somewhat inadequate. Eighteenth-century Oxford had
little to offer to a rebel and an individualist so determined as
Southey, except a mild toleration of his extravagances and opportunities to read, write, and make friends, all of which he had
taken. As he received these benefits from the university, it cannot
be said that the time he spent there was wholly thrown away.
But by now it had become evident that it was useless for him to
stay there any longer: the studies of the place repelled him, its

discipline irritated him, and he had no intention of following an academic or clerical career.

He never repented this decision. Indeed, he looked back upon Oxford with dislike ("my college years were the least beneficial and the least happy of my life", he wrote in 1816), and he continued to hold the universities in low estimation ever afterwards. His severest attack on them he put into the mouth of a don showing Espriella round Cambridge, ten years after he went down from Balliol. The university, he says, "is a joyous place for the young, and a convenient place for all of us—but for none is it a happy one". The majority of the undergraduates, most of whom are to become clergymen, are "persons whom we cannot prove to be human beings by any rational characteristic which they possess; but who must be admitted to be so, by a sort of *reductio ad absurdum*, because they cannot possibly be any thing else". The only useful function of Oxford and Cambridge is "that they are the great schools by which established opinions are inculcated and perpetuated. I do not know that men gain much here, yet it is a regular and essential part of our system of education, and they who have not gone through it always feel that their education has been defective. A knowledge of the world, that is to say of our world and of the men in it, is gained here, and that knowledge remains when Greek and geometry are forgotten."

His final summary is disillusioned, with a sting in its tail: "The truth is . . . that the institutions of men grow old like men themselves, and like women, are always the last to perceive their own decay. When universities were the only schools of learning, they were of great and important utility; as soon as there were others, they ceased to be the best, because their forms were prescribed, and they could adopt no improvement till long after it was generally acknowledged. There are other causes of decline.— We educate for only one profession: when colleges were founded that one was the most important; it is now no longer so; they who are destined for the others find it necessary to study elsewhere, and it begins to be perceived that this is not a necessary stage upon the road. This might be remedied. We have professors of every thing, who hold their situations and do nothing. In Edinburgh, the income of the professor depends upon his exertions, and in consequence the reputation of that university is so high, that Englishmen think it necessary to finish their education by passing a year there. They learn shallow metaphysics there, and come back worse than they went, inasmuch as it is better to be empty than flatulent."[58]

IV

COLERIDGE

(1794-1795)

WHILE Coleridge was wandering towards North Wales, Southey returned to Bath on foot, in the company of Burnett. His determination against taking orders was backed up by Coleridge, who wrote from Wrexham in the middle of July suggesting he should, by "a month's application", qualify himself for "the office of clerk in a counting-house". For the moment he postponed consideration of this disagreeable topic. He was fortified by visions of the future in America, where such plans would be superfluous; and besides, he had something more important to think of: on 19th July he took the prospectus of *Joan of Arc* to the printer.[59]

He had begun the poem, as we have seen, a year earlier, and had completed the first draft of it in six weeks. Since then he had revised it, and now he evidently considered it almost or completely finished. His idea was to publish by subscription. No copy of this prospectus, if it was ever issued, appears to have survived; nor do we know if it called forth any response. It was at this time, too, that Southey wrote, in three mornings, a "dramatic poem" that was later to achieve an unexpected and undeserved celebrity: *Wat Tyler*. Robert Lovell took it to Ridgeway, a London publisher, who accepted but took no steps towards printing it; and there for over twenty years the matter rested.[60]

At the beginning of August Coleridge suddenly arrived at Bristol, unannounced. Southey lost no time in introducing him to Lovell and to the Fricker family. Mrs. Fricker was the widow of a small manufacturer who had failed in business, and her daughters used to help to make ends meet by going out to do needlework. Among those for whom they worked was Mrs. Southey, and the Fricker and Southey families quickly became intimate together.[61] It was natural that Robert should now introduce Coleridge to them, for Lovell was by this time married to Mary Fricker, and he was himself moving towards an engagement with her sister Edith; but the introduction took place in an ill moment. Coleridge was emerging from his unhappy love affair with Mary Evans, and in his mood of sentimental grief he

42

found a sympathetic, a too sympathetic, listener in Sara Fricker. The sequel was to be one of the greatest misfortunes of his life.

In the middle of August Southey and Coleridge set off on a walking tour, proposing to visit Burnett at Huntspill, near Bridgwater, and Thomas Poole, a wealthy tanner of strong republican opinions with whom Coleridge was already slightly acquainted, at Nether Stowey. Their first night was an uncomfortable one, graphically described by Southey :

"We reached Cheddar about ten, anticipating the delights of a good supper and comfortable inn. We inquired the best inn, and arrived at a poor pot-house in a little village. ' Can you give us a bed?' 'No: all engaged.' We went to the other house. Mine host was asleep in his chair. ' Can you give us a bed?' He snored ' No ' and turned round again. We agreed to go back to the other inn, get some supper and sleep in the stable. Down we sat, demolished the bread and cheese and cold *à la mode* beef, and petitioned for straw in the stable. They said they would make us up a bed. It was in a garret, the only piece of furniture except another bedstead, on which lay a bed and quilt. . . . Coleridge is a vile bed-fellow, and I slept but ill. In the morning I rose—and lo! we were fastened in! They certainly took us for footpads and had bolted the door on the outside for fear we should rob the house. Cheddar cliffs amply repaid us."[62]

The visit to Poole that followed marked an epoch in Coleridge's life, the beginning of an intimacy only less profitable to him than that with Wordsworth. To Southey it meant much less: Poole and he did not take to one another at first, and they were never close friends afterwards, though they came to feel mutual respect. None the less, their meeting has its importance in his biography, for it provoked Poole to write what is by far the best contemporary account of Pantisocracy that we have, prefaced by illuminating little sketches of the two friends as he saw them.

"Coleridge, whom I consider the Principal in the undertaking, . . . possesses splendid abilities—he is, I understand, a shining scholar. . . . He speaks with much elegance and energy, and with uncommon facility, but he, as it generally happens to men of his class, feels the justice of Providence in the want of those inferior abilities which are necessary to the rational discharge of the common duties of life. His aberrations from prudence, to use his own expression, have been great; but he now promises to be as sober and rational as his most sober friends could wish. In religion he is a Unitarian, if not a Deist; in politics a Democrat, to the utmost extent of the word.

"Southey, who was with him, is of the University of Oxford, a younger man, without the splendid abilities of Coleridge, though possessing much information, particularly metaphysical, and is more violent in his principles than even Coleridge himself. In Religion, shocking to say in a mere Boy as he is, I fear he wavers between Deism and Atheism.

"Thus much for the characters of two of the Emigrators. Their plan is as follows:—

"Twelve gentlemen of good education and liberal principles are to embark with twelve ladies in April next. Previous to their leaving this country they are to have as much intercourse as possible, in order to ascertain each other's dispositions, and firmly to settle every regulation for the government of their future conduct. Their opinion was that they should fix themselves at— I do not recollect the place, but somewhere in a delightful part of the new back settlements; that each man should labour two or three hours a day, the produce of which labour would, they imagine, be more than sufficient to support the colony. As Adam Smith observes that there is not above one productive man in twenty, they argue that if each laboured the twentieth part of time, it would produce enough to satisfy their wants. The produce of their industry is to be laid up in common for the use of all; and a good library of books is to be collected, and their leisure hours to be spent in study, liberal discussions, and the education of their children. . . . The regulations relating to the females strike them as the most difficult; whether the marriage contract shall be dissolved if agreeable to one or both parties, and many other circumstances, are not yet determined. The employments of the women are to be the care of infant children, and other occupations suited to their strength; at the same time the greatest attention is to be paid to the cultivation of their minds. Every one is to enjoy his own religious and political opinions, provided they do not encroach on the rules previously made, which rules, it is unnecessary to add, must in some measure be regulated by the laws of the state which includes the district in which they settle. They calculate that each gentleman providing £125 will be sufficient to carry the scheme into execution. Finally, every individual is at liberty, whenever he pleases, to withdraw from the society.

"These are the outlines of this plan, and such are their ideas. Could they realise them they would, indeed, realise the age of reason; but, however perfectible human nature may be, I fear it is not yet perfect enough to exist long under the regulations of such a system, particularly when the Executors of the plan are taken from a society in a high degree civilised and corrupted. America is certainly a desirable country, so desirable in my eye that, were it not for some insuperable reasons, I would certainly settle there. At some future period I perhaps may. But I think a man would do well first to see the country and his future hopes, before he removes his connections or any large part of his property there. I could live, I think, in America, much to my satisfaction and credit, without joining in such a scheme as I have been describing, though I should like well to accompany them and see what progress they make."[63]

A week after they had started on their walking-tour, they were back at Bristol. By this time Southey was engaged to Edith Fricker, and it is clear that he considered Coleridge as definitely betrothed to her sister, for on 22nd August he writes: "Our females are beautiful, amiable and accomplished, and I shall then [i.e. when Pantisocracy is established in America] call Coleridge my brother in the real sense of the word."[64] The evidence on this point is important, since Southey has often been accused of pushing a reluctant Coleridge into a marriage he had never intended and so of being primarily responsible for one of Coleridge's greatest disasters: as will appear, this is a perversion of the truth.

Coleridge left Bristol for London on 2nd September, taking with him the manuscript of a drama in verse that Southey and he had just written jointly, *The Fall of Robespierre*.[65] (The subject was highly topical, for Robespierre had been executed on 27th July.) It had originally been intended that Coleridge should write the first act, Southey the second, and Lovell the third; but Lovell's production was considered unsuitable, and Southey in the end supplied the third act as well as the second. The play was published at Cambridge later in the same year under Coleridge's name. As we should expect, it has little merit—the whole thing was sketched out in forty-eight hours: it contains some blank-verse lines of delightful bathos, such as:

They took from me my ticket of admission;

but the final speech, by Barère, is tolerable rhetoric.

In London, Coleridge lost no time in pushing forward the cause of Pantisocracy. He expounded it to George Dyer—Lamb's friend, "the gall-less and single-minded"—who "was enraptured" and expressed the opinion that Dr. Priestley, whom he knew, would join in the scheme as soon as he heard of it. Coleridge spent his evenings at the "Salutation and Cat" in Newgate Street, discoursing to a mixed company that included Lamb and some of the senior boys of Christ's Hospital. Among his audience, he reported, was "a most intelligent young man, who has spent the last five years of his life in America and is lately come from thence as an agent to sell land". Not unnaturally, he gave Coleridge a very rosy impression of the country, especially of the region watered by the Susquehanna (the name delighted Coleridge, and the district recommended itself too "from its excessive beauty and its security from hostile Indians"). As to finance, £2000 would be adequate capital, their passage should not cost them more than another £400, and credit in America was easy to come by. "Literary characters make *money* there", adds Coleridge wistfully. "He never saw a *bison* in his life, but has heard of them: they are quite backwards."

After a fortnight of intoxicating mental activity in London, Coleridge went on to Cambridge, whence he immediately wrote to Southey: "My God! How tumultuous are the movements of my heart. . . . America! Southey! Miss Fricker! Yes, Southey, you are right. Even Love is the creature of strong motive. I certainly love her. I *think* of her incessantly with unspeakable tenderness—with that inward melting away of soul that symptomatizes it."

Meanwhile, his activities had been causing some disquiet in Bristol. He appears to have written to Southey only once while he was in London, and not at all to any of the Fricker family. His first letter from Cambridge crossed one from Southey, chiding him for his silence. To this he replied quite temperately the next day, and he seems to have written to Sara at the same time. But still Southey was anxious—and indeed it is hardly surprising, for Coleridge's reply had been evasive and unsatisfactory. He therefore wrote to Samuel Favell, a Grecian at Christ's Hospital who had been of the company at the "Salutation and Cat", asking for news of Coleridge. When this came to Coleridge's ears a week later, he was "beyond measure distressed and agitated", and at once wrote off another, equally vague, reply, ending: "I am in the queerest humour in the world, and am out of love with everybody." This can hardly have been reassuring, but Southey had for the moment to remain content with it: he had probably failed so far to realise the true explanation, for he was not suspicious by nature.

And however worried he might be about Coleridge's conduct,

he had other things to think about and other problems of his own to solve. In collaboration with Lovell, he was preparing to publish a small collection of poems. It appeared in the course of this autumn, a thin volume containing some 21 poems by Southey and 11 by Lovell, published by Cruttwell of Bath, who had issued Bowles's *Fourteen Sonnets*, so greatly admired by Coleridge five years earlier. The most important of Southey's contributions was "The Retrospect". At the end of the book appeared an advertisement of *Joan of Arc*.

During this autumn he also made his first appearance in the London press. Long afterwards he recollected how his mother had come home from Bristol one day in the "long coach" with a stranger who insisted on reading her a poem he had very much admired in the *Morning Chronicle*: from her account Southey was astonished to recognise it as the first of his own "Botany Bay Eclogues". It had been published without his knowledge through the kind offices of Coleridge, to whom he had given a copy. "Perhaps no praise that I ever obtained in after life", he adds, "gave me so much pleasure as this same proof that I had touched upon the right string."[66]

All this time he was busy with the details of Pantisocracy, while Coleridge was airily talking about it in London and Cambridge. On 20th September he wrote an account of it to his brother Tom, now a midshipman in H.M.S. *Aquilon*: the participants were by this time to be Coleridge, Burnett, Robert Allen, a Bristol apothecary named Heath, and most of the members of the Southey, Fricker and Lovell families—about twenty people in all. By the middle of the following month this number had grown to twenty-seven, but though he speaks of the plan as "in great forwardness; nor do I see how it can be frustrated", opposition had begun to show itself and the difficulties were crowding in.

Everything now seemed to turn on the question of money. It was all very well to dismiss it as "a huge evil which we shall not long have to contend with": even so, they must pay for their passage out and for the land on which they intended to settle, and the means for that were still to seek. Linked with this question in Southey's mind was the knowledge that neither Miss Tyler nor his uncle in Portugal had yet heard anything of the project and his uneasy premonition that, when they did, they would strongly disapprove of it—even though Mrs. Southey was to go with them, was indeed, according to her son, as enthusiastic about the idea as he was himself. Pantisocracy was frowned upon also in another quarter, where Southey had looked for sympathy:

Edmund Seward, after at first consenting to join the party, drew back and decided not to go, ostensibly because he did not think it right to leave his mother alone, but really, it is clear, because with his native prudence he had perceived the defects of the scheme. Southey took this very hard—it was natural that he should, for he had a high respect for Seward's opinion: possibly too, his friend's doubts spoke to something uneasy in himself. His immediate reaction to Seward's refusal was strong: "Southey seems to look upon my retraction from the scheme as a dereliction of Christianity itself", Seward reported to their common friend Lightfoot.[67]

In the middle of October the storm burst. Miss Tyler got wind of the plan. "My dear Brother Admiral [Robert writes to Tom], Here's a row! Here's a kick up! Here's a pretty commence! We have had a revolution in the College Green, and I have been turned out of doors in a wet night. . . . I was penniless: it was late in the evening; the wind blew and the rain fell, and I had walked from Bath in the morning. Luckily my father's old great-coat was at Lovell's. I clapped it on, swallowed a glass of brandy, and set off; I met an old drunken man three miles off, and was obliged to drag him all the way to Bath, nine miles! Oh, Patience, Patience, thou hast often helped poor Robert Southey, but never didst thou stand him in more need than on Friday the 17th of October, 1794."

Now it was indeed, as he said, "open war—declared hostilities" between his aunt and himself. She announced that she would never see him again (and here she kept her word) or open a letter from him: the Southeys removed Robert's younger sister and brothers from her house to Bath. Pantisocracy Miss Tyler chose to ascribe to Lovell. What angered her more than the crazy emigration scheme was the news of her nephew's engagement—to the daughter of an unsuccessful manufacturer of sugar-pans. "It rouses all the whole army of prejudices in my aunt's breast. Pride leads the fiery host, and a pretty kick up they must make there."

Southey took it all quite calmly. But he knew that the situation was now serious, and his prospects bleak. He had mortally offended the one relative in England who might have been willing to help him—who had, in addition, been contributing substantially to the maintenance of the rest of his family; he could hope for no favourable reception for his plans from his Uncle Hill; he had not even a small fixed income of his own, and his chances of a good career were poor; his mother, his sister, and his two younger brothers needed his help; he was engaged to Edith Fricker, and could see little prospect of being able to marry her. All this had a sobering effect upon him and upon his attitude to Pantisocracy.

For different reasons, and without fully realising it themselves, both he and Coleridge were now beginning to withdraw from the plan. With Southey it was due to his personal difficulties, which were making him more cautious, to the influence of Seward's adverse opinion, to his incipient doubts of Coleridge's reliability and of his intentions towards Sara Fricker. To one of Southey's temperament, Coleridge's conduct must indeed have been unaccountable and most provoking. On 21st October he began a letter with a long extract from a very forthcoming one, he had just received from Mary Evans, with whom he had formerly been much in love: he confessed that this had greatly moved him, and went on to say that he had sought relief from his thoughts of her in the company of an attractive Miss Brunton, hoping that "her exquisite beauty and uncommon accomplishments might have cured one passion by another. The latter I could easily have dissipated in her absence, and so have restored my affections to her whom I do not love but whom by every tie of reason and honour I ought to love". This was ominous enough—though perhaps it was less plain to Southey than it would have been to most men, for even at this early age he had an unusually high sense of duty: to him it commonly coincided with inclination, and when it did not, duty as a rule prevailed. Judging by his own standard, he may still not have realised quite how far Coleridge was from wishing to marry Sara.

Coleridge's attitude to Southey, meanwhile, was changing. He did not like being put in the wrong (even though he had remarked in September, "I am *delighted* to feel you superior to me in genius as in virtue"), and he accompanied his uneasy statements about himself and his affairs of the heart with a double attack on Southey himself. First, he suggested that Southey was self-righteous and inclined to judge others over-hastily. This was a just criticism, showing characteristically deep penetration: "Southey! Precipitance is wrong. There may be too high a state of health, perhaps even *virtue* is liable to a *plethora*. I have been the slave of impulse, the child of imbecility. But my inconsistencies have given me a tarditude and reluctance to think ill of any one. . . . Your undeviating simplicity of rectitude has made you rapid in decision. Having never erred, you feel more *indignation* at error than *pity* for it. There is *phlogiston* [φλογιστον=

' something inflammable '?] in your heart. Yet am I grateful for it. You would not have written so angrily but for the greatness of your esteem and affection. The more highly we have been wont to think of a character, the more pain and irritation we suffer from the discovery of its imperfections."

He followed this up with a protest against some of Southey's ideas on Pantisocracy. It had been intended from an early stage that Shadrach Weeks, Miss Tyler's manservant, and his wife Sally should join the party. "SHAD GOES WITH US. HE IS MY BROTHER", wrote Coleridge with enthusiasm. But presently it appeared that Southey and his Bristol friends meant the Weeks to accompany them as servants, not as full Pantisocrats. Coleridge instantly protested against the idea of taking with them "these unequal equals, these Helot Egalités": nevertheless, "I will most assuredly go with you to America, but remember, Southey, this is *not our plan*, nor can I defend it." Later on in the same letter he started another objection, of still greater importance. "The hearts of the women are not *all* with us. I do believe that Edith and Sara are exceptions, but do even they know the bill of fare for the day, every duty that will be incumbent upon them?" In November, he came right out into the open. "I wish, Southey, in the stern severity of judgment, that the two mothers were *not* to go, and that the children stayed with them. . . . *That* Mrs. Fricker! We shall have her teaching the infants *Christianity*,—I mean, that mongrel whelp that goes under its name,—teaching them by stealth in some ague fit of superstition."

Early in November he accepted the offer of a Cambridge friend to drive him up to London in his phaeton, intending to stay there only ten days and then to go on and visit Southey at Bath. But once in Newgate Street, surrounded by his old circle of admiring disciples, he found it difficult to tear himself away. In December he did pay a short visit to Bristol, during which he heard of a new alteration in the plan of Pantisocracy. Southey now proposed that, as money was still not forthcoming for the expensive emigration project, the scheme should be tried out first not in America but in Wales. This idea seems to have originated with the sensible Wynn, who, it is hardly necessary to say, had never been a Pantisocrat, but who always kept a kind and wary eye on his friend's doings. To this suggestion Coleridge gave a qualified approval—or was it only the easy assent of one who was no longer really interested in the plan?—and then quickly returned to London, to the delights of Lamb's company in "that nice little smoky room at the ' Salutation ', . . . with all its associated train of pipes, tobacco, egghot, Welsh rarebits, metaphysics and poetry".[68] All this time he continued to think of, and to write to, Mary Evans, until on Christmas Eve he brought himself to recognise that she had finally rejected him and to terminate the correspondence. But he could not refrain from dilating once more to Southey on her virtues with tactless insistence: "My ideal standard of female excellence rises not above that woman. But all things work together for good. Had I been united to her, the excess of my affection would have effeminated my intellect. . . . To lose her! I can rise above that selfish pang! But to marry another. O Southey! bear with my weakness. Love makes all things pure and heavenly like itself—but to marry a woman whom I do not love, to degrade her whom I call my wife by making her the instrument of low desires, and on the removal of a desultory appetite to be perhaps not displeased with her absence! Enough! These refinements are the wildering fires that lead me into vice. Mark you, Southey! *I will do my duty.*"

After such a series of plain statements from his friend, extending over a period of three months, it must at length have become clear to Southey that he was at least reluctant to fulfil his engagement to Sara. Accordingly, early in the New Year, after he had once more announced his intention of coming down and failed to do so, Southey made up his mind to go to London and fetch him back to Bristol himself. He went up about the middle of January and, apparently without any difficulty, persuaded Coleridge to return with him. It was probably on this short visit, which was otherwise uneventful, that Southey first met Lamb.

At Bristol, Coleridge and Burnett shared lodgings together in College Street.[69] By the beginning of February, Southey had moved over from Bath to join them; on the 8th he wrote to Bedford with a characteristic flourish: "Coleridge is writing at the same table; our names are written in the book of destiny, on the same page." Disagreement between the two was for the time being at an end, and the most fruitful period of their collaboration now opened. They were both hard pressed for money, and both casting round for ways of earning some: their ambition did not rise above a joint income of £100-£150 a year, on which they proposed to marry and settle in the country, writing and practising agriculture until they were able to go to America. For a start, they thought of taking jobs on the *Telegraph* and of producing a "Provincial Magazine" for the publication of their own and their friends' verses, but neither of these plans matured. They found help in another quarter, by other means.

Southey had recently become acquainted, through Lovell, with Joseph Cottle, a rising young Bristol bookseller, and he now hastened to introduce Coleridge to him. Cottle has been much derided as a vain little provincial, with a foolish desire to climb to fame on other men's backs; and it is true that his memoirs, which should from their material have been among the most interesting in the language, are disappointing and unsatisfactory, for his recollections were muddled and his notions of editorial method quite shocking. But none the less he was a really kind and warm-hearted man, and he rendered a most essential service to Southey and Coleridge at this important stage in their careers. He behaved to them with a generosity exceeding anything for which he could expect a return, and it fully entitles him to the comfortable reflection of his old age that it was "a gratifying circumstance to me to have been the publisher of the first volumes of three such poets as Southey, Coleridge and Wordsworth; such a distinction might never again occur to a provincial bookseller". It certainly never has.

Southey's personality appealed to Cottle instantly. "Tall, dignified, possessing great suavity of manners; an eye piercing, with a countenance full of genius, kindliness, and intelligence"—that was how he remembered the young poet many years after; and the sketch agrees with the impression we get from Hancock's drawing of Southey, made for Cottle in 1796 and now in the National Portrait Gallery. It shows him in profile, the hair hanging loose almost down to his shoulders, the nose curved and prominent, the eye looking upward in that "aspiring" manner later noted by De Quincey and caught, with his unerring insight, by Lawrence in his portrait of 1828. It is clear that he struck both Cottle and Hancock as at once proud, distinguished, and agreeable.

Cottle quickly made the two friends a definite proposal: he would pay each of them thirty guineas for the copyright of a volume of poems—a generous sum, for the highest bid that Coleridge had been able to get from a London publisher had been six. But this was not all. One evening Southey read to him some of *Joan of Arc*, which still lay in manuscript without prospect of publication. Cottle offered to give him fifty guineas for the poem and fifty free copies, which he could sell at his own profit to those who had already subscribed for it. Moreover—and this must have tempted any young author, above all Southey—the poem should appear in quarto, printed in new type specially obtained for the purpose, on hot-pressed paper; it should be "the handsomest book that Bristol had ever yet sent forth".[70] The bargain was struck at once.

At the same time Southey and Coleridge, again with Cottle's help, found another source of income: they started to give lectures in Bristol. Coleridge began at the "Plume of Feathers" in Wine Street with a series of three diatribes against the repressive measures of the Pitt government, two of which were published later on in the same year as *Conciones ad Populum*. He followed them up with more lectures, at the Assembly Coffee-House in Prince's Street, on political and theological subjects. Of Southey's lectures we learn details from the prospectus of one series of them which has been preserved.[71] There were to be twelve in all, given at seven in the evening on dates between 14th March and 21st April: the price of admission was one shilling for each lecture, or half a guinea for the whole course, and tickets were to be had at Cottle's bookshop. Southey proved a competent and attractive lecturer, but, as we should expect, far less brilliant than Coleridge. One critic remarked that "his gesticulation and attitude when he is speaking in public is not the most pleasing, his body is always too stiff, his features are apt to be distorted":[72] on the other hand, the loyal Cottle records that his lectures "evinced great self-possession in the lecturer [and] a peculiar grace in the delivery", and that they were greatly admired by "a polite and discriminating audience".

In one respect Southey was undeniably superior to Coleridge: he did deliver the lectures he had promised. Years later, when he was giving his famous lectures in London, Coleridge would sometimes fail to turn up altogether, and the audience would have to disperse unsatisfied. This was ascribed, like so much else, to opium. But even now, when he was not a drug-addict, he did the same thing. On one occasion it precipitated a fierce quarrel with Southey—which had, indeed, been brewing for some time. He had asked permission to deliver a lecture on "the Rise, Progress and Decline of the Roman Empire", which was set down in Southey's course for 3rd March, on the ground that it was a subject he had studied with particular care: perhaps with some misgiving, Southey had agreed. At the appointed time, Coleridge did not appear: there was no lecture that evening.

The next day, as it happened, had been fixed for a little excursion to Chepstow and Tintern arranged by Cottle for his two friends and their *fiancées*. All went well at the start: they crossed by the Severn ferry, made their way to Chepstow, visited the castle and retired to dine at the Beaufort Arms. But after dinner, Southey—whose "regular habits", as Cottle truly remarks, "scarcely rendered it a virtue in him never to fail in an engagement"—took it upon himself to rebuke Coleridge for his delinquency the previous evening. A heated argument ensued, in which the women presently joined, each on the side of her lover, and Cottle had considerable difficulty in quelling the storm. However, he did succeed eventually in patching things up, and they all set off for Tintern. The quarrel had wasted a great deal of time: night came down before they had reached their destination, and they lost their road. They must have made a quaint procession, and Cottle's account of their wanderings is exceedingly funny. They had one horse between them, which after a time Coleridge insisted on riding (was he not an ex-dragoon?): "Mr. Southey marched on like a pillar of strength, with a lady pressing on each arm, while the relator lagged in the rear, without even a pilgrim's staff to sustain his tottering steps." At length, after they had floundered about in a wood, and Coleridge, on the horse, had been sent out scouting in several directions, they stumbled upon the road to Tintern, where they slept, returning to Bristol next day.

This had not been a mere passing squabble. Southey and Coleridge were in truth too deeply antipathetic to live together in harmony for long. Southey complained that his earnings were four times Coleridge's and that he contributed much more than his share to the upkeep of their joint establishment, when Coleridge was perfectly capable, if he had not been so idle and unmethodical, of making as much money as he. We now know enough of Coleridge and his ways of working to realise that he was certainly not lazy: his lectures, his letters, the Gutch notebook, and the numerous miscellaneous works he produced, or half-produced, at this time are clear enough evidence of that. Yet Southey's mistake was a very natural one, for he knew his friend's powers and he saw him sponging on Cottle and on himself. Coleridge later summarised the situation perfectly in one sentence: "The truth is, you sat down and wrote; I used to saunter about and think what I should write."

But this was not the only trouble. Each of them was uneasy in his own mind about Pantisocracy, each steadily receding from his first enthusiasm, and each unwilling to be the first to admit it, either to himself or to the other. At a "strawberry party" at Long Ashton, which may reasonably be placed in June, Southey proposed to Burnett that community of property should be abandoned

⌣ ⸃pt for a single jointly-owned farm of five or six acres. Coleridge, as well as Burnett, was righteously indignant: "in short", was his scornful comment, "we were to commence partners in a petty farming trade". Southey followed this up by proposing to go out and earn money for fourteen years, only then returning to join in Pantisocracy.

Still this was not the worst. Some time in the spring, Southey received a letter from his uncle, written from Lisbon on 24th January, mild and kindly in tone, suggesting that he should pay a short visit to Portugal until a reconciliation could be effected with Miss Tyler.[73] In August, Mr. Hill followed his letter in person: he did what he could to answer his nephew's scruples about taking Holy Orders and repeated his invitation to Lisbon. At about the same time, Wynn offered Southey an annuity of £160, to begin as soon as he came of age in October, 1796. (This was really generous of him, for he was a younger son and not at all rich by his own standards.) Very sensibly, Southey made up his mind to accept both these offers—though he refused to take Orders and proposed to study law instead. Very humanly, he attempted to justify this decision and to show that it was not inconsistent with his previous conduct. Very humanly again, Coleridge found the temptation to rebuke one who had so often rebuked him too strong to resist: he indulged it to the full.

Other causes also contributed to make a breach inevitable. Lovell, for instance, did not pretend to approve of Coleridge as a husband for his sister-in-law. It seems likely, though there is no direct evidence for this, that Southey's temper shortened and his sympathies narrowed as a result of anxiety and grief—anxiety about his own uncertain future, grief for the death of Edmund Seward, which occurred on 10th June. This was a deep sorrow, which he never forgot, and he continued to refer to it for many years after.[74]

The final break with Coleridge was slow to come: the joint *ménage* does not seem to have been dissolved until the end of August, when Coleridge began to rent a cottage at Clevedon in preparation for his marriage, to which he once more looked forward with pleasure, and Southey returned to his mother's house at Bath.[75] In spite of the irritation they continually felt with one another, their seven months' residence in College Street had been profitable to both of them. Both had got through a great quantity of miscellaneous reading, the stuff of future works.[76] Coleridge had made for himself a considerable reputation in Bristol. Southey had undoubtedly benefited from his friend's liberal—at times officiously liberal—strictures on his poetry: he claims, with some exaggeration, that Coleridge benefited to the same degree from his own criticism. He advanced in other ways, too. "Last night in returning from Bristol (on foot)", he writes to Bedford on 1st October, "I for the first time saw the whole process of the moon rising, and very lovely it was. An accurate observation of the appearances of nature has improved me much in description."[77] It is easy to see who had been his tutor there. During this period he revised a great deal of *Joan of Arc* for publication, incorporating in it 255 lines contributed by Coleridge, and wrote, or revised, the first book of a new epic, *Madoc*, besides producing a number of minor poems.[78]

It was at this time, probably in September, that he first met Wordsworth, who was staying with the Pinneys at Bristol on his way to Racedown. "His manners pleased me exceedingly", Wordsworth wrote to his friend Mathews, "and I have every reason to think very highly of his powers of mind. . . . I recollect your mentioning you had met Southey and thought him a coxcomb. This surprises me much, as I never saw a young man who seemed to me to have less of that character." But by the following March he had come to agree with Mathews.[79]

On 4th October Coleridge was married to Sara at St. Mary Redcliffe. They at once moved out to Clevedon for their honeymoon. In the later stages of his engagement he seemed to have recovered all his early love for her, now expressed in the "Lines Written at Shurton Bars" and "The Eolian Harp". Looking back, wise after the event, we know that the match proved a disaster. But could that reasonably have been predicted then? Ought Southey to have foreseen it, and to have done what he could to break the engagement? Surely this would have demanded an insight into character and a maturity of judgment that few men could be expected to possess at the age of twenty. It is unfortunately true that an understanding of character was never among Southey's more conspicuous gifts, though he was not wholly impercipient or without shrewdness in this respect. But he is not to be blamed for that: it is a gift that many greater men have lacked. His assumption throughout was, as usual, straightforward: Coleridge had quite voluntarily, without pressure from any one, proposed marriage to Sara Fricker; he was a perfectly rational human being—and it should not be forgotten that he was nearly two years older than Southey; he had taken no steps to break off the engagement himself; therefore, both in his interests and in Sara's, the marriage should go forward. It is too much to expect that Southey, at his age and with all his own pre-occupations at the time, should have understood the devious ways of Coleridge's most remarkable mind, that he should have realised the full significance of Coleridge's "queerest humour in the world", of his regretful backward glances at Mary Evans and his flirtation with Miss Brunton, of his references to "her whom I do not love, but whom by every tie of reason and honour I ought to love". Southey's real error lay in making Coleridge in his own image, in crediting him with a rigid sense of duty and a decision of judgment equal to his own: and who will condemn him for that?

He now divided his time unequally between Bristol and Bath, passing five days or more in the week with the hospitable Cottle, so as to be able to see as much as possible of Edith. "I bear a good face, and keep all uneasiness to myself", he reported to Bedford: "indeed, the port is in view, and I must not mind a little sickness on the voyage." That voyage must still have appeared a long one to him; for he had now made up his mind to go to Portugal with his uncle. "I would have refused," he says, "but I was weary of incessantly refusing all my mother's wishes, and it is only one mode of wearing out a period that must be unpleasant to me anywhere." Fortunately, during all this difficult summer and autumn, he had *Joan of Arc* to occupy his mind: most of the poem was altered at the proof stage, and now at the end he had still the preface to write. The date of publication was fixed for 1st December, a week or two after he expected to leave England.

He and Coleridge saw little of one another now, though Coleridge was in and out of Bristol a good deal: their relations were strained to breaking-point—one day they went so far as to cut each other in the street. Some time in October, Coleridge wrote to Southey advising him strongly against acquiescing in his uncle's wishes and taking Holy Orders: the advice was superfluous, for Southey's mind had long been made up and never changed, as his correspondence shows. This was followed, on 13th November, by an immense letter—it is over 5000 words long—in which he attacked his friend's conduct from every side, pouring out his long pent-up fury and his resentment at Southey's self-righteous criticism. It must have given him intense pleasure to write "You are *lost* to *me*, because you are lost to Virtue", and, still more, to fire off this parting shot: "May God Almighty bless and preserve you! and may you live to know and feel and acknow-ledge that unless we accustom ourselves to meditate admiringly

on Him, the source of all virtue, no virtue can be permanent."
Southey at his worst was never more self-righteous than that. It
was the end of Pantisocracy.

On the day after this letter was written, Saturday, 14th
November, Southey and Edith Fricker were married secretly. The
wedding took place "with the utmost privacy" at St. Mary
Redcliffe, witnessed by Cottle and one of his sisters. At the church
door the husband and wife parted, to meet again for a final leave-
taking the day after. While he was away, she was to live with the
Cottles, wearing her wedding-ring around her neck and keeping
her maiden name until the news of the marriage leaked out.

The reason for this step were clearly stated by Southey when
he reported the news to Bedford: "Why did I marry, do you ask?
It is, Grosvenor, a satisfaction to myself. If the tongue of malice
should whisper that I have forsaken her (and calumny has been
busy with me), there is now an answer that will make it dumb.
And what is more of consequence, if I should not return alive she
has a claim upon the protection of those I am now satisfying [by
going to Portugal] for the ' bitter little that would then be left
of life '. . . . She still keeps her own name, for it may not be
convenient for us to live together immediately upon my return."[80]
To Cottle he added a third reason: if he had not married her,
"there might have arisen feelings of an unpleasant nature at the
idea of receiving support from one not legally a husband". It
was a characteristic arrangement: odd though it may now appear,
it was probably the best that could be made at the time.

The following Thursday he and his uncle set off in the coach
for Falmouth. They stayed for some days, while waiting for the
packet, at Nanswhyden near St. Columb in Cornwall, a magnificent Georgian house belonging to a Christ Church contemporary
of Mr. Hill's, the Rev. Robert Hoblyn. Hence, while the two
clergymen were "uttering aristocracy", Southey wrote to Bedford
on Sunday, "for two reasons, one to escape church, the other
because to write to a dear friend is to me like escaping from
prison".[81] By the time they reached Falmouth he learnt, with
small concern, that the news of his marriage was already known
in Bristol. At last, after further delays, on 8th December the
packet sailed.

V

PORTUGAL AND THE LAW

(*1795-1800*)

SOUTHEY HAD no very clear objective in his mind when he set out. His main reasons for going with his uncle were those he had stated: to please his relations and to pass the time until, with the help of Wynn's annuity, he could afford to set up house with his wife. A further motive was provided by the invaluable Cottle, who had asked him to write a book describing his travels, undertaking to publish it, as usual on generous terms. But he felt at first little enthusiasm for the journey, and when after five days he saw the cliffs of Spain, the uppermost feeling in his mind was merely one of relief that the end of a stormy and unpleasant voyage was in sight. At five in the afternoon of 13th December he landed at Corunna.[82]

The first things to strike him, typical Englishman that he was, were the smells, the filth, the fleas, and the disagreeable cooking— "Oh, their foul oils and wines!" But he was quickly cheered by striking up an acquaintance with Major Alexander Jardine, the British consul, an interesting man who had published some *Letters from Barbary, France, Spain and Portugal*, which Southey had read. The day after he arrived, they took a walk together "among the rude scenery of Galicia—little green lanes, between stony banks, and wild and rocky mountains; and, although I saw neither meadows, or hedges, or trees, I was too much occupied with the new and the sublime, to regret the beautiful". From the highest of these hills they had a splendid view out over Ferrol and Cap Ortegal to the Bay of Biscay beyond.

On the 17th, after satisfying the Spanish customs officials and military authorities, he set out for Madrid in a coach and six with his uncle and one or two fellow-travellers. Although they started before dawn each day and travelled till after it was dark, their journey was very slow: they took eighteen days and a half to cover the 400 miles. The inns were wretched beyond description, but the people proved civil and hospitable.

They arrived at Madrid to find the King and Queen about to leave for Badajoz, where they were to meet the King and Queen

59

of Portugal. This was bad news, for it meant that they would have to travel in the wake of the court, which in eighteenth-century Spain still exercised the rights of purveyance and embargo. On the whole, Madrid made an unfavourable impression upon Southey. He found it very expensive, and he disliked the extremes of its climate: on the other hand, the absence of suburbs was pleasant, the city was reasonably clean, and its best streets were, he admitted, very fine. At this moment, the inhabitants were afraid that the court might be going to move elsewhere permanently, for "they dislike that place, and the Queen (a woman very ugly, very abandoned, and very unpopular) has seldom entered it since some seditious washerwomen insulted her two years ago. ' You amuse yourself with your *cortejos* and dress yourself in your jewels, while we are in want of bread ', cried the old girls; and they are now in perpetual confinement."

On 12th January they set off again, ten days behind the court, taking with them a stock of provisions so that they should not starve by the way. This proved to have been an unnecessary precaution, as they were able to get game with ease on their journey; but they continually heard piteous complaints of the royal exactions, of how "His Majesty and his retinue have burnt the trees, cut up the roads, dirted the linen and devoured the provision." At Badajoz, on the frontier, they saw the encampments of the two sovereigns: they did not stop to gaze, but made their way straight on into Portugal. The end of their journey was dramatic: "We were fifteen days on the road to Lisbon, where I arrived after crossing the Tagus at night in a high wind —to the disappointment of finding no packet had arrived from England since we left it, and to be awakened at five the next morning by an earthquake, the severest that has been felt since the great one [of 1755]. The people are very much alarmed: it is the seventh shock since the beginning of November."

Southey remained at Lisbon for three months and a half. He did not like the place at first. It was once again the filth that appalled him. "An English pigsty is cleaner than the metropolis of Portugal." "Every kind of vermin that exists to punish the nastiness and indolence of men multiplies in the heat and dirt of Lisbon." "All my friends expect some account of Portugal; but it is not pleasant to reiterate terms of abuse, and continually to present to my own mind objects of filth and deformity." A terse sentence appears at the head of a letter written on 24th February: "Lisbon, from which God grant me a speedy deliverance."

Not only was the city squalid. The government of the country appeared to him contemptible, and the morals of its ruling class to the last degree abandoned. Above all, he learnt from what he saw in the Peninsula to despise and hate the Roman Catholic church: this was, indeed, one of the most important effects the journey had upon him. Before he left England, he had displayed no very strong feelings on the subject—he may even, like many other young Englishmen, have found Catholicism a little romantic. Now, after seeing it at close quarters, he was permanently cured of any such tendency: he swung over to an extreme position on the other side, to which he held with perfect consistency ever afterwards. Monasteries, processions, superstitions, images—he poured scorn on all of them alike, making a single partial exception in favour of the convent of Arrabida, which he visited in March. In that place, set very high among cypresses and olives, looking down over the Atlantic, his feelings softened towards monastic life: "You will forgive me", he said, "if for a moment I almost wished to be a hermit".[83]

He made one other excursion from Lisbon: early in April, with his uncle and a friend, he rode up to Cintra, which captivated him at once and for ever. His first description of it is a little stilted and literary, but it shows clearly enough how deeply he was fascinated: "I cannot without a tedious minuteness describe the ever-varying prospects that the many eminences of this wild rock present, or the little green lanes over whose bordering lemon gardens the evening wind blows so cool, so rich! ... I shall always love to think of the lonely house, and the stream that runs beside it, whose murmurs were the last sounds I heard at night, and the first that awoke my attention in the morning". He was to return to Cintra again, and to think and dream of it often for the rest of his life.

Otherwise his stay in Lisbon was uneventful. "I read very hard and spend every evening in company", he reports in the middle of February, and those seem to have been his main occupations during the whole of his visit. The *Letters* bear witness to the extent of his reading, in Spanish as well as in Portuguese. By the time he went home he read both languages well and spoke Portuguese fluently, if with no great accuracy or elegance. Snatches of news, meanwhile, reached him from England, of Coleridge's tour in the Midlands to get subscribers for *The Watchman*, a rumour of the success of *Joan of Arc*: it is easy to see that his mind was never long away from home. He managed to get on quite well with his uncle, though he complained

privately to Bedford that he was still being urged to take Orders
and that he was pressed to give up Miss Fricker (it does not seem
to have been known at Lisbon that he was already married, though
his mother was certainly aware of it).[84] Mr. Hill was indeed a
wise and tolerant man, and he showed great tact and skill in
handling his difficult nephew, whose character at this time he
estimated shrewdly: "He is a very good scholar, of great reading,
of an astonishing memory: when he speaks he does it with
fluency, with a great choice of words. He is perfectly correct in
his behaviour, of the most exemplary morals, and the best of
hearts. Were his character different, or his abilities not so extraordinary, I should be the less concerned about him; but to see a
young man of such talents as he possesses, by the misapplication
of them lost to himself and to his family, is what hurts me very
sensibly. In short, he has everything you would wish a young
man to have, excepting common sense or prudence". Apart from
the last sentence, this is a very just analysis; and even there,
though it was never really true at any time that he lacked a
fundamental discretion, it had been so much overlaid that his
uncle may be forgiven for failing to perceive it.

But it was already beginning to emerge more clearly into the
open. The events of the past year—his intimacy and quarrel with
Coleridge, his strong reaction from what he thought Coleridge's
fecklessness, his marriage and the responsibilities it had brought
—had combined to make a breach with his old impulsive, somewhat irresponsible, attitude to life inevitable. He understood this
himself, for in a letter written less than a fortnight after his
return to England he remarked: "How does time mellow down
our opinions! Little of that ardent enthusiasm which so lately
fevered my whole character remains".

A similar alteration had begun to take place in his political
views. It would be truer to say that they developed than that
they changed: there was no catastrophic revolution in them,
nothing that was inconsistent with what had just gone before.
The Terror and the execution of the Girondins, with whom he
had sympathised, had shown him that revolutionaries could
commit crimes as great as the aristocrats': now, his first trip
abroad had brought home to him the merits of his own country.
"Of what advantage has this journey been to me?" he wrote to
Wynn. "Why, I have learnt to thank God that I am an Englishman: for though things are not quite so well there as in El
Dorado, they are better than anywhere else." He continued to
regard Pitt and his government with abhorrence; but he had

taken the first steps along a road that, in the course of the next six years, led him quietly and naturally into complete sympathy with England and the Tory point of view.

On 5th May he left Lisbon. He arrived at Portsmouth nine days later, and went straight on to Bristol. The joy of his return was somewhat offset by the news, which met him, that his brother-in-law Robert Lovell had died at the beginning of the month. This distressed him more on the Frickers' account than his own, for he confided to Wynn that Lovell had "much sunk in my esteem". He at once undertook to edit a collection of Lovell's best poems, to be sold on behalf of his widow: a characteristic action, the first of several such gestures he was to make in later life.[85]

In every other respect his homecoming was pleasant. He was able to live with his wife, even though it was only in lodgings at first, and he could now enjoy the success of *Joan of Arc* and the modest degree of fame it had brought him. On the whole, it had been very favourably received, not only in Bristol, where the author was already known, but in London also. There was a laudatory notice by Dr. Aikin in the *Analytical Review*, another in the *Critical* and a third in the *Monthly*; but this was to be expected, for, as Professor Haller has pointed out, all these magazines were Foxite or revolutionary, and so in sympathy with the politics of the poem. Still, Southey had no complaint to make of its reception by his opponents. "The aristocracy have behaved with liberality to *Joan of Arc*; and if they will favour me by forgetting that I have ever meddled too much with public concerns, I will take care not to awaken their memories."

In North Wales, too, and in Lichfield, it found enthusiastic readers: it so pleased the Ladies of Llangollen that they presented a copy to Miss Seward, who sang its praises in her accustomed manner. She thought that its "poetic beauties are so numberless, so intrinsic, that its poetic defects, however conspicuous, are as dust in the balance. Its author is a born poet and of the very highest class". At the same time she noted the "disgusting arrogance of his well-written preface", and the political tone of the poem, it need hardly be said, found no favour in Lichfield Close: it was dreadful to discover that "the work seeks to brand, with deepest stains of injustice and cruelty, the memory of our gallant Henry V and turn to deadliest Aconite the laurels of Agincourt!".[86]

The preface also offended a greater critic than Anna Seward. Wordsworth found it "a very conceited performance" and thought that "the poem, though in some passages of first-rate excellence, is on the whole of very inferior execution". On the other hand, Lamb was delighted with it. "I had not presumed to expect anything of such excellence from Southey", he wrote to Coleridge "Why, the poem is alone sufficient to redeem the character of the age we live in from the imputation of degenerating in poetry. . . . On the whole, I expect Southey one day to rival Milton. I already deem him equal to Cowper, and superior to all living poets besides."[87]

With most of its earliest readers *Joan of Arc* was an undoubted success; and though it is not a good, still less a great, poem, it is easy to see why. It made a strong appeal to the romantic taste, by its freshness and originality as well as by its political sentiments: it was something new, and that was welcome to a public that had had enough of the tedious works of Dr. Darwin and the affectations of the Della Cruscans. The epic, too, was almost as unfamiliar to that generation as it is to ours: more than half a century had gone by since the appearance of Glover's *Leonidas*, the last successful poem in that form.

Meanwhile, Southey was hard at work on the volume of travels that he had undertaken to write before he left England. He was able to support himself and Edith at this time, a good deal earlier than he had hoped, chiefly on advances made to him by Cottle in respect of this work.[88] He also produced a number of short poems, of which the most important was a "Hymn to the Penates", and in the summer he began to write for the *Monthly Magazine*, at the not very generous rate of five guineas a sheet of sixteen pages. One of his fellow contributors was William Taylor of Norwich, whose translations of "Lenore" and another ballad by Bürger appeared in the July number and greatly interested him—while in Edinburgh they stimulated the young advocate Walter Scott to make better versions of his own.

A list of Southey's projected works, drawn up for Bedford at this time, includes *Madoc*, which was often in his thoughts but was not resumed seriously until the next year, "my Oriental poem of the Destruction of the Dom Daniel" (the ancestor of *Thalaba*), "my novel, in three volumes, of Edmund Oliver", and a tragedy entitled "The Banditti". This last he mentions several times: he hoped to get it produced, and by that means to earn enough to furnish a house for himself. It does not seem to have been completed, and we cannot much lament the loss, for his genius was in no sense dramatic.

Early in the autumn came an imperfect reconciliation with

Coleridge. The first move seems to have been made by Southey, who sent him a note containing a quotation from Schiller: "Fiesco! Fiesco! thou leavest a void in my bosom, which the human race, thrice told, will never fill up." At this Coleridge relented, and they went off for a walk together in the country, afterwards calling upon Cottle. But the breach between them was incompletely healed, for on the last day of the year Coleridge could write: "The *enthusiasm* of friendship is not with S. and me. We quarrelled and the quarrel lasted for a twelve-month. We are now reconciled; but the cause of the difference was solemn, and blasted oak puts not forth its buds anew! We are *acquaintances*, and feel kindliness towards each other, but I do not *esteem* or *love* Southey . . . and vice versa Southey and me."[89]

The time was now coming for Southey to leave Bristol, in order to begin his legal studies in London. He looked forward to the prospect with distaste; but there seemed no help for it, and he accepted the necessity without grumbling. He put the last touches to the *Letters Written during a Short Residence in Spain and Portugal* on 2nd January; in the course of the same month he received the first instalment of Wynn's annuity; on 7th February he was admitted a member of Gray's Inn.[90]

Soon afterwards his wife joined him in London, and he began to settle down to the law in earnest, keeping *Madoc*, on which he had resumed work, for the evenings. But he managed to get through a good deal of miscellaneous writing besides: he was still a contributor to the *Monthly Magazine*, he published some short poems in the *Telegraph* and the *Oracle* (among them his ballad "Mary the Maid of the Inn"), and in March he accepted a commission from Cadell the publisher to translate part of Necker's new work *De La Révolution françoise*. This was finished by the end of April.

His *Letters* and his new volume of poems had now been published. Both were successful. Of the poems Cottle printed only 500 copies, and the whole of this number had been sold by July. A new edition of 1000 came out in the early autumn, and by Christmas three-quarters of that had gone too.[91] The *Letters* also proved popular, and were out of print by November: a second edition appeared in 1799, and a third in 1808. Miss Tyler's comment on them was characteristic: "My aunt told Peggy [his cousin Margaret Hill] it was pretty well in me to write a book about Portugal who had not been there six months: for her part, she had been there twelve months, and yet she could not write a book about it."

S.   E

The life of the young couple was not entirely taken up with literature and with each other: they found time to see their friends as well. Before long they were on dining terms with Godwin and Mary Wollstonecraft (who were married at the end of this March). Southey did not care much for him, and he had outgrown his first enthusiasm for his works; but he was captivated by Mary's charm. Before they had ever met he had dedicated a poem to her, and now he found her "of all the literary characters the one I most admire. . . . She is a first-rate woman, sensible of her own worth, but without arrogance or affectation". Many years later he told Caroline Bowles that "she was a delightful woman, and in better times or in better hands would have been an excellent one. But her lot had fallen in evil days, and the men to whom she attached herself were utterly unworthy of her".[92] At the Godwins' he was also introduced to Gilbert Wakefield the revolutionary scholar, who had "a most critic-like voice, as if he had snarled himself hoarse": they were to meet once again, in different circumstances.

The pleasures of literary society were never rated very highly by Southey; he disliked London just as much now as when he first saw it nine years earlier; his wife was unwell. And so in April he decided to try and find a cottage by the sea where they could spend the summer, during which he was required to dine only once at Gray's Inn. The following month he and Edith set out on this quest, going first to Southampton, which made a very unfavourable impression upon him: "Its inhabitants are people connected with shipping, and sharking shopkeepers," he reported to Bedford, "its visitors the very top scum of aristocracy, the carrion that these vultures feed upon".[93] They then moved on westward through the New Forest, but the coast was still "infected by visitors" until they reached the neighbourhood of Christchurch. Here, at the village of Burton, suitable lodgings were found in the middle of June.

They were now happy and at ease once more. They liked Burton: the country round afforded "fine fishing, fine swimming, pleasant walks, and excellent prospects"; it was watered by "a congregation of rivers, the clearest you ever saw"; best of all, there was the sea. Soon after he had left, he sketched it in some pleasant verses that show again how much, under the influence of Coleridge, his powers of description had developed:

> . . . The scenes of simplest character,
> The hill that from the water'd vale abrupt

Starts up, upon whose dark and heathy side
Often at evening I have laid me down,
And dwelt upon the green and goodly vale,
Its mazy streams and tufted villages,
Rich in the sunshine now, now half embrown'd
By the long sweeping shadows, till my soul
Had entered in the deep and quiet joy
All its hush'd powers. . . .

       . . . Nor have I left
The unfrequented field unsorrowing,
Over whose wooded limits the church tower
Arose in single majesty: its bank
Was edged with feathery fern, that seem'd to form
A little forest to the insect tribes
Who lived there, and were happy; and the sun
O'er the red ripeness of the bending grass
Pour'd a glad smile. . . .[94]

At Christchurch too he struck up a new friendship, with John Rickman—"a sensible young man, of rough but mild manners, and very seditious", so he described him to Cottle. He was three years older than Southey and had come down from Lincoln College, Oxford, in 1792, since when he had been living at home. He and Southey were to find much in common, above all in politics: at that time they were both strong opponents of Pitt—"this sorry drunkard", as Rickman called him in 1800—but in later years they both developed into equally strong Tories, and for similar reasons. Rickman soon afterwards settled down to a life in the public service: he was wholly or partly responsible for the direction of the first five censuses of Great Britain (1801-1841) and became an eminent statistician. Besides Southey, he numbered among his friends Telford the engineer and, perhaps more surprising, Charles Lamb, whom he first met in 1800. His exterior was formal and rather pompous; but behind it lay an interesting mind and a good heart.[95]

All this summer Southey was busy revising *Joan of Arc* for a new edition, in which the principal changes were that he omitted the whole of Book IX, which appeared separately as "The Vision of the Maid of Orleans", and all the lines contributed by Coleridge. He was also working at *Madoc*, and in the course of this year he reached to the end of the fourth book. Of the law we hear less.

Early in July they had a short visit from Cottle, who brought with him a copy of the new volume of poems by Coleridge, Lamb, and Charles Lloyd that he had just published, on which Southey's comment was enthusiastic: "I know no volume that can be compared to it." He also came for the special purpose of consulting Southey about a projected edition of the works of Chatterton, for the benefit of the poet's sister and niece, who were said to be destitute. They carried the work through jointly, Cottle undertaking most of the editorial part and Southey contributing advice and a preface. The edition appeared at the beginning of 1803. It has no critical value, and has been described by Chatterton's modern biographer as "too patently an object of charity rather than of intelligent respect". Still, the gesture showed characteristic generosity and good feeling on the part of the two editors.[96]

Towards the end of July there came a letter from Coleridge, now settled at Nether Stowey, friendly and even affectionate in tone and containing the beautiful poem "This Lime-Tree Bower my Prison". He mentioned that he had had a visit from Lamb, pressed the Southeys to come and stay with him, and conveyed an offer to them from Wordsworth of a part of the great house at Alfoxden into which he and Dorothy had just moved from Racedown. Nothing came of this suggestion, but it shows that Wordsworth's dislike of the preface to *Joan of Arc* did not prevent him from wishing to be better acquainted with Southey: on the contrary, Coleridge now reported that he was "very solicitous to know" him.

On 14th-15th August they had a sudden fleeting visit from Lamb, who came down from London with Lloyd. He himself could stay only one night, but he left his companion at Burton. Lloyd, who was the son of a Birmingham banker and had been a devoted disciple of Coleridge, was at this time greatly wrought up over a love-affair with an heiress, Sophia Pemberton, whom he wished to carry off and marry at Gretna Green. A few days afterwards he set off for Birmingham with this intention, and Southey went with him, no doubt as a restraining influence. Lloyd did not fulfil his threat of abducting Miss Pemberton: they were married in the ordinary way in 1799. Many years later, this episode, enlivened and distorted with the passage of time, was to provide material for a piquant passage in De Quincey's *Literary Reminiscences*.[97]

Three weeks after his return from the Birmingham expedition, Southey left Burton for Bath, taking his family and Lloyd with him. Lloyd and Southey were now on very friendly terms. Both of them had formerly been fervent admirers of Coleridge, and both were now disillusioned: no doubt they exchanged stories about him, and it may have been from Southey that Lloyd got some of the material for the unattractive portrait of Coleridge that he drew in a novel he was writing at this time. It is at all events certain that its title was wholly of Southey's invention, for it was none other than *Edmund Oliver*, which had figured in his own list of projected works in July, 1796.

Echoes of his quarrel with Coleridge were still to be heard. "I never did and I never shall make Coleridge a single enemy", he wrote in September. "I never attacked his character, but I have defended my own, though seldom, and never of my own accord." Their relationship at this time remained cool, but it was no longer hostile. They praised one another's works quite sincerely, and it is evident that Southey was permitted to see not only *Osorio* but also Wordsworth's *Borderers* in mauscript, for on 22nd September he announced to Wynn: "Coleridge has written a tragedy, by request of Sheridan. It is uncommonly fine, though every character appears to me to possess qualities which cannot possibly exist in the same mind. But there is a man whose name is not known in the world, Wordsworth, who has written the great part of a tragedy, upon a very strange and unpleasant subject, but it is equal to any dramatic pieces which I have ever seen." And when, towards the end of the year, Coleridge heard that Southey supposed himself burlesqued in the "Nehemiah Higginbottom" sonnets, which were really aimed at Lloyd and Lamb, he was careful to deny any such intention.[98]

Southey may well have been particularly sensitive in this respect, for he had just been parodied in good earnest in the first number of the *Anti-Jacobin*, which was launched on its brief and brilliant career on 20th November, 1797. Its editor was William Gifford, who had ridiculed the Della Cruscans in *The Baviad* and *The Mæviad* and was afterwards to edit the *Quarterly Review*: its best contributors were George Canning and John Hookham Frere, two of the Etonian group responsible for that *Microcosm* which had inspired *The Flagellant* six years earlier. The wit of the *Anti-Jacobin* satirists was especially directed against the "Jacobin" poets: each issue contained a section devoted to poetry, on principles set out by Canning in the first issue: "We shall select from time to time, from among those effusions of the *Jacobin* Muse which happen to fall in our way, such pieces as may serve to illustrate some one of the principles, on which the poetical, as well as the political, doctrine of the NEW SCHOOL is established—prefacing each of them, for our Readers' sake, with a short disquisition on the particular tenet intended to be enforced or insinuated in the production before them—and accompanying it with an humble effort of our own, in imitation of the poem itself, and in further illustration of its principles".

The "humble effort" that followed this manifesto was a wonderful parody of Southey's "Inscription for the Apartment in Chepstow Castle, where Henry Marten, the Regicide, was imprisoned thirty years", which had appeared in his volume of 1797. It took the form of an "Inscription for the door of the cell in Newgate, where Mrs. Brownrigg, the Prentice-cide, was confined previous to her Execution", and Southey's

> Dost thou ask his crime?
> He had REBELL'D AGAINST THE KING, AND SAT
> IN JUDGMENT ON HIM

was paralleled by the *Anti-Jacobin*'s

> Doth thou ask her crime?
> SHE WHIPP'D TWO FEMALE 'PRENTICES TO DEATH,
> AND HID THEM IN THE COAL-HOLE.

The second number contained one of the most famous parodies ever written, "The Friend of Humanity and the Knife-Grinder", a set of Sapphics of marvellous bathos, copying only too faithfully Southey's poem "The Widow":

> Needy Knife-grinder! whither are you going?
> Rough is the road, your Wheel is out of order—
> Bleak blows the blast;—your hat has got a hole in't,
>   So have your breeches! . . .

A fortnight later, in the fifth issue, it was the turn of Southey's Dactylics, "The Soldier's Wife":

> Come, little Drummer Boy, lay down your knapsack here;
> I am the Soldier's Friend—here are some Books for you;
> Nice clever Books, by Tom Paine the Philanthropist.

> Here's Half-a-crown for you—here are some Hand-bills too—
> Go to the Barracks, and give all the Soldiers some:
> Tell them the Sailors are all in a Mutiny . . .

Then, with one further hit at the unfortunate Dactylics in the following week, the *Anti-Jacobin* turned its fire for the time being on other targets. But it is significant that Southey should thus have been singled out for special attack: it shows that he was now becoming something of a public figure, in a small way.[99]

After spending a fortnight at Bristol he returned to London. It was his intention to go to a special pleader at the beginning of the New Year, working with him from ten in the morning to eight at night. Before entering on this drudgery he determined to finish the revision of *Joan of Arc*, consulting some books necessary for its annotation at Dr. Williams' Library. At the same time he began to write for the *Critical Review*, "at the low rate of three guineas a sheet", he recalled afterwards; "my work was not worth more. It brought me from £50 to £100 yearly, a very acceptable addition to my straitened income".[100]

It was now that he first met Dorothy Wordsworth. She and William had come up to London to offer *The Borderers* to the management of the Covent Garden theatre. She—and presumably her brother, though he says nothing of it—dined with Southey three times and called upon him once or twice. "I know a good deal of his character from our common friends", she wrote. "He is a young man of the most rigidly virtuous habits, and is, I believe, exemplary in the discharge of all domestic duties, but though his talents are certainly very remarkable for his years (as far as I can judge) I think them much inferior to the talents of Coleridge."[101]

Early in January, 1798, he was established at No. 12, Lamb's Conduit Street; but it was not long before his wife was ill again. It seems that she found London as uncongenial as he did himself, and that they both longed for the country whenever they had to stay or live there. So in the middle of February, having kept another term at Gray's Inn, he took her back to Bath. Before he left, he contracted to supply verses to the *Morning Post*, to be published without his signature, at a guinea a week.

He spent the spring at Bath and Bristol, looking after his wife and his mother, who was also ill, and working at law and poetry. But he had other activities as well. He had begun to interest himself in the poor, and he was now engaged in pressing forward a number of schemes for improving their condition. The plans themselves are of no great importance, and they do not appear to have come to much. There was one for establishing a Convalescent Asylum for patients discharged from hospitals, so that they should not have to return, while they were still weak, to "unwholesome air, scanty and bad food, cold and filth": another society in which he was concerned "have hired a room, where they hear the story of all the beggars who choose to apply, and get them relieved, either by making the parish officers do their duty, or assisting them themselves". He urged upon Wynn the necessity of reforming the Poor Law; but here he was more than thirty years before his time, and in any case Wynn was hardly the right man for the job. Nevertheless, ineffective and amateurish though his efforts in this direction may have been, they have their own importance; for they show that his old Utopian, theoretical republicanism—his "Communist phase", if one may so call it—had passed. This was the direction his reforming energies were to go on taking for the rest of his life. Theories of progress came to interest him less and less, practical measures of reform more and more; and the condition of the working classes was a subject of which he never lost sight from this time forward.

In the latter part of May he took a short trip up to Norfolk. He went first to Yarmouth, where George Burnett was now a Unitarian minister. After the break-up of Pantisocracy, he too had quarrelled with Coleridge: in due course he had made up his differences with Southey, who had entrusted his brother Henry, now fourteen years old, to him as a pupil. At Yarmouth Southey was given an introduction to William Taylor, one of the leading figures in the literary society of Norwich, who asked him to spend a few days there on his way back. This was a welcome invitation: he already admired Taylor as the translator of Bürger's ballads, and Norwich was at that time the centre of an interesting intelligentsia, whose views were in many ways similar to his own.

It was then, what it still is to-day, the unchallenged provincial capital of East Anglia. No other English city has preserved intact so many memorials of the Middle Ages; not even York or Lincoln.[102] And it has been the good fortune of Norwich, and the whole of East Anglia, to be immortalised by the most fresh and delightful of English landscape painters: the Norwich School. From them we know just how the country and the city looked—and they have changed very little since—when Southey drove up at the end of May, 1798: the flat Broads, their edges thick with reeds, the great church-towers of stone and flint, the windmills, the enormous sky overhead.

But if early nineteenth-century Norwich stands for Crome and Cotman to us, to Southey and his contemporaries it meant that coterie of intellectuals he was about to meet. The group had a

pronounced character of its own: Radical in politics, Unitarian
or Quaker in religion, its life centred on the fine Octagon Chapel,
which still stands as one of the best products of eighteenth-
century Nonconformity. Its most interesting members were
Amelia Opie, the Martineaus, the Gurneys, and William Taylor
himself.

Taylor may legitimately claim to be the founder of modern
German scholarship in England. As a young man—his father was
one of the wealthy manufacturers of Norwich—he had travelled
extensively on the Continent, and in the course of a year passed
at Detmold had become an enthusiastic admirer of the German
language. In 1782 he met Goethe at Weimar. After his return to
England, having spent some uncongenial years in his father's
business, he turned to translating and to literary criticism. He
was the first to produce an English version of *Iphigenie in Tauris*.
In later years he was to teach German to George Borrow, who
has left a picture of him in *Lavengro*, and to sum up his main
life's work in the three volumes of his *Historic Survey of German
Poetry*. He was an eccentric thinker, often on most unorthodox
lines—he held, for instance, that "the apocryphal book, commonly
called the Wisdom of Solomon, was written by Jesus Christ
Himself after the Crucifixion".[103] But he was also a kindly, warm-
hearted and intelligent man, and he remained one of Southey's
friends without interruption, in spite of all differences of opinion,
until his death in 1836.

After a few pleasant days at Norwich, Southey set out for
home. Within a fortnight he had moved house again, taking his
wife, his mother and his young cousin Peggy Hill out to a small
house at Westbury-on-Trym, two miles north of Bristol. "Martin
Hall"—so they named it, from the number of swallows that nested
in its eaves—was a converted ale-house, with large rooms, a well-
stocked garden and a delightful view: like most other antiquities
in that neighbourhood, it has now disappeared. He afterwards
looked back to the year that he passed there as one of the happiest
times of his life.[104] During that period he almost completed the
first draft of *Madoc*, prepared the second edition of his *Letters from
Spain and Portugal*, and wrote a great number of minor poems:
"I never before or since", he says, "produced so much poetry in
the same space of time". These little pieces are interesting. They
include one of his most enduring things, "The Holly Tree",
another good poem in a similar mood, "The Ebb-Tide", the
beautiful sonnet on Winter, and several of his best-remembered
ballads: "Bishop Hatto", "St. Michael's Chair", "The Well of

St. Keyne", "The Battle of Blenheim". Among them there are one or two pieces of little intrinsic value, which are however interesting as indications of his new-found mood of English patriotism—such as "The Spanish Armada", with its obvious glances at Napoleon's projected invasion:

> . . . O fools, to think that ever foe
>   Should triumph o'er that sea-girt land!
> O fools! to think that ever Britain's sons
>   Should wear the stranger's yoke!
>
> For not in vain hath Nature rear'd
>   Around her coast those silvery cliffs;
> For not in vain old Ocean spreads his waves
>   To guard his favourite isle!
>
> On come her gallant mariners!
>   What now avail Rome's boasted charms?
> Where are the Spaniard's vaunts of eager wrath?
>   His hopes of conquest now? . . .

What with all this work, his reviews and his contributions to the *Morning Post*, it is not surprising that there was less time for legal studies: he does not appear to have done much more than keep his formal terms at Gray's Inn and his name on the books.

The new edition of *Joan of Arc* was out by the beginning of July. Its format was a contrast to the great quarto of 1796: two slim duodecimos, with a crude little print of the Maid as a frontispiece, included for the sake of giving a job to Robert Hancock, the artist who drew Wordsworth, Coleridge, Lamb, and Southey himself.

At the same time the *Anti-Jacobin* had its final fling at him. On 9th July, in its last issue, appeared the long poem "New Morality", in the course of which Larevellière-Lépaux, one of the five French Directors and the high priest of the new sect of "Theophilanthropists", came in for particular scorn:

> . . . *Couriers* and *Stars*, Sedition's Evening Host,
> Thou *Morning Chronicle*, and *Morning Post*,
> Whether ye make the Rights of Man your theme,
> Your Country libel, and your God blaspheme,
> Or dirt on private worth and virtue throw,
> Still blasphemous or blackguard, praise LEPAUX!

> And ye five other wandering Bards that move
> In sweet accord of harmony and love,
> C——DGE and S—TH—Y, L——D, and L—BE and Co.
> Tune all your mystic harps to praise LEPAUX!

The *Anti-Jacobin* was promptly succeeded by the *Anti-Jacobin Review and Magazine*, the first number of which contained a cartoon by Gillray in illustration of this passage of "New Morality": among the English worshippers of Justice, Philanthropy, and Sensibility are Southey and Coleridge, with asses' heads, and Lloyd and Lamb, represented as a toad and a frog. This was a little hard on Lloyd and Lamb, who had never been revolutionaries and who had both, like Southey, quarrelled with Coleridge. Lloyd was moved to publish a protesting *Letter to the Anti-Jacobin Reviewers*: Lamb saved up his venom, to use it against Canning in *The Champion* in 1820.[105]

Southey and Lamb were now coming into closer friendship, under the influence of their common disenchantment with Coleridge. From this same July dates the earliest of Lamb's letters to Southey that has been preserved, the first of a fine series of twelve, running up to April, 1799. In them he criticises his friend's short poems, which were submitted to him one by one as they were written, sends some of his own work in return, and talks of the old authors they both loved so much, Marlowe and Wither and Quarles.

In the middle of August Southey took his wife up to Hereford by way of a holiday, hoping that the change of air and scene might be good for her. They stayed with William Bowyer Thomas, a friend he had made in Portugal. They also spent a few days at Dilwyn, a pretty black-and-white village some ten miles north-west of the city: it was of special interest to him as the place "from whence one part of my ancestry [the Tylers] sprung, where they were some two generations back the great people, where their old mansion-house is now untenanted and in ruins, where I am visiting a stranger among strangers".[106]

This trip had a threefold importance for his work. It was in Herefordshire that he first sketched out the plan of *Thalaba*: "You know my tale of the ' Adite ', in the garden of Irem", he wrote to Cottle. "I have tacked it on to an old plan of mine upon the destruction of the Domdanyel, and made the beginning, middle and end. There is a tolerable skeleton formed. It will extend to ten or twelve books, and they appear to me to possess much strong conception in the Arabian manner. It will at least prove that I did not reject machinery in my Epics, because I could not wield it. This only forms part of a magnificent project, which I do not despair of one day completing, in the destruction of the Domdanyel. My intention is, to show off all the splendour of the Mohammedan belief. I intend to do the same to the Runic, and Oriental systems; to preserve the costume of place as well as of religion." Had he not planned such a series of epics, one on each of the great mythologies of the world, before he left school?

At Hereford, too, in the Cathedral Library, he came upon the story of the Old Woman of Berkeley. He found it in the *Flores Historiarum*: "the circumstantial details in the monkish Chronicle impressed me so strongly", he says, "that I began to versify them that very evening. It was the last day of our pleasant visit at Hereford; and on the following morning the remainder of the Ballad was pencilled in a postchaise".[107]

Again, it was in Herefordshire that he read Cottle's latest publication, the *Lyrical Ballads*. Before he went home, on 5th September, he wrote to William Taylor, asking if he had seen them. "They are by Coleridge and Wordsworth, but their names are not affixed. Coleridge's ballad of ' The Ancient Mariner ' is, I think, the clumsiest attempt at German sublimity I ever saw. Many of the others are very fine; and some I shall re-read . . . whenever I am afraid of writing like a child or an old woman." Unfortunately for his subsequent reputation, he made up his mind to review them for the *Critical*. His article appeared the following month. Certain sentences from it have been doomed to a wretched immortality; but if the comment is taken as a whole it is less unfavourable and unjust than has often been supposed. This is its substance, omitting the lengthy extracts from the poems themselves that are given in illustration of the argument:

"The majority of these poems, we are informed in the advertisement, are to be considered as experiments. . . . Of these experimental poems, the most important is the Idiot Boy. . . . No tale less deserved the labour that appears to have been bestowed upon this. It resembles a Flemish picture in the worthlessness of its design and the excellence of its execution. . . . The other ballads of this kind are as bald in story, and are not so highly embellished in narration. With that which is entitled the Thorn, we were altogether displeased. The advertisement says, it is not told in the person of the author, but that of some loquacious narrator. The author should have recollected that he who personates tiresome loquacity, becomes tiresome himself. The story of a man

who suffers the perpetual pain of cold, because an old woman
prayed that he might never be warm, is perhaps a good story for a
ballad, because it is a well-known tale: but is the author certain
that it is ' *well authenticated* '? and does not such an assertion
promote the popular superstition of witchcraft? In a very
different style of poetry is the Rime of the Ancient Marinere, a
ballad (says the advertisement) ' professedly written in imitation
of the *style*, as well as of the spirit of the elder poets '. We are
tolerably conversant with the early English poets; and can
discover no resemblance whatever, except in antiquated spelling
and a few obsolete words. This piece appears to us perfectly
original in style as well as in story. Many of the stanzas are
laboriously beautiful, but in connection they are absurd or unintelligible. . . . We do not sufficiently understand the story to
analyse it. It is a Dutch attempt at German sublimity. Genius
has here been employed in producing a poem of little merit.
With pleasure we turn to the serious pieces, the better part of the
volume. The Foster-Mother's Tale is in the best style of dramatic
narrative. The Dungeon, and the Lines upon the Yew-Tree Seat,
are beautiful. The Tale of the Female Vagrant is written in the
stanza, not the style, of Spenser. . . . Admirable as this poem is,
the author seems to discover still superior powers in the Lines
written near Tintern Abbey. On reading this production, it is
impossible not to lament that he should ever have condescended
to write such pieces as the Last of the Flock, the Convict, and
most of the ballads. In the whole range of English poetry, we
scarcely recollect any thing superior to a part of the following
passage [Southey here quotes lines 66-112]. The ' experiment ', we
think, has failed, not because the language of conversation is
little adapted to ' the purposes of poetic pleasure ', but because
it has been tried upon uninteresting subjects. Yet every piece
discovers genius: and, ill as the author has frequently employed
his talents, they certainly rank him with the best of living
poets."[108]

    To-day, when any text-book will tell us the historic importance
of the *Lyrical Ballads*, that may seem a lukewarm appreciation;
but to Southey's contemporaries—whose taste had been formed,
it must be remembered, on the standards of the eighteenth
century—it cannot have appeared ungenerous. At the same time,
it is not to be denied that his criticism, and especially that of
"The Ancient Mariner", was largely founded on personal malice.
No doubt he honestly held the opinions he expressed, and they
agree with the views he maintained in private to his friends; but

standing in the relation he did to the authors, and particularly to Coleridge, it was a pity he should have made those opinions public.

There has always been a slight element of uncertainty as to whether it was really Southey who wrote this review. The evidence in favour of his authorship, though very strong, is only circumstantial: Sir Edmund Chambers and Mr. Hanson, Coleridge's latest biographers, regard the question as still open. But a passage in one of Southey's letters to Wynn, which has—perhaps significantly—remained unpublished, puts the matter beyond any doubt. Writing on 17th December, he says: "The *Lyrical Ballads* are by Coleridge and Wordsworth. 'The Nightingale', 'The Dungeon', 'The Foster-Mother's Tale' and the long ballad of the Old Mariner are all that were written by Coleridge. The ballad I think nonsense, the Nightingale tolerable. The other two are pieces of his tragedy. For Wordsworth's poems, the last [' Tintern Abbey '] pleases me best, and though 'The Idiot Boy' is sadly dilated, it is very well done. *I reviewed them two months ago.*"[109] No notice of the *Lyrical Ballads*, except that in the *Critical*, appeared before December.

Three protests were raised against Southey's review. Lamb sent him a famous remonstrance on 8th November: "If you wrote that review in ' Crit. Rev.', I am sorry you are so sparing of praise to the ' Ancient Marinere '; so far from calling it, as you do, with some wit, but more severity, ' A Dutch Attempt ', etc., I call it a right English attempt, and a successful one, to dethrone German sublimity. . . . You allow some elaborate beauties—you should have extracted 'em." The authors' comments were, each in its own way, equally characteristic. Coleridge threw off a somewhat laboured epigram, addressed "to a Critic who extracted a passage from a poem without adding a word respecting the context, and then derided it as unintelligible". Wordsworth wrote to Cottle: "Southey's review I have seen. He knew that I published those poems for money and money alone. He knew that money was of importance to me. If he could not conscientiously have spoken differently of the volume, he ought to have declined the task of reviewing it. The bulk of the poems he has described as destitute of merit. Am I recompensed for this by vague praises of my talents? I care little for the praise of any other professional critic, but as it may help me to pudding."[110]

Within a fortnight of the publication of the book, and before it had been reviewed anywhere, Cottle sold off the bulk of the impression of 500 copies, at a loss, to the London firm of J. and

A. Arch. He had already done the same with two of Southey's works, transferring the second editions of *Joan of Arc* and the *Poems* of 1797 to Longman for £370. Southey knew this, and remarked on it, with perhaps a hint of annoyance, in a letter to his brother Henry of 14th July: "I should have sent you a copy of *Joan of Arc* to give your friend, but Mr. Cottle has disposed of the whole edition to a London bookseller and I cannot therefore get them with the same ease, nor under the booksellers' price." The history of Cottle's publishing transactions is too obscure, largely because his own account of them is so muddled, for us to be certain of the motives behind them; but he was thinking of retiring from the publishing trade—he sold his business outright to Longmans in the following year—and it seems most probable that he was simply disposing of his assets in the ordinary way. There is, at any rate, no evidence to show that in so hastily ridding himself of the *Lyrical Ballads* he acted on Southey's advice. Still, the episode shows Southey in an unattractive light. All that can be said for him is that, in the course of another forty years of reviewing, he never again wrote a criticism out of personal malice. Nor, it may be noted, did he ever review another book by Coleridge.[111]

He spent most of the autumn on a walking-tour with a friend in South Wales. They visited Llanthony,[112] and in the middle of October he wrote to his wife from Bwlch in Brecknockshire, praising the country, the cream, and the civil manners of the Welsh. They had come up from Merthyr by way of Brecon and were then on their way to the Black Mountains and St. David's.

This trip seems to have been taken for the sake of his health; but here it was a failure, and at the end of the year he was ill at Westbury, complaining to Taylor of heart trouble. Thomas Beddoes, the famous Bristol doctor (and the father of T. L. Beddoes, the poet), diagnosed the complaint as nervous, said it was due to his sedentary way of life, and prescribed for him as much exercise as possible. This advice he took, to the necessary detriment of his work. A projected visit to London at the beginning of February had to be cancelled: "the journey might not possibly have hurt me", he explained to Bedford, "but I did not feel equal to it. The fatigue appeared tremendous to me in my present state, and I was fearful of fixing a cough which I am getting rid of."[113] He speaks of taking frequent doses of ether, very much against his will. On the other hand, when Taylor took too grave a view of his illness, he was at pains to put him right, adding at the same time an interesting estimate of his own nervous condition: "At one time I was apprehensive of some local complaint of the heart, but there is no danger of its growing too hard, and the affection is merely nervous. The only consequence which there is any reason to dread is, that it may totally unfit me for the confinement of London and a lawyer's office. I shall make the attempt somewhat heartlessly, and discouraged by the prognostics of my medical advisers: if my health suffers, I will abandon it at once. . . . Literary exertion is almost as necessary to me as meat and drink, and with an undivided attention I could do much. Once, indeed, I had a mimosa-sensibility, but it has long been rooted out: five years ago I counteracted Rousseau by dieting upon Godwin and Epictetus; they did me some good, but time has done more. I have a dislike to all strong emotion, and whatever could excite it; a book like *Werther* gives me now unmingled pain. In my own writings you may observe that I rather dwell upon what affects than what agitates".

He was now busy on a new plan. Taylor had remarked, in the course of a letter in the previous September, that some one should undertake an English "Almanack of the Muses", on the French and German models, "an annual Anthology of minor poems—too unimportant to subsist apart, and too neat to be sacrificed with the ephemeral victims of oblivion". Two months later Southey took up the idea and began to work at it, asking his friends for short poems and considering which of his own to use. During the spring the first issue of this *Annual Anthology* was put together, under his editorship. It appeared in the summer: among the contributors were Southey himself, who wrote about half the poems, under a variety of signatures, Taylor, Bedford and Joseph Cottle.[114]

Another of them was Humphry Davy, the brilliant young Cornishman, who had just come to Bristol to work under Dr. Beddoes at his "Pneumatic Institution". Davy is now remembered exclusively as a scientist, but in his early years he displayed remarkable literary talent too. He quickly became a friend of Southey's: they kept in touch for some years, until Davy went to London and became, as Southey and others thought, too grand to know his old friends. Even then, Southey always spoke of his genius with the greatest admiration.

By the beginning of May he felt sufficiently recovered to be able to go up and keep two more terms at Gray's Inn. This formality detained him in town three weeks, during which he found his greatest pleasure, as on so many subsequent visits to the great cities of England and Europe, in rummaging the book-

GRETA HALL

From a photograph in the possession of Mr. H. W. Howe

stalls. What with this, and seeing his friends, and writing some more of his guinea-a-week verses for the *Morning Post*, and walking in and out from the Bedfords' house at Brixton, where he was staying, he had little time to be bored or homesick. He visited Lamb once, and sent back to his wife a curious report of their conversation: "Lamb told me that he dined last week with his Anna—who is married—and he laughed and said she was a stupid girl. There is something unnatural in Lamb's levity; if he never loved her, why did he publish those sonnets? If he did, why talk of it with bravado laughter, or why talk of it at all? My opinions are for the world, but my feelings are to myself. I would proclaim the one under the gallows, but shrink from the indulgence of the other in presence of my nearest friends. . . . Lamb loves to laugh at everything—he speaks of everybody with a joke except Bishop Taylor". This seems to show that Lamb still thought more of Ann Bartram (Ann Simmons that was) than he admitted in his letters, or at least in those that have survived; and Southey's remarks on his own reticence are extremely significant and true.[115]

The lease of Martin Hall expired at midsummer, and they decided to go back to Burton if a suitable house could be found there. So on 28th June, leaving Edith at Bristol, he set out on yet another expedition. He took the Oxford Mail as far as Warminster, sitting on the box: "to a foreigner", he noted, "this would be heroic travelling, the very sublimity of coachmanship. The box motion titillates the soles of the feet like snuff affects the nose".[116] The rest of the fifty-odd miles he walked, observing as he crossed the downs to Shaftesbury how "the lark seems to live only for enjoyment: up he mounts, his song is evidently the song of delight; and when they descend, it is with outspread wings and motionless, still singing. They make the great amusement of down-walking". He managed to find a house, after some difficulty, at Burton; but it would not be ready for them to occupy until the autumn, and in the meantime they were homeless. They were able, however, to make the Danvers's house at Bristol their headquarters; and here, on 12th July, the first version of *Madoc* was at length completed, and *Thalaba* begun the very next morning.[117]

A fortnight later they were both off on another walking-tour, this time to North Somerset and Devon. They made their way out through Bridgwater and over the Quantocks to Watchet, which Southey described as "the most miserable collection of man-sties I ever beheld. The Cornish boroughs are superb to it". At Minehead Edith again fell ill, suffering from "extreme debility,

S.

F

pains in the back and bowels, and a wasting away, with sleeplessness and total want of appetite". Here, while he was anxiously
waiting for her to recover, he received a touching letter.

Coleridge had been in Germany since the previous September,
first with the Wordsworths and then on his own at Göttingen.
Towards the end of July he returned to England: he may perhaps
have been in time to meet the Southeys as they passed through
Stowey on their way from Bridgwater, and that meeting may
once again have been cold. At all events, he quickly made up his
mind to try for a more complete reconciliation with his brother-
in-law, and on the 29th he wrote to him. After referring to "an
affection which (' though fallen, though changed ') has played too
important a part in the event of our lives and the formation of
our character, ever to be *forgotten*", he went on: "I am perplexed
what to write, or how to state the object of my writing. Any
participation in each other's moral being I do not wish, simply
because I know enough of the mind of man to know that [it] is
impossible. But, Southey, we have similar talents, sentiments
nearly similar, and kindred pursuits; we have likewise, in more
than one instance, common objects of our esteem and love. I
pray and entreat you, if we should meet at any time, let us not
withhold from each other the outward expressions of daily
kindliness; and if it be no longer in your power to soften your
opinions, make your feelings at least more tolerant towards
me."

No doubt Sara was partly responsible for this overture. While
her husband was away, their nine-months-old son Berkeley had
died: Southey had taken charge of the funeral arrangements, and
while she was recovering from this shock she had stayed with him
and Edith at Westbury.[118] Some further explanations having
passed, with the tactful assistance of Poole the breach was once
more healed, early in August.

On the 8th, Edith apparently being better though not yet fit
for walking, Southey went over to Porlock, staying alone at the
"Ship": "the bedroom reminded me of Spain, two long old dark
tables with benches and an old chest composed its furniture: but
there was an oval looking-glass, a decent *pot de chambre* and no
fleas!" Next day he walked along the coast —rather incongruously,
in the company of a natural son of one of the Royal Dukes—to
Lynmouth, which made a deep impression on him: "the finest
spot, except Cintra and the Arrabida, that I ever saw", he called
it. In the Valley of Rocks he had a strange thought. "A palace
of the pre-Adamite kings, a city of the Anakim, must have

appeared so shapeless, and yet so like the ruins of what had been shaped after the waters of the flood subsided": we have here a momentary glimpse of the fantastic inner world of his mind, in which the weird scenery of his epics was shaped. On the 12th he was back with Edith at Stowey.

Here he spent "some days wholly immersed in conversation" with his brother-in-law, finding that "the hours slip away and the ink dries upon the pen in my hand". (It was a sensation that must have been familiar to many people who listened to that wonderful voice.) A fortnight later they all went on together to Ottery St. Mary for a visit to Coleridge's relatives. While they were there, he and Southey walked over to Budleigh Salterton. "Also we went to Sidmouth, a nasty watering place, infested by lounging ladies, and full of footmen." On 2nd September Southey and his wife moved to Exeter, where they stayed five weeks.

He was too much of a Somerset man to say anything very good about Devon, maintaining that "those travellers who praise it so highly must either have come from Cornwall, or have slept through Somersetshire".[119] He admired the north coast, and he admitted that Totnes and Dartmouth, which he saw with Coleridge in the middle of September, were finely situated; but the inland scenery, including that of Dartmoor, failed to please him because "the character of the whole is bald high hills, with hedges and no trees, and broad views that contained no object on which the eye could fix". As for Exeter, he thought it was "the filthiest place in England". Still, it boasted two good bookshops and a useful library, in which, with an eye to *Thalaba*, he read the travels of Fryer and Chardin. He also met William Jackson, the cathedral organist, an accomplished musician, a painter and writer besides, a friend of Sheridan and Gainsborough. Jackson imparted a touch of distinction, of the metropolitan, to what was otherwise an old-fashioned and very provincial society (Southey noted that there were still people there who were in the habit of referring to the Americans as "the rebels").[120]

At the beginning of October they moved to Christchurch. The second volume of the *Annual Anthology* was now well under way, and Southey begged Coleridge to let him have "Christabel" for it, promising that it should be the opening poem. This application was unsuccessful: in its place he received "This Lime-Tree Bower my Prison", "Lewti", and a few other small pieces. At the same time he renewed acquaintance with Gilbert Wakefield— in the gaol at Dorchester, where he was serving a two years' sentence for a seditious attack on Bishop Watson of Llandaff. At the end of the month they at last got into their new home at Burton.

They now thought they were settled for the time being; but after all their preparation, they were not to remain there long. No sooner had they moved in than Southey fell ill again, and more seriously than before. "Something ails me at heart", he wrote to Davy on 12th November. "I have, except the first few morning hours, a settled, dull, obtuse aching there, as if a rib against which it pressed were bruised. For a fortnight this has been the case, and within the last five days a diarrhœa, with consequent fever and sleeplessness, has reduced me to an almost palsied debility." Early in December he was thoroughly nervous about himself and went back to Bristol, where Beddoes once more "recommended exercise, as little application as possible to any study, and by no means the leaning posture of writing. My chest he said was by no means of a consumptive make".[121]

By Christmas time he had decided that he "must go abroad, and recruit under better skies". This time, of course, Edith would accompany him, and he proposed that the Coleridges should join them. Perhaps it was as well that this plan fell through. Coleridge said he could not go because he had a biography of Lessing on his hands, which he felt he must complete: still, "that being done, I would accompany you, and see no impossibility of forming a pleasant little colony for a few years in Italy or the South of France". "Davy! Davy!" he exclaimed on 1st January, 1800, "if the public good did not iron and adamant you to England and Bristol, what a little colony might we . . . not make. Tobin, I am sure, would go, and Wordsworth, and I—and Southey. Precious stuff for dreams—and God knows, I have no time for them!"[122] Was it *really* necessary for Southey to go abroad? "We might most assuredly continue to fix a residence somewhere, which might possess a sort of centrality", he wrote to his brother-in-law. "Alfoxden would make two houses sufficiently divided for unimpinging independence." These were some of the last echoes of Pantisocracy, and they died away as suddenly as they had come.

Instead, Southey began to think of going back to Portugal, and wrote to his uncle to ask if a suitable house could be found for them. He looked back on the country with affection, but he had a more compelling reason for returning there too: in the course of this autumn he had made up his mind "to undertake one great historical work, the History of Portugal". For this he would need to spend some time in Portuguese libraries and collections of manuscripts, and in touring the country so as to get the scenery clear in his mind, as the necessary background for relating its history. In the course of March he received a letter from Mr. Hill approving of his plan, and he at once made his arrangements for starting. Only one obstacle remained: because of his illness, he had been obliged to give up journalistic work for some time past, and he was in financial difficulties. But this was opportunely solved by his friend Elmsley, who made him a present of £100, enough to pay for the journey out and to clothe him and Edith in Portugal for a year.

It was in a solemn mood that they left Bristol on 14th April. Edith was "miserably unwell, and overcome by the prospect of leaving her sisters". Without any undue alarm, Southey was very seriously worried about his own condition. He clearly feared, in spite of Beddoes's assurance to the contrary, that he might be consumptive—the particular dread of so many of the intelligent and highly-strung in those days. "I am going for health", he wrote to Bedford, "and would not willingly be laid to rest under the cypress and Judas trees."[123]   Before he left, he appointed Coleridge his general literary executor and handed over the charge of what he hoped would be a third *Annual Anthology* (which did not in fact materialise) to a Bristol friend, Charles Danvers, and to Humphry Davy. Even if his trip did him good, and he came back from Portugal feeling better, there was still the problem of his career. He continued to think of himself as a prospective lawyer, writing to Wynn in January to suggest that he might go over to Chancery practice from the common law. But he must by now have seen that it would be difficult for him ever to make his way there: not only did he dislike the whole subject, but it tied him to London, where he was invariably ill.

Altogether, the future appeared dark and anxious as they drove down to Falmouth. When they arrived, there was the usual delay in waiting for a wind. "Six days we watched the weather-cock, and sighed for north-easterns. I walked on the beach, caught soldier-crabs, and loitered to admire the sea-anemones in their ever-varying shapes of beauty." He had with him Coleridge's poems, Burns, the *Lyrical Ballads*, and Landor's *Gebir*—"the miraculous work of a madman", which he had read, praised to all his friends, and reviewed with enthusiasm in the *Critical* that September. He also found time to write part of the ninth book of *Thalaba* before they sailed on 24th April.

VI

PORTUGAL: DUBLIN: KESWICK

(1800-1803)

THE VOYAGE was quick, but not altogether without excitement. In the early morning of the fourth day out they were borne down upon by a strange cutter, flying English colours but suspected of being a Frenchman in disguise. When she was hailed, the answer was returned in broken English. She came so near that they could see the smoke of the matches for firing her guns, sailed past them and seemed about to attack another ship with which they were in company. However, their suspense was soon over: it was discovered that she was English indeed, but manned by a crew consisting largely of Guernseymen, who spoke with a strong French accent. Southey records that he stowed his wife away in the cockpit and himself stood on the quarter-deck with a musket, which he was glad he had no occasion to use.[124]

Two days later they were off the coast of Portugal, running close enough inshore "to see the silver dust of the breakers, and the sea-birds sporting over them in flocks". A few hours more, and they were sailing up the magnificent estuary of the Tagus. It was the first time he had approached Lisbon from the sea, and the splendour of the picture drew from him an ecstatic tribute: "It is indeed a sight exceeding all it has ever been my fortune to behold in beauty and richness and grandeur. Convents and Quintas, grey olive-yards, green orange-groves and greener vine-yards; the shore more populous every moment as we advanced, and finer buildings opening upon us; the river, bright as the blue sky which illuminated it, swarming with boats of every size and shape, with sails of every imaginable variety; innumerable ships riding at anchor far as eye could reach; and the city extending along the shores and covering the hills to the farthest point of sight."

They landed on May-day and moved straight into the small house Mr. Hill had taken for them, which was "thoroughly Portuguese", with little cool rooms and a fine view across the river. Edith, who had never been out of England before, naturally felt strange and unhappy at first, what with smells and fleas and foreign servants; but the roses and the oranges soon cheered her.

Southey's spirits were momentarily damped by the changes he found in the circle of acquaintance in which he had moved five years before: "Where is one? dead. Another? in England. A third? at Madrid. A fourth? God knows where. . . . The place of every one is soon supplied, as one plant grows in the place of another." It made him think of Spenser's Cantos of Mutability.[125] But this depression did not last long: it was soon forgotten amid all the bustle of settling into a new life. Very quickly, too, he began to feel the joy of recovering his health after so many months of weakness and pain. By the beginning of July the "night-seizures" he had been troubled with had almost gone, and he felt "an everlasting sunshine of spirits". This improvement he put down almost entirely to the change of climate; but it must also have been related to the change of scene and to the fresh outburst of intellectual activity that began as soon as he arrived in Portugal. In less than two months he had finished *Thalaba* (the eleventh book was written at break-neck speed in two days): by October the revision of the poem was complete, and he was able to send copies of the manuscript to England.

The *History of Portugal* went steadily forward from his first arrival in the country. He planned "to go through the chronicles in order, and then make a skeleton of the narrative; the timbers put together, the house may be furnished at leisure". This proved more difficult and slower work than he expected. The public library at Lisbon was splendidly stocked and well arranged; but the books might not be taken away, and they were kept in wire cases, with the result that "the freedom of research is miserably shackled by the necessity of asking the librarian for every volume you wish to consult: to hunt a subject through a series of authors is thus rendered impossible". However, he was able to buy editions of some of the old chronicles published by the Portuguese Academy, and before August was over he thought he had achieved a grasp of the general facts, "a fair and accurate opinion of the chief personages, differing very considerably from their received characters, and a map of the method to be pursued". Early in 1801 he began to write the book. "My heart and soul are in the work", he told Wynn. "I hope you will like the plain, compressed, unornamented style, in which I endeavour to unite strength and perspicuity."

His life in Portugal was not eventful. When the heat of Lisbon grew intolerable, at the end of June, they moved up to Cintra, which at once renewed its spell over him: he described it to Danvers as "a place that wants only fresh butter and genial society to make it an earthly paradise". They rode about the country on donkeys, Edith showing "a great proficiency in *asswomanship*", and made a few gentle excursions, among them one to Mafra early in October. At the end of the same month they returned to Lisbon for the winter.

In March, 1801, they went with some friends on a journey of 350 miles, to Coimbra and back, visiting Alcobaça, Batalha and Pombal on the way. "All Lisbon, I believe, thought us mad when we set out", he wrote to Tom; "and they now regard our return with equal envy, as only our complexions have suffered." Hardly were they home from this exploit before Southey was off again, with only one companion this time, for an even longer tour of Alentejo and Algarve, the southern part of the country. In the course of it he visited Sagres on Cape St. Vincent, where Henry the Navigator passed his remote, dedicated life. (What a theme that would have been for Southey—the heroic, astonishing tale of Portuguese discovery!)

All the time, as the background for the *History*, he was storing up impressions of the scenery, the customs and the people of Portugal. He once thought of publishing a second set of *Letters*, and even addressed some, with that idea in mind, to his brother Tom. But this project was abandoned, and he left no formal account of his second visit to Portugal, though it was so much longer and more important than his first. Its place can, however, be supplied from his letters to his friends: to read them is to see at once how deeply interested he was in the country and how greatly his descriptive powers had advanced since his previous stay there. His style has become more flexible and free, and at the same time he commands a much greater range.

He can compass a quiet poetry, as when he describes the view from his window in Lisbon:

"The river, seen by moonlight from hence, is a far finer spectacle than art can make. It lies like a plain of light under the heaven, the trees and houses now forming a dark and distinct foreground, and now undistinguishable in shade as the moon moves on her way; Almada stretching its black isthmus into the waters, that shine like midnight snow".

He is not without humour:

"At Pombal, Waterhouse and I slept in public, in a room that served as a passage for the family. Men and women indiscriminately made the ladies' beds; one night we passed through a room wherein eight men were sleeping, who rose up to look at us, something like a picture of the Resurrection."

But it is in extended description of scenes and places—a Corpus Christi procession in Lisbon, a bull-fight, Mafra, Batalha—that he is at his best. Take, for instance, his vivid picture of Coimbra:

"I never saw a city so nobly situated, a view so altogether glorious as opened upon us from its near heights. The preceding day we had been wetted, and for three days threatened with dark and lowering clouds. Of course the sun was welcome; it dried us, and warmed us, and made everything cheerful. The country is hilly and well watered—olives and oranges everywhere, and cypresses thick as poplars about London. Mountains bounded the scene: the farthest object was one snowy summit of the Estrella, glittering in the sun. Down the southern boundary a few clouds were floating, so beamy white that they seemed like light condensed to visible shape and substance. The city, with its fine convents, shone on an eminence over the Mondego, now in the fullness of its waters.

"Coimbra is the spot of which the historian and the poet scarcely ever lose sight; whatever was interesting in the history or literature of Portugal centred here; and I looked at the city with the strong recollection of old times and old heroes. Knowing what to expect within, I was prepared for the contrast; yet was it impossible not to feel disappointment at quitting [? finding] so rich a people rendered vicious and knavish and impudent by the contagion of the University. The first object was disgusting. Passing under an old gateway, the prison fronted us, and two gallows-faced fellows, fastened with chains round their necks, were standing in the street begging. We met several other prisoners dragging their fetters through the town, on the same employment. Everywhere in Coimbra some relic of antiquity presents itself, but everywhere it is mixed with modern patches. In the monastery of Santa Cruz, one of the oldest and most famous establishments in the kingdom, I saw nothing so remarkable as the poultry yard. The royal tombs were comparatively modern and miserably poor, after what we had seen at Alcobaça and Batalha. The sword of Alfonso Henrique was mislaid; nor did I regret not seeing what I knew not to be genuine. . . . But the poultry yard was perfect; it was one of the quadrangles converted to this useful purpose, cut with canals of running water, over which were several small temples. And such geese and ducks, and another sort of wild water-bird to me unknown, so fat, they ought to have been roasted in the Alcobaça kitchen! I did long to beg, buy or steal a dinner.

"The Fountain of Tears was far the most heart-interesting

object in this vicinity. It is the spot where Inez de Castro was accustomed to meet her husband, Pedro, and weep for him in his absence. Certainly her dwelling-house was in the adjoining garden; and from there she was dragged to be murdered at the feet of the King, her father-in-law. There is a famous passage in Camoens upon this subject; it is very bad, and therefore much admired by all poetry-dabblers, being a complete specimen of false taste. But bad poetry does not affect the fact, and the loves of Inez and Pedro are historically interesting. I, who have long planned a tragedy upon the subject, stood upon my own scene. Two cedars—most magnificent, most ancient trees—stand one on each side of the fountains. I do believe, and not because I wish to believe it, that Inez sat under their shade four hundred years ago. Who is there who has not, when he stood under a fine tree, felt the littleness of man's existence? And these cedars might have been the main beams of Solomon's temple—of such luxuriant size in their growth. There is beside them one modern tree—bless the hand that planted it!—a great willow whose boughs bend into the water. Behind the fountain rises a high hill, green with corn, and spotted with the shadow of olive trees. The whole scene is in my eye, even with the vividness of actual sight."

Here is all his feeling for the past—the same feeling that moved him to undertake his epics, his histories and his biographies. It is characteristic, too, that the cypresses of Coimbra should make him think of "poplars about London": although he loved the warmth and colour of the South, he continued, as he put it, to "hunger after the bread-and-butter comforts and green fields of England". But now it was not with the anxiety and homesickness of his earlier visit. On the whole, this was a very happy interlude in his life: he had Edith with him, and in many ways he would have been glad to have stayed in Portugal longer than he did, or even to have made his permanent home there.

Among the English colony in Lisbon he formed some pleasant new friendships: with Miss Barker, who was afterwards to be his neighbour in Cumberland, "a very clever girl, all good humour, and a head brimful of brains"; with Barbara Seton of Bideford, a cousin of the Misses Berry, Horace Walpole's friends; and with Henry Koster, the son of a sugar-merchant of Liverpool and Oporto, who later wrote an interesting volume of *Travels in Brazil*.[126] His relations with Mr. Hill had grown easier with the passage of time: "my uncle with me was always the man of letters," he wrote soon after he came home, "and the many points in common to us quite hid the difference of age and the utter dissimilarity of opinions on more important but not every-day topics".[127] They continued to draw steadily closer together, united by similar interests and sympathies, and in later life Southey dedicated two of his best works to his uncle—one of them, the *Colloquies*, in terms of deep affection.

But his happiness in Portugal was by no means unclouded. He had not been out there long before he heard that his cousin Peggy Hill, to whom he was greatly attached, was in an advanced stage of consumption—and in those days that was a verdict from which there could be no appeal. Soon afterwards they were themselves directly threatened by the spread of an epidemic from Spain. Some reported it was the "black vomit", some yellow fever, some the plague; by the end of October 8000 people were said to have died from it in Cadiz. On top of this, in the spring of 1801 the Spanish Government was induced by Napoleon to declare war on Portugal, England's ally. Fearing that the country would be invaded and that they would be expelled, the English began to make their preparations for returning home. Chest after chest of the books Mr. Hill had collected—so much raw material now for the *History of Portugal*—were dispatched as opportunity offered; and Southey remarked that his own books had by this time become so numerous that they must "anchor" him at home: "they cannot follow me, and I must therefore settle with them". As the danger proved less immediately pressing than had at first been thought, it was not until June that he and Edith sailed. After a long and disagreeable passage of a fortnight they at last arrived at Falmouth, reaching Bristol on 10th July.

Southey's second visit to Portugal, like his first, saw a steady development in his political opinions. He remained in two minds about the war. Like Coleridge, he was slow to understand the full menace of Napoleon. He was still obsessed by his hatred of Pitt and of all that Pitt stood for: "England is now the bedarkening power; she is in politics what Spain was to religion at the Reformation." But in February, 1801, Pitt resigned, to be succeeded by Addington; and Nelson's victory at Copenhagen in April seemed to open the way to a peace recognising England's supremacy on the sea and France's on land. This is what he would ideally have wished for: in England, the war over and her security regained, the course of liberal reform could have been resumed; while the dominant power on the Continent would have been Revolutionary France, not England's allies, the hateful tyrannies of Austria and Russia.

In every other respect he had become increasingly English in sympathy. "One Englishman here only talks politics to me", he wrote from Cintra; "his taste is French in everything, and in all else mine is right English and anti-Gallican." Catholicism disgusted and appalled him more and more, and it put him in a dilemma known to many Liberals: "I cannot argue against toleration," he wrote to Wynn, "yet is popery in its nature so very damnable and destructive a system that I could not give a vote for its sufferance in England. I could no more permit the existence of a monastic establishment than the human sacrifices of Mexican idolatry." "I never saw the Inquisition, quiet as it is," he remarked on another occasion, "without longing to join a mob in as glorious a day as the 14th of July." For him it soon ceased to be a dilemma. He took the path away from toleration, which led him to his later high Toryism: the intolerance of the Catholic system called forth an answering intolerance in him.

He owed, then, a great deal to his second Portuguese visit: the recovery of his health, much of the material for the most grandly-conceived of his works, as well as for several lesser things, a maturing prose style, an increased knowledge and a more certain judgment of political questions. And the happiness he had known in Portugal made him look back to those fourteen months ever afterwards as a golden time, and to plan again and again to return there.

On his arrival at Bristol he found two letters from Coleridge, written from Keswick in April and May. They contained a dismal account of his health, a description of Greta Hall where he and Sara had been living since July, 1800, and a pressing invitation to the Southeys to join them there: "The house is full twice as large as we want; it hath more rooms in it than Alfoxden; you might have a bedroom, parlour, study, etc., etc., and there would always be rooms to spare for your or my visitors. In short, for situation and convenience—and when I mention the name of Wordsworth, for society of men of intellect—I know no place in which you and Edith would find yourselves so well suited."

The reference to Wordsworth was not a very happy thought, for Southey did not greatly approve of his brother-in-law's latest and most intense devotion: he thought he had done wrong, on his own account and on Sara's, in moving to so remote a part of the country, far from all their other friends, and "wholly giving himself to Wordsworth".[128] Nevertheless, he accepted Coleridge's invitation, promising to set out with Edith as soon as business would allow him and ending his letter with an outburst of the old feeling: "Time and absence make strange work with our affections; but mine are ever returning to rest upon you. I have other and dear friends, but none with whom the whole of my being is intimate—with whom every thought and feeling can amalgamate."

Before he could start, it was necessary for him to try and settle some plan for his own future. He had at length made a final decision against the law, after playing in Portugal with the idea of practising at the Indian bar, where the strong inducement of a hot climate was added to the chance of making a fortune in a short time. Instead, he made up his mind to try for some secretaryship in a legation in southern Europe, and he now offered his services, through Wynn, to William Drummond, who was about to leave for Naples as British Minister. They were not accepted, and other plans had to be made.

At the same time he was negotiating with Longman for the publication of his third epic. He offered him the choice between a completely revised *Madoc* and a Hindu romance that he had begun in Portugal under the title *The Curse of Keradon*. The price he demanded was similar to that he had received for *Thalaba* (£115), of which he wanted £50 to be paid in advance: sanguine as usual, he undertook to complete whichever poem Longman should prefer in six months. The bargain fell through, on the question of terms, to Coleridge's delight: "I am glad that Longman played the Jew with you", he wrote. "Do not, whatever you do, do not send *Madoc* hastily out of your hands. I have much (and I believe some things of importance) to talk over with you respecting that poem. I cannot but believe that it will stand unrivalled in its own kind, and that a very noble kind. I am *anxious* about that poem." This was all very well, but it did not fill Southey's purse, and in the meantime he had to fall back once more on journalism.

It was not until the very end of August that he was free to set out for Keswick. His first visit to the Lakes was a casual and rapid affair. They made no deep impression upon him at the outset: all he could think of was the superior beauty of Portugal. "These lakes are like rivers; but oh for the Mondego and the Tagus!" "This country is very beautiful, but very cold", he told Wynn. "It disappoints expectation. You will look for larger lakes and loftier mountains. The more I see them the more they become objects of admiration. But Skiddaw is a dwarf to Monchique, and I wish myself again at Cintra."[129] As for Greta Hall, which was later, as it turned out, to be his home for nearly forty years, he does not even mention it. Nor does he say anything of

Coleridge or his family. He seems to have stayed only a fortnight, after which, leaving Edith behind with her sister, he set off for a tour in North Wales with Wynn.

This was something more than a pleasure trip: it was undertaken with a view to improving the background of *Madoc* by sketches of local scenery. They started from Wynnstay up the valley of the Dee, past Llangollen (whose Ladies he was unkind enough not to visit) and Valle Crucis Abbey, which charmed him; thence by way of Bettws-y-coed to Conway, and so under Penmaenmawr to Bangor. At this point he wrote to Edith, attempting the task, so familiar to us to-day, of comparing North Wales with the Lake District, after visiting each for only a week or two. "These mountains look to me the highest, but that is probably because they are more insulated. Wales has wood, and the interest of ruins, and many recollections. Anything so simple and so severely sublime as your view to Borrowdale and Newlands, or so quietly beautiful as Grasmere and Rydal, I have not seen." They then planned to go on to Capel Curig, climb Snowdon, and return to Llangedwyn, Wynn's house in Denbighshire. There Southey found a letter that brought his holiday to an abrupt conclusion.

Rickman had just gone over to Dublin as secretary to Charles Abbot, the newly-appointed Chief Secretary for Ireland. Through his influence Southey was now offered a similar post with Isaac Corry, the Irish Chancellor of the Exchequer. His salary was to be £400 Irish (£350 sterling): half of this was set apart for travelling expenses, for he would be expected to go frequently backwards and forwards between Dublin and London. The opening seemed a good one, or at any rate the best that offered, and he accepted the post at once. After a second visit, lasting a few days, to Keswick, he set out, reaching Dublin by the middle of October.

He saw Ireland at an interesting time. Pitt's Act of Union had been passed in the previous year, and had come into force on 1st January, 1801. Without Catholic Emancipation, which George III had refused to grant, it was popular on neither side of the Channel—though Southey himself had approved of the principle of Union three years earlier.[130] The Act was passed, as the government of Ireland was habitually carried on, by corruption on a considerable scale; and among those who had been bought over from the popular side was Corry himself. He had been Chancellor of the Irish Exchequer since 1798, and in the Union debates he had been the chief Government spokesman against Grattan, with whom he had even fought a duel. He was a skilful politician, if something of a lightweight, and he had all the politician's professional charm of manner.

But Southey did not see much of him. Corry was out of Dublin when he arrived: a few days afterwards they met for "a bow and a take by the hand", and then he was off to London, leaving his secretary to follow at leisure. This suited Southey very well. He was able to begin the revision of *Madoc* in Dublin, and to make a third brief visit to Keswick on his way up to London, where he arrived in the first week of November.

He was thus in Ireland for just a fortnight, and, as it happened, he was never to see it again. Dublin appeared to him, as it must have appeared to any one at that date, "a very fine city—a magnificent city—such public buildings, and the streets so wide! For these advantages Dublin is indebted to the prodigal corruption of its own government. Every member who asked money to make improvements got it; and if he got £20,000, in decency spent five for the public, and pocketed the rest". Of the Irish his impression was necessarily superficial. "It will be difficult to civilise this people. An Irishman builds him a turf stye, gets his fuel from the bogs, digs his patch of potatoes, and then lives upon them in idleness: like a true savage, he does not think it worth while to work that he may better himself. Potatoes and butter-milk—on this they are born and bred; and whisky sends them to the third heaven at once."

But this brief visit gave him one thing of importance: an insight into administration, however superficial, and a connexion with it. That was a useful and necessary step in the development of his political ideas. "The government, acting well and wisely [what a change it is to come upon such a phrase in one of his letters, after so many years' bitter and ill-informed criticism!], control both parties, the Orangemen and the United Irishmen, and command respect from both; the old fatteners upon the corruption are silent in shame: the military, who must be kept up, will be well employed in making roads." His stay in Dublin, too, led to closer relations with Rickman and a better understanding of his character and abilities, which lay just in this administrative direction. Their association was to be profitable to both of them, and particularly to Southey, in the future.

When he got back to London, he was instructed to make some inquiries into corn laws, financial questions, and tithes—more, it seems, in order to give him something to do than for any immediately useful purpose. At the same time, Corry proposed to him that he should undertake a history of the Egyptian campaign,

lately completed by Abercromby's victory at Alexandria. Though
Rickman was in favour of this scheme, Southey was not greatly
attracted by the subject: he infinitely preferred Portugal. He was
already growing tired of such an uncongenial and pointless life.
"This foolish place under Corry cannot subsist a second year," he
wrote to Wynn on 9th December, "from no fault on my part, nor
any unwillingness. But he does not want me—I am utterly
useless to him. He is a *weak man*, and therefore an unsteady one.
Plan about me he can have had none: what he says to-day is
merely for the sake of saying something—he did not think of
it yesterday, and he will not remember it to-morrow."[131] For
this his "gentle and reconciling manners" were scant compensation.

In London, where Edith joined him, he saw much of the
Lambs, dined once with Lord Holland, and went on with *Madoc*.
At the end of the year he was suddenly called down to Bristol by
the news that his mother was dangerously ill. In less than a
fortnight she died, on 5th January. (She had had a superstition
she would die in 1802: she was born in 1752, married in 1772 and
widowed in 1792.)

Southey was very fond of his mother, to whom he was an
excellent son; but he was not passionately devoted to her—he had
been too little with her in childhood, too much with Miss Tyler,
for that. He felt her death deeply, though it was perhaps less from
personal grief than because it cut one more of the links that
bound him to his earlier years. "My ties to this country are being
daily loosened—one goes after another", he wrote to his brother
Harry. "The old leaves are dropping from the family tree, and I
see no bud upon its branches! My books grow dearer to me. I
cling to them with a comfortless feeling that it is the only safe
attachment, that they are the friends whom there is no danger
of losing, who must survive me."[132] This was a constant thought
with him, and it was to be a recurring theme in his letters, as
well as the subject of the most famous of his short poems.

Having settled up his mother's affairs in Bristol, he returned
to London, to live for a time in the Strand. Early in February he
paid a short visit to Norwich to consult William Taylor about
Madoc, and, no doubt, to see how his brother Harry was going
on. He was not without anxiety in that quarter. Harry was now
studying surgery, at Mr. Hill's expense, under Dr. Martineau of
Norwich, where William Taylor, who liked him very much, kept
an eye upon him. Robert expressed himself "uneasy lest he should
contract habits of expensiveness", and occasionally wrote him

CROSTHWAITE CHURCH AND BASSENTHWAITE LAKE, FROM THE
GARDEN AT GRETA HALL

*From an engraving by William Westall in the sixth volume of "The Life and
Correspondence of Robert Southey" (1850)*

anxious and rather solemn letters of advice. His fears were not groundless.

Besides his mother's death and Harry's tendency to extravagance, he was now faced with a third trouble in his family, more serious than either of the others. In the previous October, just before he left Dublin, Coleridge wrote him a letter breaking the news that his marriage to Sara was a failure: perhaps he felt he must state his side of the case to Southey before his wife, through her sister Edith, could put in hers. He came to the point in the first paragraph of his letter with a characteristic sidelong transition, sudden and strangely touching: "My knee is no longer swollen, and this frosty weather agrees with me—but O Friend! I am sadly shattered. The least agitation brings on bowel complaints, and within the last week *twice* with an ugly symptom— namely sickness even to vomiting—and Sara—alas! we are not suited to each other. . . . I will go on believing that it will end happily—if not, if our mutual unsuitableness continues, and (as it assuredly will do, if it continue) increases and strengthens—why then, it is better for her and my children that I should live apart, than that she should be a widow and they orphans". Again on 9th November he cries: "If my wife loved me, and I my wife, half as well as we both love our children, I should be the happiest man alive—but this is not, will not be!" In February, 1802, he was in London and dined with Southey; but though the old breach was not renewed, it is clear from their correspondence, their references—and lack of references—to each other, that the uprush of mutual affection they had felt the previous summer had once more gone. They were now beyond arguing or quarrelling, but they were both uneasily aware that this problem lay ahead, and that one day it would have to be solved.

With all these trials crowding in upon him, and his own future as unsettled as ever, a new note creeps into Southey's letters this spring: one of irritation and mild protest, very rare with him, for he was a patient man in the serious things of life. He complained to Bedford, for instance, that "the lamentable rambling to which I am doomed, for God knows how long, prevents my striking root anywhere—and we are the better as well as the happier for local attachment". In this mood of exasperation, oppressed beyond endurance by the futility of the work he was doing for Corry, he threw up his job in disgust at the end of May. Later on, he discovered why Corry had been so anxious to keep him (though Cuthbert Southey seems to be wrong in suggesting that this had anything to do with his resignation).

S.   G

"I have found it out, as Vincent says", he told Wynn. "I was to be tutor to the son, but to be called secretary to the father, in order that the tutor might be paid by the Treasury. A good specimen of ways and means."[133] This being settled, he moved back to Bristol once more.

While he was in London he met a number of interesting people: Fuseli and Flaxman, Barry the painter, Bowles and Mrs. Inchbald, Thomas Campbell, "who spoke of old Scotch ballads with contempt!". Before he left town he arranged with Longman to undertake a new book, a translation and abridgement of the Castilian romance *Amadis of Gaul*. The work was originally intended to appear anonymously, and if it proved successful it was to be one of a series of similar editions of all the great romances. But the first of these provisions fell through when the publisher, "very incautiously, though certainly with no mean motive", allowed Southey's name to appear in an advertisement of the book, and in the end he agreed to acknowledge it on the title-page, Longman raising his terms accordingly. The edition was published in four small volumes in 1803. The *History of Portugal* also went forward; but he explained to his friends that he could publish nothing for the moment as his first volume would "touch popery to the quick", and that would deny him all further access to the Portuguese archives he had not yet explored.

They spent the summer at Bristol, taking a furnished house at Kingsdown in the same row as the Danvers's. Lodgings were no longer adequate for them, for Edith was expecting a child. This at least was cheering. Their marriage had been a happy and successful one, but it had been marred by the absence of children, whom they both longed for, and by Edith's ill-health. All the winter she had been unwell: in February Coleridge reported that she was "exceedingly valetudinarian", and Southey told Danvers that her spirits were, "beyond anything that you can imagine, bad". Now there was reason to hope, as Coleridge wrote when he heard the news, "that Edith will be born again, and be a healthy woman". On 31st August she gave birth to a daughter, who was christened Margaret.[134]

It was now more than ever necessary that they should have some fixed home. They considered Richmond, where John May lived, but rejected it. Then Coleridge wrote to urge them to share his house at Keswick with Sara and himself: he may already have foreseen that as a solution to his own domestic *impasse*. "The services and benefits I should receive from your society", he wrote with a winning humility, "and the spur of your example would be incalculable." Three long accounts of Greta Hall, the expenses and management of it, followed, fascinating to lovers of that historic house, but not of immediate importance here. By the beginning of September, Southey had almost decided to go there: the climate alone, he said, caused him to hesitate.[135] But at that moment another plan turned up, in some ways more attractive: he heard of a house in the Vale of Neath—indescribably lovely then, still untouched by industry. This idea seized his imagination. He had always been attracted by Wales, it would perhaps be warmer than Keswick, and it was much less remote: "a friend who should leave Bristol by the mail at one in the midday might reach me at breakfast hour the next morning". When the landlord refused to make some small alterations in the kitchen that Southey demanded, and the negotiations had to be called off, he was seriously disappointed. He used often to speak in after years, so his son records, "with something like regret of Maes Gwyn and the Vale of Neath".

Disappointed in Wales, he fell back on a plan of taking a house somewhere near Bristol for the time being. "Here in the west", he wrote to William Taylor, who had pleaded the claims of Norwich, "the intercourse with Portugal is far easier. There I must go in about two years, and there if possible I would willingly fix my final abode, and spend my life speaking Portuguese and writing English." But Coleridge, who had by now decided that he must go abroad for his health, continued to press his invitation to Greta Hall, with a persistency very unusual and striking in him. Thus in February, 1803, he wrote again: "I do warmly recommend you to go to Keswick. I shall certainly be absent—even if I live—two years. . . . You will have no furniture to buy, and all your books and, if you choose, yourselves too might go by water. And you might go to Lisbon from Liverpool. You would save at least £100 in the two years, . . . and Mrs. Southey and Mrs. Coleridge will, I doubt not, be great comforts to each other."

Equally unusual and striking was Southey's indecision. He spent nearly a year wavering between one plan and another, as if he were reluctant to go to Keswick and casting about for any eligible alternative. The only reason he ever gave for his hesitation was the Cumberland climate. Perhaps that was all he was doubtful about; but there was probably a more cogent reason as well: he too must surely have seen how a joint *ménage* with the Coleridges would inevitably end, and he was not in a position to undertake fresh responsibilities lightheartedly. Besides his own wife and child, he had three younger brothers to think of: Tom, it is true, was for the present settled in the navy, but that was no certain career, for he might at any time be put on half-pay; Harry showed an unfortunate tendency to extravagance; while Edward, the youngest, was already turning out a complete good-for-nothing, whose debts Robert was still soft-hearted enough sometimes to discharge.[136] There were also Edith's unprovided sisters to keep an eye on, and young George Fricker, her brother. How were all these people—let alone any more—to be looked after on an annual income of £160, supplemented by the uncertain profits of literature?

They were indeed very uncertain. *Thalaba*, which was published soon after he arrived back from Portugal, sold slowly, and by the spring of 1804 only 500 copies had gone.[137] Its sale may have been helped a little by Jeffrey's notice, unfavourable though on the whole it was, which appeared in the first number of the *Edinburgh Review* the following October; but a second edition of the poem did not appear until 1809. Although the *Poems* of 1797, with the second volume added two years later, continued to be popular, a third edition appearing in 1800 and a fourth in 1801, the royalties on them cannot have been important. The staple of his income from writing continued to be journalism: "I am reviewing for Longman, reviewing for Hamilton, translating: perhaps about again to versify for the *Morning Post*—drudge, drudge, drudge", he told William Taylor in January, 1803.

In the summer he went up to London to negotiate with Longman for the publication of a *Bibliotheca Britannica* under his editorship, the purpose of which, he explained to his brother Tom, was "to give an account, chronologically arranged, of all the books in all the British languages, with biography, criticism, and connecting chapters, so as to form a connected history of English literature: each volume 800 pages in quarto, each page 40 lines: terms, £150 per volume to me, as editor and manager-in-chief and absolute director; four guineas a sheet for what is written, five where the subject-author has written in Saxon, Welsh or Latin. . . . Everybody likes the scheme, which is the most important that has ever been undertaken in this country. I calculate upon writing a quarter part of each volume, upon the average, and thus clearing £250 by each". He got together a good team of contributors. At their head stood Coleridge, who took up the idea with enthusiasm and at once began to extend it to an impracticable vastness. But neither his gigantic plan nor Southey's more moderate one came to anything, for a minor financial crisis in August caused Longman to draw in his horns and think better of embarking on any such large project. It came near fulfilment only a century later, in the *Cambridge History of English Literature*.

His income, then, so far from certain and his commitments already so extensive, it is hardly strange that Southey should have hesitated a long time before consenting to go and live at Greta Hall. He knew of the friction between Coleridge and his wife; he knew that Coleridge intended to go abroad: is it not likely that he was afraid he might be called upon to add to his own burdens by becoming responsible for Sara and her three children?

As it was, he cannot be said ever to have made up his mind to go to Keswick: it was made up for him, by domestic tragedy. In July, Margaret fell ill with teething trouble. Her father was immediately anxious, especially since, as he told Rickman, " we cannot employ the means that would benefit her, because they produce such passion and fear and agitation as more than counteract the good effect. Her spirits and her appetite are gone, and she loses flesh daily". Hydrocephalus soon developed, and three weeks later she was dead. This decided them. " Edith will be nowhere so well as with her sister Coleridge", he wrote to John May. " She has a little girl, some six months old, and I shall try and graft her into the wound, while it is still fresh." They left Bristol as soon as they could (he thought of it now with a shudder: " the place was haunted, and it is my wish never to see it again"), and after a brief visit to Miss Barker in Staffordshire they reached Keswick on 7th September.

VII

GRETA HALL

SOUTHEY'S LIFE falls neatly and naturally into two distinct parts, divided at the day of his arrival at Greta Hall, 7th September, 1803. This is no mere artificial arrangement, existing solely for the biographer's convenience: it corresponds to a striking change that took place at this time, both in the outward circumstances of his life and in the inner habits of his mind. Not that he himself saw it in that light. To him this visit was a temporary one, like so many others he had paid since he married and became a wanderer eight years earlier. He still looked forward to settling down one day in some diplomatic or consular post in southern Europe. But that was never to happen: his visit at Greta Hall was to last until his death.

Hitherto his life had been a restless, somewhat unsatisfactory affair. He had moved continually from place to place, never settling anywhere for long. And he had seemed to lack strength of will: his failure to stick at the uncongenial drudgery of the law, for instance, had not been due only to illness and the atmosphere of London. This had had its counterpart in his work. Nothing he had so far written had shown any great power of concentration: the best of his early poetry had been fresh and spontaneous rather than solid or strong. This was not wholly a bad thing, and it was largely due to the extraordinary facility with which he wrote verse; but it debarred him from writing great poetry, a task for which he was in many other respects admirably equipped.

He was aware of this himself, and it was to some extent deliberate. The composition of poetry excited him, as he thought, to a dangerous degree. It brought home what was known only to himself, to his most intimate friends, and later to one or two penetrating observers from the outside: that he was a most passionate man. One of the great problems of his life at all times was how to keep this passion in check. For he was never in the least doubt that it must be fought down: to give it rein might mean complete loss of self-control—it might even ultimately lead to madness. It was just at this time, and for this reason, that he decided to abandon poetry for prose, *The Curse of Kehama* for the

History of Portugal. "I am out of humour with Kehama", he told Bedford, "for half a hundred reasons: historical composition is a source of greater and quieter and more continuous pleasure."[138] We shall see that he partly went back on this resolution, and that in the years 1808-1814 his poetical talent showed a striking revival; but this was nevertheless a vital decision, for it meant that prose, not poetry, was to be the staple of his work. There lay his highest and most satisfying achievement, and it was now that he took the path leading to it. On the way, he achieved an adequate measure of concentration; and as for will-power and industry, the capacity to stick to a job, his life at Greta Hall exhibited those qualities on an almost unexampled scale.

He had long outgrown the heady revolutionary ideas of his youth, and we have noted a gradual change in his feelings about the war with France. The first milestone for him was the replacement of Pitt by Addington; the second, the Peace of Amiens in March, 1802. Twenty years later, when he thought of dedicating his *History of the Peninsular War* to Addington, he observed that that Peace "restored in me the English feeling which had long been deadened; it placed me in sympathy with my country, bringing me into that natural and healthy state of mind upon which time, and knowledge, and reflection, were sure to produce their proper and salutary effect".[139] With the renewal of hostilities, after Napoleon's threats, in May, 1803, all Southey's doubts were over: he was for war against France to the end.

One further change was also taking place in his life at this time. Hitherto, although his reputation as a writer had stood high in his own circle of friends, and among those who sympathised with the ardent politics of his earlier years, he had not been widely known. But Jeffrey's attack on *Thalaba* in the *Edinburgh Review* had marked an alteration in this respect as well. Fierce though that attack was, no one could mistake the tone in which Jeffrey spoke of him, as of some one wrong indeed, but a considerable and important poet; and the *Edinburgh Review* reached a very wide public.[140] There, too, he had again been publicly associated with Wordsworth and Coleridge; together they formed a new "*sect* of poets"; the "Lake School" was born.

We know just what Southey looked like now, from the fortunate accident that two of his best portraits were taken at this time. In the painting of his head and shoulders by Opie, which was exhibited in the spring of 1803 and subsequently engraved for the *Life and Correspondence*, his features are strongly marked and well formed: the nose is especially prominent, though less startling than in some of his later portraits. There is nothing spruce about him: his hair is long and curly, his cravat negligently tied. Above all, he has a commanding air, he gives an impression of forcefulness and strength. Edridge's pen-and-ink drawing, which was made in 1804, is complementary to Opie's painting, though a less perfect work of art: there has been a failure in the actual portraiture—he has set the eyes too far apart and made the head too broad—and the picture is not in the same class as the splendid sketch of Wordsworth he drew two years later. Still, it manages to tell us a great deal about Southey, for it shows him seated in a chair, handling a book, as he must so often have appeared to visitors at Greta Hall. He is a little tidier here (did Opie, one wonders, in painting the wild romantic poet, deliberately heighten the careless effect of his dress?); and as he appears at full length, we can see his remarkable thinness, on which everybody who met him commented.

We have already noticed that he was a passionate man, of strong attachments and dislikes, but also with a high sense of duty. These portraits, and particularly Opie's, reveal another trait in his character: his pride. Indeed he was a very proud man —independent, reserved, self-respecting. He was also intensely proud of his own achievements, and here his pride was tinged with self-righteousness and vanity. In this lay his most conspicuous failing, which has always afforded an easy target to his detractors. It was perfectly genuine and unstudied. He never thought twice about remarking to a friend, for instance, that *Madoc* would enjoy "a fame as lasting as the English language and the passions and affections of man"; or, of *Thalaba*: "I know no poem which can claim a place between it and the *Orlando*. . . . Perhaps, were I to speak out, I should not dread a trial with Ariosto."[141] If these poems had been works of high genius, we should of course accept Southey at his own valuation: we might even admire his self-confidence, as we cannot help admiring Wordsworth's. But it is otherwise, and Southey's pride in his own work has ever since been ridiculed or scornfully written down as mere conceit.

An attentive reader of his letters—and especially of some passages from them that have remained unpublished—may, however, reach a rather different conclusion. Was he really as sure of himself as these judgments on his own work suggest? Or was he, in some measure, shouting to keep his spirits up? Most of this self-praise can be paralleled by later doubts or self-condemnation. Thus, only a year after he had expressed the high opinion of *Madoc* that has just been quoted, he could write of it:

"I suspect its merit more than I ever did the merits of either *Joan of Arc* or *Thalaba*. . . . The want of unity is a grievous fault." Again, in 1810 he remarks that in structure *The Curse of Kehama* is "far superior to *Thalaba*—in most other respects, I am afraid, I do not like it quite so well". Perhaps he was less certain of himself than he appeared to be. May not his excessive self-assurance have served as cover and compensation for his own doubts, in the same way as his calm, even frigid, exterior hid a passionate spirit behind?[142]

However that may be, he impressed the outside world as a man who was sure of his own great powers and sure that he knew his own limitations. His weaknesses, which might make that strength somewhat brittle, were yet unseen. So now, in his reaction to Margaret's death, he appeared grieved, but not very deeply wounded. He looked after his wife with his usual tender care, supervised every detail of their removal to Keswick, and was quickly back at work, with hardly more than a hint even to his close friends of how much he had suffered. Only in May, 1804, when another daughter had been born to him who seemed likely to thrive, did he lift the curtain a little: in a letter to William Taylor he said that he would love this child "with the wary wisdom of *second* love, for now I may tell you that the first loss almost broke my heart".[143]

It was well for them both that this loss was soon repaired; for Edith Southey had felt it, in her own less intense way, as acutely as Robert in his. She was not a woman who left a strong impression of personality behind her, and it is difficult for us to form any very clear picture of her now. At the best we can only hope to see her in the rather faded tints of one of those pale, delightful water-colours her contemporaries painted. Her nephew Hartley, after her death, referred to her with sympathy: "Poor Aunt—I trust it is well with her. A melancholy close was hers, of a day never bright, even when the sun shone most serenely upon it. Never knew I a being in whom a pure and benevolent spirit was so little joyous; a morbid sensitiveness to pain and an almost apathy to pleasure, an intellect sensible and not uncultivated, but of little activity, sink beneath afflictions which coarser minds cry out in a few weeks, and in which livelier natures might, after the first pangs were over, discover topics of hope and consolation."

From the first she had been low-spirited (doubtless this had a physical explanation), and her interests were purely domestic: she was devoted to her husband—though she made no pretension to understand or share in his work—to her children, and to her house. "Dreary, dreary," exclaimed her brother-in-law Coleridge, "would be the hours passed with her—amusement, and all the detail of whatever cheers or supports the spirits, must be sought elsewhere." But for all that, her husband was very deeply attached to her, as he showed most pathetically throughout her long and dreadful last illness. And Nathaniel Hawthorne noted that she was remembered in Keswick as late as 1855: the sexton at Crosthwaite told him of "her charity to the poor, and how she was a blessing to the neighbourhood".[144]

Her sister Mrs. Coleridge was an altogether more robust character. By great good fortune, she corresponded with Thomas Poole, and he, being a man of method, kept her letters. They have recently been published, and they throw a fascinating light on herself, her family, and the whole of the Greta Hall circle. They reveal her as the perfect *petite bourgeoise*. She has the standards we should expect of her class and upbringing. She is sublimely unaware of her husband's greatness: "You will also be sorry for another thing respecting him—Oh! when will he ever give his friends anything but pain [she writes in 1816]? he has been so unwise as to publish his fragments of ' Christabel ' and ' Koula-Khan.' Murray is the publisher, & the price is 4s. 6d.— we were all sadly vexed when we read the advertizement of these things." She is shrewd and sharp and loves gossip; but she is likeable, too, and above everything vividly alive, *clichés* and all:

Dear and kind friend,
　　Your very interesting letter of the 10th March must *first* be acknowledged with many, and grateful thanks, before I begin upon the *old subjects* of *myself* and *surrounding objects.* . . .
　　The whole account of your dear niece is very interesting: Southey knows the Bishop by Character: the family are highly respectable: Wordsworth believes it is of *ancient* respectability from the name, and he told me his reason for thinking so, but I shall mangle the thing if I attempt to write it, it was something about an *inscription on a Gate*—n'importe: they are decidedly persons of talent. . . .[145]

There were now three Coleridge children: Hartley, born in September, 1796; Derwent, four years younger; and Sara, born in December, 1802. Hartley was already a most remarkable boy, showing every sign of inheriting a measure of his father's genius:

he quickly won a place in his uncle Southey's heart, which through all the vicissitudes of his career he was never to lose. The children were looked after by Mrs. Wilson (Hartley's beloved "Wilsy"): she fulfilled the double function of nurse to them and housekeeper to Mr. Jackson, the Coleridges' landlord, who lived under the same roof with them but in a separate part of the house. The *ménage* was completed by a third Fricker sister, Mrs. Lovell, whom Edith Southey brought with her.

So much for the household.

The house itself has often been described, for in the first forty years of the nineteenth century it was visited by many English writers, not to mention other distinguished persons—artists, politicians, bishops, Frenchmen, Americans. And it still stands to-day, comparatively little changed from what it was when Coleridge became its tenant in 1800 and Southey arrived there in this September of 1803.

You first catch sight of it from the Cockermouth road, at the western end of Keswick. It is placed on a little hill above the winding Greta, and even now, when other houses have been built close to it, it appears somewhat aloof, withdrawn: it must have looked much more solitary then. From the road below you see it rising tall and square among trees, the roof low-pitched and the windows in the top storey rather too small. The general effect is a little gaunt and forbidding. But when you get closer, this impression changes. You then see that the house has a most unusual architectural feature, which is invisible from the road below and does much to redeem it from bareness: at each side is a wing of two stories—the centre of the building has three—curving backwards in symmetry.

Inside, the rooms are square and plain, perhaps rather smaller than you would expect. It is only when you go upstairs and look out of the windows—especially those of the room that was Southey's study on the first floor—that you realise the full glory of the house: its wonderful position, and the views it commands. Ahead lies Derwentwater, with the mountains of Borrowdale beyond; to the right, Bassenthwaite; behind, Skiddaw. "My God! what a scene!" cried Coleridge. "Right before me is a great *Camp* of single mountains—each in shape resembles a giant's tent; and to the left, but closer to it far than the Bassenthwaite Water to my right, is the lake of Keswick, with its islands and white sails and glossy lights of evening—*crowned* with green meadows, but the three remaining sides are encircled by the most fantastic mountains that ever earthquakes made in sport; as fantastic as if Nature had *laughed* herself into the convulsion in which they were made."

Lamb's similes were equally apt and striking when he told his friend Manning of the visit he paid to Greta Hall in the late summer of 1802. "Coleridge", he says, "dwells upon a small hill by the side of Keswick, in a comfortable house, quite enveloped on all sides by a net of mountains: great floundering bears and monsters they seemed, all couchant and asleep. We got in in the evening, travelling in a post-chaise from Penrith, in the midst of a gorgeous sunshine, which transmuted all the mountains into colours, purple, etc., etc. We thought we had got into Fairy Land. But that went off (as it never came again—while we stayed we had no more fine sunsets); and we entered Coleridge's comfortable study just in the dusk, when the mountains were all dark with clouds upon their heads. Such an impression I never received from objects of sight before, nor do I suppose I can ever again. Glorious creatures, fine old fellows, Skiddaw, etc. I never shall forget ye, how ye lay about that night, like an intrenchment; gone to bed, as it seemed, for the night, but promising that ye were to be seen in the morning. Coleridge had got a blazing fire in his study; which is a large, antique, ill-shaped room, with an old-fashioned organ, never played upon, big enough for a church, shelves of scattered folios, an Æolian harp, and an old sofa, half-bed, etc. And all looking out upon the last fading view of Skiddaw and his broad-breasted brethren: what a night!"

A detailed description of the interior of the house, as it was then arranged, is given in one of the letters Coleridge wrote to Southey when he was pressing him to come and live there: "The house consists—the first floor (or rather, ground floor) of a kitchen and a back kitchen, a large parlour and two nice small parlours; the second floor of three bedrooms, one a large one, and one large drawing-room; the third floor or floors of three bedrooms—in all twelve rooms. . . . If it suited you, you might have one kitchen, or (if Edith and Sara thought it would answer) we might have the two kitchens in common. You might have, I say, the whole ground floor, consisting of two sweet wing-rooms, commanding that loveliest view of Borrowdale, and the great parlour. . . . We should have the whole second floor, consisting of the drawing-room, which would be Mrs. Coleridge's parlour, two bedrooms, which (as I am so often ill, and when ill cannot rest at all, unless I have a bed to myself) is absolutely necessary for me, and one room for you if occasion should be, or any friend of yours or mine. The highest room in the house is a very large one intended for two, but suffered to remain one by my desire. It would be a capital healthy nursery."[146]

At the outset the two brothers-in-law divided the rent equally between them, paying a little over £20 a year each. In 1809, when it was clear that Coleridge had abandoned the place, Southey became the sole tenant, on a lease of twenty-one years. Ten years later he had thoughts of buying the whole Greta Hall estate; but he abandoned the plan, probably because he found difficulty in raising the necessary capital. His rent had by then risen to £75 (though this included a small quantity of furniture): on the renewal of the lease in 1830, it was reduced to £50.[147]

This, then, was the setting for the rest of Southey's days, and the company in which they were mainly passed. His life at Greta Hall was quiet, simple, remote; static, though not stagnant; punctuated by births and deaths, the visits of friends and occasional trips to other parts of England or to the Continent; above all, given over to books, by choice as well as from necessity: one of the most even, admirable careers English literature can show.

VIII

RISING REPUTATION

(1803-1809)

A T THE TIME of the Southeys' arrival at Keswick, Coleridge was away in Scotland. He had set off on a long-planned tour with Wordsworth and Dorothy in the middle of August. In his extremely neurotic condition, he must have been a trying companion even to such devoted friends, and when they reached the head of Loch Lomond Wordsworth suggested they should separate. Coleridge then walked on into the heart of the Highlands alone, through Glencoe to Fort William and Inverness and so back to Perth—a distance, he tells us, of 263 miles in eight days. Here he learnt of Margaret Southey's death. He was deeply affected and at once hastened on to Edinburgh to take the coach for Penrith. At Edinburgh he was delayed for two or three days, to his great vexation: "I cannot chitchat with Scotchmen", he wrote to Southey, "while you are at Keswick, childless." On 15th September he was home.

His sympathy for his brother-in-law and his desire to comfort him were quite genuine, and they got on very well together for the time being. But he found Mrs. Southey and Mrs. Lovell "a large, a very large Bolus"; and the constant irritation of living with them and his wife was soon too much for him. He was by now very ill indeed—"my bowel and stomach attacks frequent and alarming", he reported at the end of November— and he quickly decided that he must get away from England into some warmer climate. With that object he set out from Greta Hall on 20th December.[148]

He went alone, leaving his wife and children in Southey's care. Whether they made any kind of fixed arrangement, or whether it was done tacitly, we do not know. In either case it threatened a formidable increase in Southey's responsibilities, at a time when, as we have seen, he could very ill afford it. But he bore the new burden quite uncomplainingly, and very much more efficiently than Coleridge. The financial situation is far from clear, but it seems that Coleridge paid off his debts before he left England for Malta the following April, and that in his absence his wife was able to draw freely upon the annuity of £150 he received from the

Wedgwoods. In March, 1803, he had also taken the precaution of insuring his life for £1000, besides making a will, by which he left his family in Poole's, or if Poole were dead in Wordsworth's, guardianship. So that at first they cannot have been any very considerable financial charge on his brother-in-law.[149]

The cloud of grief that lay upon Southey and his wife when they arrived at Greta Hall soon began to disperse. Much of it was lifted with the birth of a second daughter on 30th April, 1804. Like Margaret, she was at first a frail child: she was not christened until June, 1805, when she received the names Edith May at Crosthwaite church.[150] Her health caused her parents a good deal of alarm : they were both over-anxious by temperament, a tendency that must have been strengthened by Margaret's death. But gradually she grew stronger, and they began to breathe more easily. On 11th October, 1806, another child was born—to Southey's great delight a son, who was called Herbert, no doubt after Mr. Hill. He was from the beginning, as every one could see, his father's favourite child. His sisters were never in the least neglected or under-valued; but Southey's love for him was always of a peculiar intensity.

What with these children and the little Coleridges, Greta Hall soon became a gay and noisy place. It was an ideal house for a large family, and Southey's a proper spirit to preside over it. He treated his sisters-in-law—particularly Mrs. Coleridge, who was his special butt—with continual banter, and the children with a very reasonable indulgence. From the first, moreover, he delighted to receive his friends there, and as he was always willing to show civility to their friends too, his circle of acquaintance rapidly grew larger.

In May, 1804, his wife safely delivered of her child, he went off to London on a business visit. During his journey up, which took 48 hours, the coach stopped at Oxford. It was just after sunrise, and while the horses were being changed he walked about the city: "I went under the windows of what had formerly been my own rooms; the majesty of the place was heightened by the perfect silence of the streets, and it had never before appeared to me half so majestic or half so beautiful."

In London he stayed with Rickman, now the Speaker's secretary, at his house in Palace Yard. His main object was to see Longman, with whom he discussed his plans for future works. *Madoc* was now almost finished. The whole poem had been revised, extensively, competently, and quickly. Soon after he reached Keswick he reported that "not one line in five stands as

originally written"; four months later, "the first part (about
3600 lines) is clean, corrected, and fit to be read to Spenser himself
if he were upon earth". The book at last appeared, as a huge
quarto appropriately dedicated to Wynn, in April, 1805.

But though he might believe that his epics would be the
corner-stone of his permanent reputation, he knew by now that
for immediate financial profit he must look elsewhere. He continued to draw the bulk of his income, apart from Wynn's annuity,
from reviewing. When he arrived at Keswick he had just completed a series of papers for the *Annual Review*. This was a fresh
venture set on foot by Longman, and it became Southey's main
stand-by for the next few years, until it was replaced by the
Quarterly and the *Edinburgh Annual Register* from 1809 onwards.
It was edited by Arthur Aikin, an old acquaintance of Southey's,
and one of the purposes of his present visit to London was to
arrange for a cargo of books to be sent down to Keswick to keep
him employed for the next few months.

He always called reviewing, and journalism of all kinds,
"task-work", and he often referred to it in deprecatory terms—
"I am manufacturing a piece of Paternoster Row goods, value
three guineas, out of Captain Burney's book." But his work in
this field (which always appeared anonymously) reached a high
standard: he was a conscientious, hard-working reviewer, who
rarely dealt with a book that lay outside the range of his knowledge. Though he was a severe critic, who found much contemporary literature unattractive or pernicious and never hesitated
to say so, he was seldom unfair, and his work is quite free from
any such disgraceful episodes as the *Blackwood* and *Quarterly*
articles on Keats.[151] More than once he used his position to bring
into notice obscure writers he thought deserving, like Lucretia
Davidson and Mary Colling; and though his judgment here was
erratic and his verdicts have generally been reversed by posterity,
his disinterested kindness was none the less admirable.

He also had two new prose works to discuss with his publisher.
Less than two months after his arrival at Greta Hall he had told
Tom that he was going to write "the volume of letters which
you have heard me talk of—an omnium-gatherum of the odd
things I have seen in England". During the next year the book
took shape as the *Letters from England by Don Manuel Alvarez
Espriella* (a fictitious Spaniard invented by Southey).

Before coming up to London he had suggested to Longman the
publication of a sequel to George Ellis's *Specimens of the Early
English Poets*. Now he renewed the proposal, at first putting

SOUTHEY IN 1804

*From a drawing by Henry Edridge in the National
Portrait Gallery*

forward Charles Lamb as a suitable editor. Whether Longman rejected this suggestion, or whether Lamb declined, it was Southey who in the end agreed to prepare the book. His wide reading and retentive memory qualified him for the task very well; but unfortunately he hit upon the idea of taking Grosvenor Bedford as co-editor, partly because he lived in London and could therefore get at the rarer books with ease, and partly as a way of initiating him into the pleasant paths of literature. Now Bedford —an intelligent man and in other ways a blameless, attractive character—had one incurable fault: his mind was lethargic, he was inclined to be lazy. The effect on the *Specimens of the Later English Poets* was unhappy. In spite of careful instructions on method and procedure, as well as much spurring, from Southey, the book was not ready to appear until 1807, and then the text was, full of printer's errors and faults of every kind: it is the only really unsatisfactory piece of work with which Southey is associated. His correspondence with Bedford on "the damned specimens", as he ended up by calling them, may stand as an awful warning to collaborators;[152] but a measure of the blame must rest on both of them for embarking upon a work they had not fully discussed together, living as they did at opposite ends of England.

In less than a month he was back at Keswick. That summer brought visits from Humphry Davy, "stark-mad for angling", and his young brother Henry, who was with him for some months. He had got into trouble at Norwich the previous year: Dr. Martineau had refused to keep him because he was so idle, and he had contracted a debt of £48, which his long-suffering brother had to help him discharge.[153] He was now packed off to continue his medical studies at Edinburgh, where he turned over a new leaf, achieving his M.D. in 1806.

Pleasant though his life was, and much as he liked Greta Hall, Southey was far from regarding himself as settled there. At the beginning of 1805 a rumour got abroad that England was about to send an expedition to Portugal under Sir John Moore: this looked like the opportunity he had been waiting for, and he snatched at it eagerly. He asked Bedford to put him in the way of securing an appointment as a civil inspector of accounts with the expedition, for which he thought he was adequately qualified. But the rumour soon proved to have been ill founded, and the chance faded away. He prepared to remain at Keswick for the time being.

One result of his living there was that he renewed acquaintance

with Wordsworth, on more cordial terms than before. Little
more than a month after his first arrival, Wordsworth came over
from Grasmere. His main purpose then was to see Coleridge, but
the visit also caused him to revise his previous unfavourable
estimate of Southey: he found him "very pleasant in his manners,
and a man of great reading". After this meeting they continued
to keep in touch, and now disaster brought them closer. In the
second week of February Southey heard of the death of John, the
poet's beloved younger brother. He had been captain of an East
Indiaman, the *Earl of Abergavenny*, which was wrecked off the
Dorset coast. At first he thought that he would actually have to
break the news to Wordsworth, who was coming over to Keswick,
but in fact it had already reached Grasmere. Though he does not
seem ever to have met John Wordsworth, he was deeply moved.
"In such circumstances", he wrote to Wynn, "I believe we feel as
much for others as for ourselves. . . . I am writing to you merely
because this dreadful shipwreck has left me utterly unable to do
anything else. . . . Of all deaths it is the most dreadful, from the
circumstances of terror which accompany it." Wordsworth now
showed how his feelings for Southey had changed by turning to
him for help. "If you could bear to come to this house of mourn-
ing to-morrow," he wrote the day after the news arrived, "I should
be forever thankful. . . . Your conversation, I know, will do me
good." Southey did as he was asked, went again a few days later,
and once more in April for a day or two. Such a crisis showed
him at his best, and it marked the beginning of his friendship
with Wordsworth.[154]

This same year 1805 also brought him acquainted with another
of his great contemporaries, Walter Scott. Elmsley came up to
visit him, and bore him off early in October for a short visit to
Edinburgh. On the way they spent three days at Ashestiel. This
does not seem to have been his first meeting with Scott: he had
probably seen him in August, when he passed through Keswick
on his way to stay with Wordsworth at Grasmere. Scott (who
was, almost to a day, three years older than Southey) was now
in the first full tide of fame: *The Lay of the Last Minstrel* had been
published at the beginning of the year, and it was meeting with
a success then unparalleled. But nothing ever turned his head,
and he received his less-successful fellow-poet with unaffected
kindness. "I saw nothing in Southey's manners like literary
jealousy", he told Miss Seward, "and should think him above it;
certainly they are not always and altogether so pleasing as those
of Wordsworth, but I think it is mere manner."[155] Southey for his

part found it "impossible not to like" Scott; and looking back on this visit he contrasted him very favourably with the literary pundits of Edinburgh, whom he now went on to meet.

His opinion of them was certainly not flattering. Jeffrey and Brougham seemed to him "pygmies", then and always. "Perhaps I am not a fair judge," he adds, "having been accustomed to live with Coleridge and Wordsworth; but the plain truth is that, compared with such men as these, the Scotch *literatuli* are very low indeed." He had no personal dislike for Jeffrey, in spite of his treatment of *Thalaba*: the little man (he was five foot one) travelled back in the coach with them and came to supper at Greta Hall. Nor were such remarks as these made *pour faire effet*: they were perfectly sincere. "Edinburgh Reviewers" and "Lake Poets" were already separating into opposite camps—the terms are wide and loose, but they are legitimate symbols. It was much more than a mere matter of critical opinions. They belonged to two different worlds of ideas, in life, in politics, in literature; and the gulf that separated them was too wide ever to be bridged.

Scott was one of the few great writers of that generation who never belonged to either party. There were many reasons why he stood aside. In the first place, his sympathies were divided. He was a loyal Scot and a personal friend of Jeffrey's: he enjoyed the wit and brilliance of the *Edinburgh Review*, and was quite happy to write for it occasionally. But unlike his fellow-contributors, he was also a poet: he appraised the works of the "Lake School" with a poet's eye, little as he agreed with some of their principles, and he understood Jeffrey's shortcomings and limitations as a critic.[156] He held aloof in wider senses too. He was a strong, straightforward Tory, a supporter of Pitt and Dundas without qualification. That of course divided him from the Whigs of the *Edinburgh Review*; but it also put him at a distance from the ex-Jacobins of the Lakes. Of their long and often bitter pilgrimage, enshrined for ever in the *Prelude*, his sturdy, uncomplicated spirit knew nothing. Above all, he was a man of the world, and his large mind disliked all quarrels other than the ancient warfare of political parties. He always had a slight disdain for literary controversy, as if it were something of a storm in a teacup, an affair of Tweedledum and Tweedledee.

Back at Keswick, Southey fell upon his "task-work", which occupied him for the best part of four months. He also began upon *Espriella's Letters* in good earnest, writing to ask several of his friends for information to include in them. On cookery and music he applied to Miss Barker, on pugilism to Rickman, on the navy to Tom. His brother Henry when in London paid a special visit to the Swedenborgians' chapel, on which Letter LXII was based; while Letter XXIII, on the monuments in Westminster Abbey, seems to have been mainly written by Richard Duppa—an old friend of Southey's, an artist and the author of a biography of Michelangelo.[157] With so many fingers in the pie it is surprising that the book should have appeared homogeneous in the end, as it undoubtedly does.

At the same time, *Madoc* out of the way, he was making some slow progress with another epic—that Hindu poem he had conceived during his second visit to Portugal. *The Curse of Keradon* had now become *The Curse of Kehama*. It was apparently begun in blank verse, but in May, 1805, he told Bedford of a change in this plan: "Wynn will show you the first book of *Kehama* beryhmed. . . . My notion of the metre is only to rhyme it in parts, either to increase the bustle or to give ornament to what in itself is least interesting, the greater part remaining unrhymed."[158] He showed an unusual hesitancy, however: over a year later he reported that "Elmsley advised me to go on with it; and the truth is, that my own likings and dislikings to it have been so equally divided that I stood in need of somebody's encouragement to settle the balance". Altogether, the poem made fitful progress until, as we shall see, another poet roused him into completing it.

That winter brought great political events, which affected Southey even in remote Keswick. Napoleon was everywhere victorious in Europe: in October, 1805, the Austrian army surrendered to him at Ulm; six weeks later came his resounding triumph at Austerlitz. Only on the sea was he worsted, and there the victory of Trafalgar seemed at the time to lose half its value through the death of Nelson. The prospect was bleak indeed when the new year opened, and on 23rd January Pitt died.

He was not lamented by Southey, who always spoke of him with a narrow rancour. This may appear strange to us, for Pitt had been the driving-force of the war against France, which Southey now approved with all his heart. Stranger still, he never ceased to respect Fox, though Fox had long been a defeatist and anxious for peace. These two estimates were relics of his liberal youth that he never grew out of: he could not forgive Pitt for his repressive measures against the Jacobins, or condemn Fox when he remembered his consistent defence of them.

The new government was a predominantly Whig coalition, headed by Fox and Lord Grenville. Among its minor members was Wynn, who became Under-Secretary for the Home Department. This seemed to Southey to open up a chance of securing some appointment abroad such as he had long wanted. His thoughts were naturally still fixed on Portugal. There were two suitable posts there, one of which was likely to become vacant soon, and Lord and Lady Holland both promised to speak for him; but the weeks went by and nothing happened. It may have been with the object of hastening a decision by appearing in person that he made another short visit to London in April. If this was the idea in his mind, his journey was wasted. Moreover, he had an interview with Longman, in which he learnt that his total profits on a year's sale of *Madoc* had amounted to £3 17s. 1d.: altogether it was a depressing trip. With a sourness unusual in him he noted that "Wordsworth flourishes in London, he powders and goes with a cocked hat under his arm to all the great routs. No man is more flattered by the attentions of the great, and no man would be more offended to be told so."[159]

Before returning home he went down to Taunton to see his Uncle Thomas, his father's younger brother. John, the eldest member of the family, had died a rich bachelor the previous year, leaving the bulk of his money to his brother Thomas and none to his nephews. With this uncle—who was in his late fifties and likewise unmarried—Robert was on rather better terms: he had stayed with him for two or three days in 1802, and described the experience to Wynn wryly and vividly. "He was very civil, powdered his wig, which is only done on Sundays, changed his coat, and moved into the best parlour. I found a strange man living a comfortless life: his dress shabby, his manners boorish, a strong understanding wasted, and good feelings habitually suppressed till they have been almost destroyed. He keeps no company, and his establishment is almost miserly. . . . I talked with him, laughed with him and made him laugh, he pushed the bottle, loaded my plate with fruit, broached his best beer for me—still it was not comfortable: I heard the click of the clock, and the hum of the gnats at evening, and the crumbling of a wood fire, and a man never hears these sounds if he is enjoying himself.[160] On this second visit the old man so far forgot his nature as to give his nephew £25. They never met again.

After this unprofitable expedition to the south, the summer at Keswick brought many enjoyments. Henry, straight from his degree at Edinburgh, came down for another long holiday, and in July he took his brother off for three days' stiff walking. They climbed Great Gable, saw the Isle of Man from the top, drank five quarts of milk when they got down again, and ended up at Greta Hall "as fresh as larks after a walk of eleven hours". Some weeks later, they were joined by Tom: it was the first time the three brothers had been together since they were children.

When they left him in September, Robert turned to reviewing once more. But he did other things at the same time. He completed an edition of the sixteenth-century Portuguese romance *Palmerin of England*. This was not a wholly new translation, but a revision of the earlier versions: it proved troublesome work and cost him much labour before it finally appeared, in four volumes, in 1807.

This winter also brought him two fresh tasks. At the end of October he heard of the death of a young *protégé* of his, Henry Kirke White. This lad, the son of a Nottingham butcher, had attracted his attention three years earlier with a small volume of verse, *Clifton Grove*. An unsympathetic, though by no means a savage, notice of the little book appeared in the *Monthly Review* and excited Southey's great indignation. He wrote to Kirke White and at once began to interest himself in the boy. It seemed that he had published the book in the hope of making a little money to help him towards going to the university. This he at length achieved: with the assistance of Wilberforce and Simeon he entered St. John's College, Cambridge, as a sizar in October, 1805. (He was a precocious Evangelical—a trait that did not commend itself to Southey.) At Cambridge he developed consumption: it drove him to over-work, and in a year he was dead, at the age of twenty-one.

Southey at once volunteered to do for him what he had helped Joseph Cottle to do for Chatterton, and in the course of the winter he received from the boy's relatives all his papers that were to be found. Working with remarkable speed, he produced a selection from them with a full biographical introduction, and two volumes of *The Remains of Henry Kirke White* were published in the autumn of 1807. The profits from the sale of the book were generously made over by Southey to the White family. Ironically, it came nearer to being a "best-seller" than anything else he ever produced: it ran through ten editions in sixteen years. In 1822 he added a third volume, containing a further selection of poems and letters.

This success, as Southey himself knew, was not primarily owing to public admiration for Kirke White's poetry: it had other extraneous causes—the sentimental appeal of his pathetic life, his religiosity, so dear to certain types of Evangelical. But there was also support for Southey's view that he had the stuff of a fine poet in him, and from unlikely quarters. Among Kirke White's contemporaries it would be hard to name a witness less sympathetic to him by temperament than Byron. Yet in 1809 he praised him in *English Bards and Scotch Reviewers*:

> Unhappy White! while life was in its spring,
> And thy young muse first waved her joyous wing,
> The spoiler swept that soaring lyre away,
> Which else had sounded an immortal lay.

While in 1811 he remarked to his friend Dallas that " with a great deal of cant, which in him was sincere (indeed, it killed him . . .), certes there is poesy and genius".[161]

Reading Kirke White to-day, he seems very small beer indeed: he· was unquestionably not a Chatterton or a Keats. But if one can disregard his unpleasing type of piety, it is possible to catch an occasional glimpse in him of a vein of genuine, if minor, poetry. It may be added that everything a modern critic can find to say in his favour has been well said by John Drinkwater.[162]

The other new work Southey now undertook was a very much larger affair. He had continued to make substantial progress with the *History of Portugal*: in the summer of 1806 he told John May that he had reached the death of John III (1557), and that the history of the Portuguese in India was complete to 1539. His plan for the whole work was on a great scale: three volumes were to be devoted to the history of Portugal itself, two or three to the Portuguese in Asia, two more to the literary history of the whole Iberian Peninsula, and one each to Brazil, to the Jesuits in Japan, and to the Monastic Orders—" in all, ten, eleven, or twelve quarto volumes". Unhappily, the splendid design was never completed—it was little more than begun. A great deal of the material for it had been collected by his uncle during his long residence in Portugal. In the summer of 1801, when the threatened French invasion of that country drove him home, he brought his papers with him and settled down in the comfortable Herefordshire living of Staunton-on-Wye. By 1806 the times, as Southey said, were " South American mad"; Mr. Hill had in his hands manuscripts and notes containing much information that was not otherwise obtainable in England; it occurred to him to offer them to the government. Lord Grenville answered that the information they supplied " seemed to relate to the wrong side of South America", but he urged nevertheless that a history of Brazil should be written without delay on the basis of these materials. Southey took this advice, and laying aside the main work sat down to his new task on 1st February, 1807.[163]

No doubt he acted on Lord Grenville's suggestion because it seemed good in itself: it would be pleasant to produce a topical book for which there would be some demand. But he may also have thought that by doing as he was bidden he would increase his chances of securing one of those diplomatic or consular posts he coveted. He still thought of Portugal with longing. "Cintra! Cintra! . . ." he exclaimed to his brother Henry. "That place is the only place in the world which I love better than this, and very probably I shall never quit this unless it be to reside in Portugal, where I would willingly go and take up my abiding-place for the remainder of my days. It is not possible to tell you how deeply I love that country. . . . Here my happiness proceeds wholly from my mind—there I have an animal and bodily happiness for which my soul thirsts whenever I remember it."[164] But the chances of returning there seemed as far away as ever, and it now became necessary for him to decide whether he was to continue living at Greta Hall or to leave it.

Coleridge had returned from Malta in the previous August, and after a good deal of procrastination had come down to visit his family in November. Like the Wordsworths, Southey had been shocked by his appearance. "His countenance is more changed for the worse than I could have believed possible", he told Danvers. "The eyes have lost all their life, partly from fat and still more from the quantity of laudanum which he takes, and the quantity of spirits. Nothing intoxicates him, and he is not sensible and will not be easily convinced that he drinks enough to kill anybody—frequently when he was at home nearly a bottle of rum in a day. Do not talk about this, for it is better kept to ourselves, but he is every way the worse for his long absence, except in his understanding." He had now determined on separating from his wife, and every one agreed that that was the best course—except Mrs. Coleridge herself, whose respectable soul was outraged at the idea: "everybody will talk", was her constant complaint. His plan was that the children should be with him for their education, spending their holidays with her. For this purpose she would obviously need a home, and it may have been for her sake as much as for his own convenience that Southey decided to remain at Greta Hall. It certainly suited him best that way: it meant that if he should decide to go to Portugal alone, as he thought of doing, his family would not be homeless; and it saved him the expense of a move, which he could ill afford.[165]

It was soon out of Lord Grenville's power to serve him even if he wished to, for at the end of March his government fell. It had been tottering for weeks past, and Wynn had determined to try and secure some perquisite for his friend while he was still in a position to do so. At the last moment in the frantic scramble he managed to get Southey offered the choice between a pension of £200 a year as a man of letters and the Registership of the Vice-Admiralty Court of St. Lucia, which carried a salary of £600. There was no time to consult Southey as to his preference, or both might be lost, so Wynn on his own responsibility accepted the former, with Southey's subsequent approval. Financially it made little difference to him—and what difference it did make was for the worse. He had hitherto received an annuity of £160 from Wynn: this he now gave up as a matter of course. The pension amounted to only £144, £56 being deducted for income-tax, to his great indignation. Looking back on his past history, he was amused to find himself a government pensioner. "And yet", he reflected, "mine has been a straight-onward path! Nothing more has taken place *in* me than the ordinary process of beer or wine—of fermenting, and settling, and ripening." That summarises his own view of his career in a sentence: he had matured and developed; there had been no violent change in his opinions, still less any apostasy.

The year 1807 saw the publication of no less than four of Southey's works: the editions of *Palmerin* and Kirke White, the unhappy *Specimens of the Later English Poets*, and *Espriella's Letters*. All of them appeared under his own name except the last. In this case he was anxious to try and keep up the fiction that the book really was by a Spaniard, since that would give greater weight to the views it expressed. To Danvers he added another reason: he hoped that the *Letters* might "pass as a translation with those reviewers who criticise my books with no other object than to injure me". In the event, the reception of the book gratified him. He had succeeded in piquing the curiosity of the public, and with the aid of a friendly "lift" in the *Courier* the first edition sold quickly and another had to be prepared almost at once. When the secret came out—as it inevitably did quite soon—the sale fell off, though the book was again reprinted in 1814, besides receiving the compliment of three American editions and of translation into French and German. It thoroughly deserved this modest success, for it is a most lively and readable sketch, giving a brilliant impression of life in early nineteenth-century England.[166]

Now that *Palmerin* was off his hands, he was able to press forward with the translation of another and a finer romance. The heroic career of the Cid Campeador is among the greatest glories of Spanish history. It is recorded in the twelfth-century *Poem of the Cid*, in the prose chronicle of Alfonso the Wise, and in a number of medieval ballads. Southey's *Chronicle of the Cid* represents a fusion of material from all these sources, skilfully welded into a single plain, clear narrative. It was published as a quarto in 1808 and has been among the most widely admired of his works.[167]

What the Cid is to Spain, Roland is to France and King Arthur to England. It was natural that Southey, with his passion for romances, should next think of editing Malory's wonderful book, and in November, 1807, he began to cast about for the materials. He applied to Wynn and to Richard Heber, the great collector, for the loan of rare books. Barely had he written when he learnt that the same idea had simultaneously occurred to Scott, who told him that he was "thinking of publishing a small edition of the Morte Arthur, merely to preserve that ancient record of English chivalry". Without delay Southey wrote back, telling Scott of his own more elaborate plan—"to give the whole bibliology of the Round Table in the preliminaries, and indicate the source of every chapter in the notes". Scott at once stepped gracefully aside with a characteristic gesture: "I am very glad the Morte Arthur is in your hands; it has long been a favourite of mine."[168] But Southey seems to have made little progress with the work, and two years later we find him writing to Scott again: "Your views about the Morte d'Arthur are wiser ones than mine. I do most formally and willingly resign it into your hands. . . . A very limited edition is sure to find purchasers, and nothing need be sacrificed to ensure success." Nevertheless, it was Southey who in the end produced the book. It was set up from a transcript of the Caxton edition, made from Earl Spencer's copy, and Southey's part in it was confined to an introduction (in which he expressly states that he was not responsible for the text) and some notes. *The Byrth, Lyf, and Actes of King Arthur* made its belated appearance in two quarto volumes in 1817.

Southey was now at the height of his powers. The years 1807-1816 were the best of his life. Not only did they bring his finest works, in verse and in prose: they gave him domestic happiness too—precarious, but real enough while it lasted. His family grew steadily: four more daughters were born to him in rapid succession—Emma in 1808, Bertha in 1809, Katharine in 1810, and Isabel in 1812. Emma died when she was little more than a year old, but the rest proved stronger.

De Quincey has left us an unfading portrait of Southey, founded on his intercourse with him in these years, in his *Literary Reminiscences*. It was drawn more than a quarter of a century afterwards; it has suffered from the dimming of his memory and from his constitutional inaccuracy in matters of fact; it has been coloured by estrangement (though it is less malicious than the similar sketches of Wordsworth and his family): but these are small faults compared with its vividness and its poetic truth.

De Quincey first met Southey in November, 1807. He had escorted Mrs. Coleridge up from Bristol by way of Liverpool and had just had his first meeting with the Wordsworths, whom he accompanied on an expedition over the Kirkstone Pass into Patterdale and so along Ullswater to Penrith. Wordsworth had business to attend to there, and De Quincey walked slowly over to Keswick by himself. "It was about seven o'clock when I reached Southey's door", he recalled in 1839; "for I had stopped to dine at a little public house in Threlkeld, and had walked slowly for the last two hours in the dark. The arrival of a stranger occasioned a little sensation in the house; and, by the time the front door could be opened, I saw Mrs. Coleridge, and a gentleman whom I could not doubt to be Southey, standing, very hospitably, to greet my entrance. Southey was, in person, somewhat taller than Wordsworth, being about five feet eleven in height, or a trifle more, whilst Wordsworth was about five feet ten; and, partly from having slender limbs, partly from being more symmetrically formed about the shoulders than Wordsworth, he struck one as a better and lighter figure, to the effect of which his dress contributed; for he wore pretty constantly a short jacket and pantaloons, and had much the air of a Tyrolese mountaineer. . . .

"His face I profess myself unable to describe accurately. His hair was black, and yet his complexion was fair; his eyes I believe to be hazel and large; but I will not vouch for that fact: his nose aquiline; and he has a remarkable habit of looking up into the air, as if looking at abstractions. The expression of his face was that of a very acute and aspiring man. So far, it was even noble, as it conveyed a feeling of a serene and gentle pride, habitually familiar with elevating subjects of contemplation. And yet it was impossible that this pride could have been offensive to anybody, chastened as it was by the most unaffected modesty; and this modesty made evident and prominent by the constant expression of reverence for the great men of the age (when he happened to esteem them such), and for all the great patriarchs of our literature. The point in which Southey's manner failed the most in conciliating regard was in all which related to the external expressions of friendship. No man could be more sincerely hospitable—no man more essentially disposed to give up even his time (the possession he most valued) to the service of his friends. But there was an air of reserve and distance about him—the reserve of a lofty, self-respecting mind, but, perhaps, a little too freezing—in his treatment of all persons who were not among the *corps* of his ancient fireside friends. Still, even towards the veriest strangers, it is but justice to notice his extreme courtesy in sacrificing his literary employments for the day, whatever they might be, to the duty (for such he made it) of doing the honours of the lake and the adjacent mountains."

The next day Wordsworth came on to Greta Hall from Penrith. De Quincey's curious and penetrating eye at once noted the contrast between the two poets, and the picture he drew of their imperfect sympathy with one another is a classic. "I could read at once, in the manner of the two authors, that they were not on particularly friendly, or rather, I should say, confidential terms. It seemed to me as if both had silently said—' We are too much men of sense to quarrel because we do not happen particularly to like each other's writings: we are neighbours, or what passes for such in the country. Let us show each other the courtesies which are becoming to men of letters; and, for any closer connexion, our distance of thirteen miles may be always sufficient to keep us from *that*.' In after life, it is true—fifteen years, perhaps, from this time—many circumstances combined to bring Southey and Wordsworth into more intimate terms of friendship: agreement in politics, sorrows which had happened to both alike in their domestic relations, and the sort of tolerance for different opinions in literature or, indeed, in anything else, which advancing years and experience are sure to bring with them. But at this period, Southey and Wordsworth entertained a mutual esteem, but did not cordially like each other. Indeed, it would have been odd if they had. Wordsworth lived in the open air: Southey in his library, which Coleridge used to call his wife. Southey had particularly elegant habits (Wordsworth called them finical) in the use of books. Wordsworth, on the other hand, was so negligent, and so self-indulgent in the same case, that, as Southey, laughing, expressed it to me some years afterwards, when I was staying at Greta Hall on a visit—' To introduce Wordsworth into one's library is like letting a bear into a tulip-garden '."[169]

De Quincey's statements on the relations between the two poets, as those of a particularly acute observer, are of the greatest value; but it must be remembered that he was writing many years afterwards, and that as an artist he always tended to heighten his contrasts. Wordsworth and Southey were both reserved by nature: this seems to have misled De Quincey, to some extent at least, into thinking that their feelings for one another were less cordial than they really were, and into seeing what were mere differences between the two men as antagonism.

Just after De Quincey's visit, Southey was approached through Scott with an invitation to become a contributor to the *Edinburgh Review*. It was a tempting proposal, for the remuneration offered was more than double what he was getting from the *Annual*. " I am certain you may add £100 a year, or double the sum, to your income in this way with almost no trouble", wrote Scott; "and, as times go, that is no trifle." It was no trifle indeed to Southey, whose entire income at this time, including his pension, barely exceeded £300 a year. And an even more important consideration lay behind: "the advantage to have been gained from the civility which would have been ensured [in the *Edinburgh Review*] to my future publications was still greater than this increase of immediate pay". Yet he decided, with little hesitation, to turn the offer down. In his reply to Scott he expressed personal civility to Jeffrey; "but it was impossible for me", he told Bedford, "to coalesce with a man whom I consider as ' a bad politician, a worse moralist, and a critic in all matters of taste equally incompetent and unjust '. Those were the words I used."170

He quickly wrote off to Coleridge to tell him of the plan, and to suggest that they should join together to attack Jeffrey, either in a verse satire, to be called *The Man in the Moon*, or in a series of letters. At the same time he expressed a wish that Coleridge should start a new journal in opposition to the *Edinburgh*: " Clarkson has probably talked to you about a new review. Were it possible that you could undertake the management (oh that I thought this were possible!) you might secure to yourself an income of £500 a year. My co-operation might be drawn on to any extent. With my brother Harry I challenge all England for good spirits and making a noise. With you I would challenge all the critics in England and make open war upon them."171

Coleridge already had some such project as that in his mind. According to Cottle, he had been considering the plan of a " New Review", with himself as editor, only a month or two before. In the early summer of 1808 he gave Wordsworth some details, and

in August he came down to stay with him at Grasmere. The
Wordsworth family having now grown too big for Dove Cottage,
they had just moved into Allan Bank—a new house, large and
plain, superbly situated to the north of the village and above it,
commanding the whole Vale. Here, away from the distractions
of London, and looked after with tender care by the Wordsworths
and Sara Hutchinson, Coleridge began to think of ways and means
of carrying the plan into effect. It matured at length as *The
Friend*, the unique periodical that ran its erratic course from 1st
June, 1809 to 15th March, 1810. At the outset, Southey gave the
scheme every encouragement, until he realised that its success
was hopeless from the faulty plan on which it was grounded and
from Coleridge's irregularity as an editor; but he burdened
himself nevertheless with the thankless task of reading the
proofs.[172]

Moreover, in spite of all discouraging precedents, he went
into partnership with his brother-in-law in the preparation of one
more book. This was a discursive collection of miscellaneous
anecdotes and comments on literary and philosophical subjects,
which duly appeared in 1812 under the title *Omniana, or Horae
Otiosiores*. It was an admirable idea, for it displayed the extraordinary learning of both authors to advantage and it was
exactly suited to Coleridge's peculiar mental habits, turning his
spasmodic methods of composition to good account.[173]

Southey's wish for a new anti-Whig review was soon fulfilled.
In expressing his discontent with the *Edinburgh*, his anger at its
politics, he was airing the opinion of the overwhelming majority
of English conservatives, and of all who were in favour of the
whole-hearted prosecution of the war. In the spring he made a
journey to London: there he found "a base and cowardly feeling
abroad, which would humble this country at the feet of France".
He "declared himself unqualifiedly for the war", reported Crabb
Robinson, whom he now saw for the first time.[174] In this spirit
he went on to Bristol, where he met a fellow-poet who felt as
strongly on the subject as he did himself: Walter Savage Landor,
whom he had longed to know ever since *Gebir* had fallen into his
hands nine years before. They found many things in common,
political ideas prominent among them. Landor was nothing if
not a bellicose character, and he and Southey now encouraged
one another in violence.

Their excitement rose to a higher intensity in May with the
news of the uprising of the Spanish people against Joseph
Bonaparte and the French army of occupation, the beginning of

the Peninsular War. In the summer Landor went off to fight as a volunteer in the Spanish army. "I have never seen anything so marvellous as that man", wrote his new friend: "if he be present when King Joseph is taken, King Joseph will be hanged upon the first tree."[175]

The Portland government had now made up its mind to abandon the policy Britain had hitherto pursued in the war, that of attacking France primarily in her overseas trade and colonies, and to send a substantial expeditionary force to Portugal in order to help the insurgent people of the Peninsula. On 1st August Sir Arthur Wellesley's troops began to disembark in Mondego Bay. On the 21st they won a considerable defensive victory at Vimiero. But its fruits were thrown away by Wellesley's inept superiors on the spot, and on the 30th the so-called Convention of Cintra was signed, allowing the French army to be shipped out of Portugal unmolested. There was much to be said for thus gaining time for the British forces to consolidate themselves, and Lisbon was now secured to us without a blow; but far too many of the French demands were weakly conceded, and when the news of the Convention reached England there was an immense public outcry. It was caught up, in terms of extravagant violence, at the Lakes. "Had I been minister", wrote Southey, "I would have followed the Roman example in such cases—annulled the treaty, and delivered up the generals who signed it to the French, with ropes round their necks." For, as he put it on another occasion, the signing of the Convention had "abandoned our vantage ground . . . by degrading into a common and petty war between soldier and soldier, that which is the struggle of a nation against a foreign usurper, a business of natural life and death, a war of virtue against vice, light against darkness, the good principle against the evil one". This was the lofty spirit of indignation that Wordsworth so splendidly voiced in his *Tract on the Convention of Cintra*, which appeared in its final form the following May.[176]

Holding such views as these on the Spanish war, Southey's anger at the line taken by the *Edinburgh Review* may easily be imagined. It had maintained for some time past that Britain should make peace, on the ground that France was invincible. Now, quite consistently, while paying lip-service to the heroism of the Spanish people, it gloomily prophesied the defeat of their efforts. "Upon the case as it is at present before the country," we read in the July number, "the sounder opinion seems to be that which is unhappily too melancholy to contemplate with calmness,—that the Spaniards will be defeated, after a gallant and most sanguinary struggle." Another paper, by Jeffrey, in the following number gave even greater offence, particularly by such passages as this: "Something, we would fain hope, may be done, even yet, *to protract the defeat* of that great and good cause, and to obtain better terms for the patriots, if they ultimately fail. . . . But is there no possibility of gaining even more than the utmost probable success can secure, by availing ourselves of the offer lately made to open a negotiation?" On reading this article, Scott told Constable to remove his name from the list of subscribers.[177]

The idea of a rival quarterly, run on similar lines to the *Edinburgh* but with opposite politics, seems to have originated with Murray. John Murray II was a very able man of business, with a real feeling for literature and a desire to play the part of Maecenas to the distinguished authors of his day in London, as Constable was managing to play it so successfully in the Scottish capital. In September, 1807, he wrote to Canning, commenting on the "radically bad" principles of the *Edinburgh* and going on to remark that "some means equally popular ought to be adopted to counteract their dangerous tendency". Nothing came of the idea for the moment; but a year later, in the course of a visit to Ashestiel, he laid before Scott a more detailed plan for a new review, proposing as its editor William Gifford, the former editor of the *Anti-Jacobin* and a long-standing associate of Canning's.[178]

Grosvenor Bedford was among Gifford's close friends, and it was through him that Southey was approached at the beginning of November with a request that he should become a contributor to the new journal. He agreed at once, stating that he thought himself particularly well qualified to deal with three subjects: history, biography and travel. He added, for Gifford's benefit, a concise statement of his political views: "I despise all parties too much to be attached to any. I believe that this country must continue the war while Buonaparte is at the head of France, and while the system which he has perfected remains in force; I therefore, from my heart and soul, execrate and abominate the peace-mongers. I am an enemy to any further concessions to the Catholics; I am a friend to the Church establishment. I wish for reform, because I cannot but see that all things are tending towards revolution, and nothing but reform can by any possibility prevent it". This is an important statement in the evolution of Southey's political ideas: it illuminates the path he had already taken, and it foreshadows the future development of his mind.

WORDSWORTH IN 1805
*From a drawing by Henry Edridge in the possession of
Mrs. H. D. Rawnsley*

Murray's project quickly went forward, and the first number of the *Quarterly Review* appeared in February, 1809. It included a paper by Southey on the subject of Christian missions in India, for which he received the good fee of £21 13s.[179] This was the first of the series of 95 articles, of varying length and effectiveness, that he was to contribute to the *Review* during the next twenty-nine years. For the rest of his active life it continued to provide the backbone of his literary income. The fees he received for his work there gradually rose, and on the whole he was generously and fairly treated by Murray. At the same time he was certainly not over-paid, for it was his steady support, united to Gifford's competent editorship, that founded the reputation and prosperity of the *Quarterly Review*.

Yet he never wholly approved of its management or its principles.[180] Of the very first number he wrote to Scott: "The *Quarterly* is a little too much in the temper of the *Edinburgh* to please me. No man dips his pen deeper in the very gall of bitterness than I do . . . but I do not like to see scorn and indignation wasted on trivial objects—they should be reserved like the arrows of Hercules for occasions worthy of such weapons." In May, 1809, he heard from John Ballantyne that Canning's friends talked of "unmuzzling" Gifford, by which they meant allowing him to revert to his old Anti-Jacobin line. "I simply told him in either of these cases I should withdraw from the journal, ' being of any party rather than the Anti-Jacobin '. I might have told him that I would rather be hanged without that Anti to my denomination than pensioned with it."[181] How far he was from that docile, orthodox high Toryism for which he was reviled by his enemies!

The papers he wrote for the *Review* were all of a pattern, the conventional pattern established by the *Edinburgh* and familiar to us from Macaulay's *Essays*: they took the form of long articles, on texts provided by some book or books recently published. But they were something more than merely elaborate reviews: the best of them were independent essays, clear and well argued in a style rather more trenchant than that of his books. And from an editor's point of view he had certain merits to be highly prized. "Two things I can promise", he himself told Gifford: "perfect sincerity in what I write, without the slightest assumption of knowledge which I do not possess; and a punctuality not to be exceeded by that of Mr. Murray's opposite neighbours at St. Dunstan's." His relationship with the *Review* was never an easy one. Again and again he was angered by the mutilation his papers suffered at Gifford's editorial hands: he often grew restive,

S.   I and several times he threatened to withdraw altogether. For thirty years, as Andrew Lang remarked, "he, like Pistol, ' ate and swore ' at the source of his provender".[182] But he could never afford to do without the income the *Quarterly* brought him, while Murray and its successive editors valued his contributions too highly ever to let him go. It was a *mariage de convenance*, and it lasted for the rest of his active life.[183]

At the same time, in December, 1808, Southey received a prospectus of the *Edinburgh Annual Register* from James Ballantyne the printer, then about to set up with his brother and Walter Scott as the ill-fated firm of John Ballantyne & Co. He agreed in a casual way to become a contributor, sent some small things for inclusion in the first issue, and thought no more of the matter. In the following August he was asked to write for it an account of the history of Spain during the previous year; and then, soon afterwards, came a further proposal that he should be responsible for the whole historical part of the *Register*, at the handsome salary of £400 a year. This would more than double his income at a stroke, and the work was congenial, for it gave him a chance to speak his mind on public affairs: he can hardly have thought of refusing. But it imposed on him a new and severe task, to be performed against time: the narrative of the year 1808 had to be completed as soon as possible—though actually it was not published until the autumn of 1810. He continued to write for the *Register* for over three years. Then, in the winter of 1812-1813, he abandoned it owing to John Ballantyne's dilatory and evasive methods of payment. The firm was already in difficulties, and Southey suffered along with its other various creditors: he did not receive the last of the sums he was owed until November, 1818. But he was not the sort of man to sit down meekly under such treatment. He complained in peremptory terms both to Ballantyne himself and to Scott; and in private he was wont to refer to Ballantyne as "Sir Shuffler", "a dirty fellow", and "a scoundrel".[184] However, for two or three years the *Register* did bring in a large addition to his income, and later on he was able to use some of the material he had contributed to it as the basis of his *History of the Peninsular War*.

The year 1808, then, marks another important milestone in his career. The *Quarterly* and the *Register* did three things for him, in return for the great services he rendered them. First, they gave him a measure of economic security: from this time onwards he was never in acute financial difficulty, even if it was to be many years yet before he became comfortably off. Secondly, by the work they demanded they turned him from a hack reviewer, putting months of activity into ephemeral little articles for the *Annual* and such journals, into an essayist whose papers were substantial enough to be worth reprinting as they stood, or to form a solid basis for future books. Thirdly, and at first sight rather strangely, his anonymous contributions to the *Quarterly* and the *Register* added immensely to his reputation. He became a rumour among their readers, and that rumour soon became a certainty—"Southey's prose is so good that every one detects him", said Gifford.[185] His views were listened to with respect, and in time he achieved a certain political importance. He had found his feet at last.

IX

SUCCESS AND FAME

(*1809-1816*)

OR ALL his recent preoccupation with prose, Southey was still continuing to write poetry. Disheartened by the slow sale of *Thalaba*, he had put aside *The Curse of Kehama* for a time, and we hear little of it in 1806 and 1807. But in March, 1808, he paid his exciting visit to Landor at Bristol. His new friend inquired after his poems, and learning that they were laid by because he "could not afford to write them", exclaimed, with characteristic impulsiveness and generosity, "Go on with them, and I will pay for printing them, as many as you will write and as many copies as you please". This offer touched him to the quick: he could not think of accepting it, but neither could he let the challenge go unanswered. He set out at once to complete *Kehama* by working at it exclusively before breakfast, "for the sake of showing him poem after poem, and saying, 'I need not accept your offer, but I have done this because you made it'". The work was at last finished on 25th November, 1809, and it was published the following year. He also carried through a heavy revision of *Thalaba* at the same time. And furthermore, this rediscovery of his poetic faculty joined with his passion for Spain, now at its height in the Peninsular War, to inspire one more epic, on a subject he had long contemplated: Pelayo and the restoration of the Spanish monarchy in the eighth century. A week after finishing *Kehama*, he began on the poem that was to become *Roderick, the Last of the Goths*.[186]

These were indeed years of concentrated industry: in a literary sense, they were the most satisfactory of his life. Besides *Kehama*, 1810 brought the publication of the first volume of the *History of Brazil*. His work was interrupted only by occasional short visits —to Durham, where his brother Harry was now in practice, to the Lloyds at Old Brathay by Ambleside, to De Quincey or to the Wordsworths at Grasmere.[187]

Coleridge paid his last two visits to Greta Hall in the summer of 1810 and in February, 1812. We have seen what assistance Southey had given to his literary work. He now made a final attempt to recall Coleridge to a sense of his responsibilities towards his family. At the beginning of 1811 he sent him "a short letter in plain but proper terms, asking him if he did not himself feel how idle it was to go about looking for external aid, . . . urging him to return here, this being the best place for him whether he adopts a wiser mode of life or persists in his present destructive one, and beseeching him to let me be his task-master for three months. . . . Something too I said about his children. He has given me no answer, which is easily accounted for, for I have no doubt that this letter, as well as two former ones which I have written him, is still unopened." Whether it was eventually answered or not, the appeal was fruitless.[188]

We do not know the exact amount of the liabilities Southey incurred on behalf of his brother-in-law's wife and children. The late E. H. Coleridge, who spoke with unique authority on the subject of his family, estimated Mrs. Southey's income at £105 a year. Southey refused to allow her to live in a cottage at Amble-side, where the boys were educated, insisting that she should remain at Greta Hall, and giving the whole family board and lodging. In the later years of her life there, she seems to have paid him something, but certainly not enough to cover the whole cost of her family's keep.[189]

Finance was not the only consideration, however. Southey's kindness was even more strikingly displayed in the way he treated his sister-in-law and her children—in every respect as members of his own family. He succeeded as far as any one could in supplying Coleridge's deficiencies, both as a husband and as a father. When Hartley was to go up to Oxford in 1815, it was he who secured the money for his expenses, from other members of the family and from friends. Hartley's subsequent failure, though it disappointed his uncle, did not at all diminish his kindness: there were no recriminations. Perhaps, therefore, considering his history and his position as a dependent relative, his tribute is the most remarkable Southey ever received from any one. "Sometimes", he confessed to his mother in 1836, "I may have said things about dear Uncle to you, which I should have [been] very angry if anybody else had said, but then—it was when you used his name as a reproach to me, or advanced his conduct or opinion as a rule. Now if you want to make a man hated, hold him up as an example. It is an extraordinary proof of the loveli-ness of Southey's character, that though his name was rife in every objurgation and every admonition I received, I never could help but love him." There could hardly be higher praise than that.[190]

After his trip to London in 1808, Southey did not go there again until the summer of 1811. This visit was made memorable by a meeting with Blake, whose pictures (then on exhibition in Golden Square) Southey went to see. Twenty years later he told Caroline Bowles that he had found Blake "so evidently insane, that the predominant feeling in conversing with him, or even looking at him, could only be sorrow and compassion. . . . Some of the designs were hideous, especially those which he considered as most supernatural in their conception and likenesses. In others you perceived that nothing but madness had prevented him from being the sublimest painter of this or any other country. You could not have delighted in him—his madness was too evident, too fearful. It gave his eyes an expression such as you would expect to see in one who was possessed." After meeting Blake, he went on to a party at Lamb's. Crabb Robinson, who was also there, noted that Southey "admired both his designs and his poetic talents, at the same time that he held him for a decided madman. Blake, he says, spoke of his visions with the diffidence that is usual with such people, and did not seem to expect that he should be believed. He showed Southey a perfectly mad poem called *Jerusalem*—Oxford Street is in Jerusalem".[191]

He left London with Edith towards the end of July. Their return journey to Keswick was leisurely and roundabout, for they stopped to see several of their friends on the way. In August they visited Landor and his newly-married wife (poor pretty, empty-headed Julia Thuillier) at Llanthony. They spent three nights among the grey Cistercian ruins of that enchanted monastery, deep in the folds of the Black Mountains. More than forty years afterwards, Landor recalled how

> Along Llanthony's ruined aisles we walkt
> And woods then pathless, over verdant hill
> And ruddy mountain, and aside the stream
> Of sparkling Hondy. Just at close of day
> There by the comet's light we saw the fox
> Rush from the alders, nor relax in speed
> Until he trod the pathway of his sires
> Under the hoary crag of Cwmioy.

We know nothing else of the visit, but from the letters of both men it is clear that it was an unqualified success. With Landor that could never be taken for granted, for he was one of the most quarrelsome men who ever lived. But no coolness was ever to come between him and Southey, in spite of many differences of opinion: a remarkable tribute in its way to them both.[192]

From Llanthony they went on to Ludlow and thence, after a visit to Miss Barker in Staffordshire, to Wynn's Llangedwyn. The weird splendour of the Black Country impressed Southey deeply: "There is something very striking in that sort of hell above ground—hills of scoria, an atmosphere of smoke, and huge black piles, consisting chiefly of chimneys and furnaces, grouped together in the finest style of the damnable picturesque." After leaving Wynn, they went on to see the Kosters at Liverpool, stopping on the way to dine with the Ladies of Llangollen, and so at the beginning of September they reached home.[193]

Two months later, unknown to Southey, there arrived at Keswick a devoted lover of his poetry: the young Shelley, bringing with him Harriet Westbrook, whom he had rashly married in Edinburgh that August. Shelley was now at his most idealistic and visionary—he was only nineteen—and one of his objects in coming to Keswick was to see the Lake Poets whose work he so much admired. He never met Wordsworth or Coleridge—a fact that Coleridge at least regretted in after years, for he felt that he might have been able to handle him sympathetically;[194] but Southey he did meet, at the Calverts' house Windy Brow, about Christmas time.

Before he saw Southey, he thought of him as "a *really* great man"; though, being an ardent Radical, he already disliked Southey's politics. "I shall see him soon", he wrote in mid-December, "and I shall reproach him for his tergiversation. He to whom Bigotry, Tyranny, Law was hateful has become the votary of these idols in a form the most disgusting." But after talking to Southey, his opinion changed for a time. "A man must possess high and estimable qualities, if with the prejudices of such total difference from my sentiments I can regard him [as] great and worthy. In fact Southey is an advocate of liberty and equality. . . . Southey, though far from being a man of great reasoning powers, is a great Man. He has all that characterises the poet—great eloquence, though obstinacy in opinion, which arguments are the last thing that can shake."[195]

On his side, Southey treated Shelley with all his accustomed kindliness, entertaining him at Greta Hall, discussing philosophical and political questions with him, lending him books to support the arguments he put forward.[196] He was greatly struck by Shelley at once, as anybody must have been who met him;

not only by his genius, which he was quick to perceive, but by the remarkable resemblance he bore to what he had himself been in youth. (Had not Shelley been expelled from University College, Oxford, for publishing a pamphlet called *The Necessity of Atheism*, just as Southey had been expelled from Westminster for his contribution to *The Flagellant*?) "Here is a man at Keswick", he exclaimed, "who acts upon me as my own ghost would do. He is just what I was in 1794." All his old distaste for Oxford authority returned upon Southey with a rush: "He is brimfull and overflowing with everything good and generous—though the Oxford men were as much shocked at him as if he had had hoofs and horns, four and forty iron teeth, and a tail with a sting at the end of it. . . . I do not say that it would have been either right or expedient to keep Shelley at Oxford, but this I will swear, that when they expelled him they sent away more genius and better principles than they kept behind—that is, better in their *roots*, and which will prove themselves so by the fruit which they will bring forth."[197]

Southey's kindness to Shelley was not limited to hospitality and good advice. It took a more practical turn too. Thinking that Rickman, as the Speaker's secretary, might well know Shelley's father, who was M.P. for Shoreham, he wrote asking if he could intercede for the boy. "If you know the father well enough to speak upon such a subject, endeavour to make him understand that a few years will do everything for his son which he ought to wish. . . . He will get rid of his eccentricity, and he will retain his morals, his integrity and his genius, and unless I am greatly deceived there is every reason to believe he will become an honour to his name and his country."

Rickman does not seem to have approached Timothy Shelley— or if he did, his intervention was unsuccessful; and it had already become clear that for all their mutual cordiality, there was little in common between Southey and his young admirer. An admirer of his poetry Shelley remained: Southey's influence is written largely over his work (most of all in *Queen Mab*, which was finished early in 1813).[198] But he soon came to think less highly of Southey's character. "I am not sure that Southey is *quite* uninfluenced by venality", he writes on 2nd January, 1812. "He is disinterested, so far as respects his family; but I question if he is so, as far as respects the world." A fortnight later he considers that Southey, "whose principles were pure and elevated once, is now the paid champion of every abuse and absurdity"; and on leaving Keswick at the beginning of February he records that he "passed Southey's house without *one* sting. He is a man who *may* be amiable in his private character, stained and false as is his public one, he *may* be amiable; but, if he is, my feelings are liars".[199]

Southey and he never met again, though some famous letters were to pass between them in the course of the next eight years.[200] It is not surprising that they should have failed to understand one another fully: what is remarkable is that after these brief, disputatious meetings, and in the course of a correspondence in which each was eagerly concerned to demolish the other's position, neither of them ever lost his temper or his respect for his adversary. Yet their debate was made of the most inflammable stuff: it was a clash between two brilliant, self-willed generations, and it was fundamentally a controversy on moral issues—on the social ethics of Shelley's conduct, on the "venality" of Southey's politics.

Harshly as Shelley judged Southey's motives in supporting the Tory government, he would have been still more shocked if he had known of the attempts that had gone on behind the scenes in the past, and were about to be resumed, to secure him a well-paid sinecure. More than two years earlier, in June, 1809, Scott, with his customary kindness in forwarding his friends' interests, had suggested that Southey should try for a university chair, offering the powerful support of Canning and George Ellis for his candidature. But this was impracticable, at least in England, for it involved subscription to the Thirty-nine Articles, to which Southey could not in conscience assent. However, in the following month he heard that an appointment, which he thought might suit him very well, was likely to fall vacant: the Stewardship of the Derwentwater Estates, belonging to Greenwich Hospital. The office, he understood, was a sinecure—like that Distributorship of Stamps to which Wordsworth was appointed later on; the salary, £700 a year. He had no hesitation in enlisting Scott's help.[201] But it soon turned out that though he had been correctly informed as to the salary, the duties attached to the post were anything but nominal: the Steward worked seventeen or eighteen hours a day; he had to be highly qualified in agriculture, surveying and mineralogy; and on top of that he was expected to be a competent lawyer. Not surprisingly, Southey remarked when he learnt this that he "would rather live in a hollow tree all the summer, and die when the cold weather should set in, than undertake such an employment".

At the same time, he had discussed a third idea with Scott.

There was, he heard, a post of Historiographer Royal, to which it was thought that a salary of £400 a year was attached. Might it not be possible for him to receive this appointment, while relinquishing his pension—it would mean a net gain for him, after income-tax had been deducted, of £134 a year? The office was then held by the Huguenot Louis Dutens, but his age was seventy-nine: his place must soon be vacant. The old gentleman held on until 1812. When he died, there was a strong attempt made to secure the succession for Southey. Lord Lonsdale applied on his behalf; Croker, unsolicited, lobbied the Prime Minister and the Lord Chamberlain; Scott wrote to ask the help of Lord Melville.[202] But it was no use: the Prince Regent had decided to bestow the prize on one of his chaplains, James Stanier Clarke. The disappointed candidate described his successful rival, maliciously but not unfairly, as "a painstaking man, and so far fit for it, but a most extraordinary blockhead, and so far unfit". He consoled himself with the discovery that the salary was only half what he had understood it to be.

Yet another effort was made in the following year; and this time Scott's persevering assistance was decisive. On 11th August, 1813, the Poet Laureate, Henry James Pye, died. This was no very distressing loss to literature, for his verse resembles nothing so much as tepid water; but it set in motion the usual scramble for succession to his place. The Laureateship was then, it is true, a somewhat equivocal distinction: since Dryden had lost it in 1689, it had been held by a string of nonentities, broken only for five years by Thomas Warton. The duties attached to the office consisted mainly in producing official odes, which invariably rendered their writers ridiculous; but its emoluments were popularly believed to be large, including the famous butt of sack, which had first been bestowed on Ben Jonson. On this occasion, to his credit, the Prince Regent made up his mind to offer the post to Scott, a really good poet. For a little while Scott hesitated. He understood the salary was £300 or £400 a year: he was not a rich man, and he had his family to think of. But he quickly decided to reject the offer. That he would be "well quizzed" if he accepted it worried him little; but he already held two public appointments, and he thought it would be greedy to take a third, "which might do real service to some poorer brother of the Muses". Accordingly, with much civility and many expressions of gratitude, he declined the proposal.

But he did not let the matter rest there. He knew a "poorer brother of the Muses" to whom the Laureateship would be very well worth having, if it could be offered to him and he be induced to accept it. When he refused the post, he wrote to Croker, asking him to use his influence to get Southey appointed in his place. And shortly afterwards he sent Southey this winning and graceful letter:

My dear Southey,

On my return here I found, to my no small surprise, a letter tendering me the laurel vacant by the death of the poetical Pye. I have declined the appointment, as being incompetent to the task of annual commemoration; but chiefly as being provided for in my professional department, and unwilling to incur the censure of engrossing the emolument attached to one of the few appointments which seems proper to be filled by a man of literature who has no other views in life. Will you forgive me, my dear friend, if I own I had you in my recollection? I have given Croker the hint, and otherwise endeavoured to throw the office into your option. I am uncertain if you will like it, for the laurel has certainly been tarnished by some of its wearers, and as at present managed its duties are inconvenient and somewhat liable to ridicule. But the latter matter might be amended, and I should think the Regent's good sense would lead him to lay aside these regular commemorations; and as to the former point, it has been worn by Dryden of old, and by Warton in modern days. If you quote my own refusal against me, I reply—first, I have been luckier than you in holding two offices not usually conjoined; secondly, I did not refuse it from any foolish prejudice against the situation—otherwise how durst I mention it to you, my elder brother in the muse?—but from a sort of internal hope that they would give it to you, upon whom it would be so much more worthily conferred. For I am not such an ass as not to know that you are my better in poetry, though I have had, probably but for a time, the tide of popularity in my favour. I have not time to add ten thousand other reasons, but I only wished to tell you how the matter was, and to beg you to think before you reject the offer which I flatter myself will be made to you. If I had not been, like Dogberry, a fellow with two gowns already, I should have jumped at it like a cock at a gooseberry. Ever yours most truly,

Walter Scott.

Abbotsford, Melrose. 1st September [1813].[203]

When this letter reached Keswick, Southey was, as it chanced, already on his way to London. It was not until he arrived there that he knew his name had been put forward for the Laureateship. Scott's suggestion had, however, been acted upon, and it was at once offered to him through Croker. He soon discovered that the salary was much less than Scott had supposed it to be—a mere £90 a year, in fact; but even that was to him worth having, and he decided to take the offer, if only the Laureate's duties could be a little modified. Might he not be excused the absurd necessity of turning out birthday and New Year odes, and write instead on any great national event or occasion that moved him? Croker primly observed to him that it was "not for us to make terms with the Prince Regent"; but he hinted that it might be possible to suggest privately the wisdom of forgoing the foolish custom. With this assurance Southey was contented: he accepted the Laureateship, as a matter of duty. He explained the reasons for his decision to Landor: "It would have been rank cowardice, and therefore rank folly, to have refused the appointment, which I could only have done because I disliked the Prince's government, or distrusted my own power of making the office respectable, or because I feared to give occasion to the jests of newspaper joke-smiths." The exiguous salary he made up his mind to invest in a life insurance for the benefit of his family. As to the official odes, the arrangement suggested by Southey was eventually adopted: it has governed the practice of Poets Laureate ever since.

It is pleasant to find that Scott ultimately benefited from this affair as well as Southey. When he declined the office, he had been afraid of offending the Prince Regent, "and perhaps losing an opportunity of smoothing the way to my youngsters through life"—an important and a perfectly legitimate consideration in those days. But it had had the opposite effect. The Regent said that "Walter Scott's charming behaviour about the laureateship had made him doubly desirous of seeing him at Carlton House"; eighteen months later Scott was presented to him for the first time; one of his earliest acts when he became King in 1820 was to confer a baronetcy upon Scott of his own accord.[204]

Southey's visit to London on this occasion lasted nearly three months. He was now able to make his headquarters with Mr. Hill, who had recently been appointed to the pleasant living of Streatham; and he spent, for him, an unusually large amount of time in visits and social pursuits. Coleridge indeed complained that he was "so *chevaux-de-frized* and palisadoed by pre-engagements" that it was difficult to get hold of him.[205] However, at the beginning of October the two brothers-in-law visited Madame de Staël together (who was not accustomed to being unable to get a word in edge-ways, and expressed her resentment in a famous sentence: "Pourtant, pour M. Coleridge, il est tout à fait un monologue").

He had one memorable experience on this visit: a meeting with Byron, which took place at Holland House on 26th September. Since the publication of the first two cantos of *Childe Harold* in the previous year, Byron had been the lion of London: his popularity as a poet had outshone Scott's, and it was enhanced by his dazzling personality, by his fame as a lover, and by whispers of his unmentionable intrigue with Augusta Leigh. Such a man was hardly likely to attract Southey, especially as he had ridiculed *Joan of Arc*, *Thalaba*, and *Madoc* in *English Bards and Scotch Reviewers* four years earlier:

> Oh! Southey! Southey! cease thy varied song!
> A bard may chant too often and too long:
> As thou art strong in verse, in mercy, spare!
> A fourth, alas! were more than we could bear.

Before being introduced to Southey, Byron was careful to make sure from Samuel Rogers that he was "magnanimous" enough to forgive such satire. When he had been reassured on this point, the two poets met, and talked agreeably enough for a little while. "I saw a man", reported Southey, "whom in voice, manner and countenance I liked very much more than either his character or his writings had given me reason to expect"; but years afterwards he vividly remembered how he felt "an insidious softness in Byron's manner which made him compare it at the time to a tiger patting something which had not angered him with his paw, the talons being all sheathed". Byron, for his part, was a good deal impressed by Southey. Writing to Tom Moore, he touched him off lightly as "the best-looking bard I have seen for some time. To have that poet's head and shoulders, I would almost have written his Sapphics". But to his journal he confided a more serious estimate of Southey: "His appearance is *Epic*; and he is the only existing entire man of letters. All the others have some pursuit annexed to their authorship.[206] His manners are mild, but not those of a man of the world, and his talents of the first order. His prose is perfect. Of his poetry there are various opinions: there is, perhaps, too much of it for the present generation; posterity will probably select. He has *passages* equal to anything."[207]

Southey's elevation to the Laureateship, faded though that honour was, did signify a real measure of public recognition: his contemporaries regarded him by this time as a major poet, one of the greatest then living. This same year 1813 also saw the appearance of the one book by which posterity has agreed to remember him: the *Life of Nelson*.

To the *Quarterly Review* for February, 1810, Southey had contributed an article on Nelson, based upon the immense biography by James Stanier Clarke (who was later to be his rival for the post of Historiographer) and John McArthur, and several other works. For this he received double pay—twenty guineas a sheet. Murray was so delighted with the result that he at once commissioned him to turn the article into a small book: "such a life of Nelson", Southey told Bedford, "as shall be put into the hands of every youth destined for the navy—a five-shilling volume, for which he gives me a hundred guineas".[208]

As usual, the work took much longer to complete than he expected, partly because of his other commitments and partly because, being at once a landsman and a very conscientious writer, he had to handle nautical matters with the greatest care. He was able, however, to make good use of his sailor brother Tom, who had fought as a lieutenant at the battle of Copenhagen, and a letter he wrote to him on 30th December, 1812, gives at once a good idea of his methods as a biographer and of the care he expended on the book. He wants all the vivid, rememberable details: "You used to speak of the dead lying in shoal water at Copenhagen; there was the boatswain's mate, or somebody, asked for, when he was lying face upward under the stern or somewhere. Tell me the right particulars of this, which is too striking a circumstance to be lost". Again: "Tell me all about your guns, and what loss they occasioned. Were they not honeycombed? Were you not saying when you pulled the triggers, ' Here goes the death of six!' This is a thing which would be felt." It is by such touches as these, which Southey, unlike many biographers, was always eager to use, that his *Nelson* has lived. At the same time he remained acutely aware of being out of his element: "I am such a sad lubber that I feel half ashamed of myself for being persuaded ever even to review the *Life of Nelson*, much more to write one. . . . I walk among sea terms as a cat does in a china pantry, in bodily fear of doing mischief, and betraying myself."

Such fears were by no means groundless: captious critics have rejoiced to point out the technical errors he made—and in the larger questions of strategy and tactics they are certainly serious.[209] But they have been corrected by scientific historians. Southey gives us something even more precious than technical accuracy; something that nobody else—not even a Mahan, for all his knowledge—has ever been able to achieve: a living picture of the man himself that speaks and moves. And that picture still colours the minds of us all when we think of Nelson: it has been well said that "the ' Nelson ' whom. we know to-day is almost as truly Southey's creation as ' Henry the Fifth ' and ' Richard the Third ' are Shakespeare's".[210]

The book had a moderate success on its appearance, even though, by an annoying miscalculation on the part of the printer, it had to be issued in two small volumes instead of one and was consequently more expensive than it should have been. Another edition was called for in the following year, and five more in Southey's life-time. With that mild irony that so often pursued him, it became truly popular only after his death: it has been reprinted at least a hundred times in England alone during the past century.

When they were discussing the Laureate's official duties together, Croker remarked that at least Southey need find no difficulty in writing an ode for the New Year of 1814. "You can never have a better subject", he said, "than the present state of the war affords you." It was true; for now at length the defeat of France was clearly approaching. Every year since 1808 had brought major disasters for Napoleon, in Spain, in Portugal, in Russia, in Germany. The names rang out like the strokes of a hammer: Talavera, Torres Vedras, Albuera, Moscow, and now in October, 1813, Leipzig. As a sincere and ferocious patriot, Southey shared to the full in the general joy. At a dinner-party in London just after the news of Leipzig had come, Crabb Robinson noted how he and the rest of the company "emulated each other in maledictions on Napoleon".[211]

Peace negotiations now began. Southey, and those who thought with him over the war, regarded them with great mistrust: the terms they wished for approximated to what we now call "unconditional surrender". In this they were not simply vindictive: they had some grounds for fearing the weakness or the misplaced clemency of the Allies. At Frankfurt this month, Metternich actually offered France peace if she would agree to give up the territory she had conquered in Germany, Italy, and Spain: this would have left Belgium in her hands—the very menace that England had gone to war to avoid. Fortunately for us, however, Napoleon, still dreaming of a world empire, could not bring himself to accept these terms. The war went on.

Southey acted on Croker's suggestion for his New Year ode. The poem was a good deal altered before it appeared. In deference to the criticisms of Rickman and Croker, he omitted from it the more violently anti-French stanzas. They pointed out that the ode was an official performance, and it was possible that before long France might become a friendly power: in that case, "can you stay in office," asked Rickman, "this *Carmen* remaining on record?" The offending section was ultimately published, with some additional lines, as an *Ode Written During the Negotiations with Buonaparte*; the official poem as *Carmen Triumphale, for the Commencement of the Year 1814*, garnished with notes including extracts from past numbers of the *Edinburgh Review*, designed to show its spirit of craven defeatism.

Napoleon succeeded in prolonging the war only until the spring. Then with the double invasion of France, by Blücher from the north-east and by Wellington from the south-west, it was clear that the game was up: on 31st March the Allies entered Paris; on 11th April the Emperor abdicated. The terms to be offered to the French now became everybody's speculation. Southey fully agreed with Landor, whose *Letters on the Preliminaries of Peace* had appeared in the winter under the pseudonym "Calvus", that this was the opportunity to repair the mistakes made at Utrecht. France should be confined to her 1648 frontiers; and in order to balance her power in Europe, a great state should be formed in northern Germany with Prussia at its head, and Italy should be unified. As to her lost colonies, Southey argued that France had no kind of right to expect to receive them back, but he suggested they might be returned to her if she bought them—the purchase money to go towards increasing the pay of British soldiers and sailors: she should also be compelled to abolish the slave trade.

The actual terms settled at the Congress of Vienna seemed to him criminally lenient; and when, with Napoleon's return from Elba in March, 1815, the war had once more to be resumed, he took a grim pleasure in saying "I told you so". His peace terms were now briefer, and more extravagantly savage, than they had been in the previous year: "Buonaparte and the Marshal [Ney] to the gallows, the rest of the army to Siberia and Cayenne! There should be nothing short of this; and if Paris be burnt in the conflict, I for one shall acknowledge the hand of righteous retribution." The end came quickly, and this time it was final: Waterloo was fought on 18th June; a month later Napoleon was on the *Bellerophon*.

To us, familiar with the course of nineteenth-century history, Southey's fanatical hatred of France may seem crude and misplaced. But was it really so inexcusable? Ever since the days of Richelieu, France had been the aggressor of Europe. Again and again she had embarked on wars of conquest. The two greatest of them she had lost; but she had been treated with studied mildness in the peace settlements that followed them, and after a short time she had resumed her career of aggression. Was there not something to be said for rejecting now the precedents of 1713 and 1763, for drawing the teeth of France once and for ever? Southey and his contemporaries could not know the truth: that France's military excesses had bled her white, that she would never again be able to challenge the whole of Europe single-handed. Ironically he welcomed the rise of that new power beyond the Rhine, which, in the succeeding century, has made the violence of Napoleon look liberal and civilised by comparison. But to-day, faced with the necessity of curbing a barbarous Germany, can we not sympathise a little with Southey's cry for a strict and exemplary treatment of the great aggressor of his age?

The news of Waterloo clearly called for some special celebration; and on 21st August a great party ascended Skiddaw to light a joyful bonfire on the top. Besides Southey himself, his wife, his eldest daughter, and his son, there was Wordsworth, with Mrs. Wordsworth and Dorothy; there was Miss Barker, who was now living at Greta Lodge, next door to Greta Hall; there was Lord Sunderlin (Edmund Malone's younger brother, aged seventy-six), Lady Sunderlin, and James Boswell the younger, who was staying with them at the time; not to mention three maids and "Messrs. Rag, Tag, and Bobtail". Arrived at the top, they had roast beef, plum pudding and punch, sang "God Save the King" round a bonfire made of tar-barrels, and rolled blazing balls of tow and turpentine down the mountain-side. "We formed a huge circle round the most intense light, and behind us was an immeasurable arch of the most intense darkness, for our bonfire fairly put out the moon." They got back to Keswick soon after midnight, some of Messrs. Rag, Tag, and Bobtail very happily drunk. Mrs. Coleridge was of course sitting up for them: "I had a very anxious time during the nine hours of their absence for I feared lest the Mists should come on, and so keep them on the heights all night, but not a Cloud came to distress them and not

S.   K one of the party were any worse for the expedition." "On the following week", she adds, consoling herself and Sara for not having been able to climb Skiddaw with the rest of them, "we had illuminations, Trans[formations?] and a balloon at Ld. S.'s on the other side the Lake, with elegant refreshments, & a great deal of good company—we took all the older children & on these occasions his Ldship always sends his carriage to fetch & carry us home."[212]

This was not the only way in which Southey celebrated the end of the war. A month later he set out on a tour of the Low Countries, to visit above all the field of Waterloo.[213] It was the first time he had been out of England for fourteen years. He took with him his wife and Edith May, by this time a girl of eleven: the rest of the party consisted of Henry Koster, Dr. H. H. Southey (who had now left Durham for a practice in Queen Anne Street) and his newly-married wife, with her mother and sister.

They crossed from Ramsgate to Ostend. Thence they made their way straight to Bruges, which at once fascinated Southey: "without exception the most striking place I ever visited", he called it in his decisive way. At Bruges they fell in with a party of their fellow-countrymen, including a deformed young artist named Edward Nash, who charmed Southey with his "uncommonly winning manners" and accompanied them for the rest of their tour: their acquaintance ripened into a firm friendship, which ended only with Nash's premature death in the winter of 1820.

Two days later they went on by canal to Ghent. It was a gentle and peaceful way of travelling—"a swan playing about the Trekschuit and looking as usual to be fed by the passengers; the water alive with fish, water-lilies (a rare sight on navigable waters, but these are perfectly still, and the canal is of such an age that nature has made it completely her own); and Bruges with its majestic towers to complete the picture". From Ghent they proceeded to Brussels, where Southey lost little time in calling upon the great bookseller Verbeyst. His shop presented an astonishing spectacle, crowded as it was from cellar to garret with books, the spoil of countless conventual libraries pillaged by the armies that had lately been campaigning in Belgium. Verbeyst's stock had overflowed into a church, which it also filled; and then, having no further storage room, he had been obliged to sell fifty tons more of books for waste paper. As a true bibliophile, he was genuinely grieved at the destruction; but it must at the same time have brought him a fortune. He and his new customer recognised each other at once as kindred spirits. "I dealt with him largely considering my slender means", noted Southey: Verbeyst always remained for him the prince of booksellers.

But other places demanded attention in Brussels besides book-shops. There were the usual sights of the city to visit—though they were largely thrown away upon Southey, who had little understanding of art or architecture, and all the dislike of the Baroque characteristic of his generation. He had too a more melancholy duty to perform. In the hospital were a number of British soldiers, wounded in the late campaign. Among them was a Keswick man, Richard Carbonell, whose parents had en-trusted Southey with a letter for him; but on inquiry it appeared that he had died six weeks before. The sight of the wounded men being taken out in waggons for an airing affected Southey deeply: "I had never before seen the real face of war so closely; and God knows! a deplorable sight it is."

On 3rd October they went out to Waterloo. It was over three months since the battle had been fought, but its traces were still evident enough: the ground was littered with shoes and belts and hats, stripped of their lace. (It must have brought back to his mind "The Battle of Blenheim", which he wrote in 1798 before he had ever seen a battlefield.) "Over the whole field", he noted, "poppies and pansies were in bloom; you saw them where the footsteps of the cavalry were still uneffaced, and in some parts upon the very graves." They had a guide to explain the positions to them and spent the night in the "Roy d'Espagne" inn at Jemappes, where Wellington had had his headquarters on 17th June, Napoleon on the 18th and Blücher on the 19th. Thence they made a circuit by way of Liége, Aachen and Louvain, and so back to Brussels. After visiting Antwerp they made their way to Calais, arriving at Dover on 28th October.

Southey's record of the trip, like all his other travel diaries, makes pleasant, unexciting reading. He was emphatically a character who was the same abroad as he was at home: curious about details, exacting in small things, but not too fastidious, philosophical over minor mishaps; on the whole a contented, easily-pleased traveller. He was not one of those who can appreciate no kind of landscape but his own. "Fresh as I am from Derwentwater," he says, "I can feel the beauty of this kind of country, and understand how it should have produced so many painters. It has everything which is soothing and tranquil—still waters, a wide horizon, delicious verdure, fertility and shade."

The *Journal* does not lack modern touches: at Brussels, for instance, he learns that "the Prussian Commandant at Paris has been murdered, that the destruction of Paris must be expected as an inevitable consequence". Again and again he hears tales of the greed and brutality of the Prussians: yet at the same time, when he meets some Prussian officers, he does ample justice to their good qualities. Altogether, the *Journal* shows him as a man of candour, good humour, and good sense.

He rounded off the trip by writing a description of his experiences in verse: *The Poet's Pilgrimage to Waterloo*. It was to some extent a matter of duty, he thought, for the Poet Laureate of England to celebrate so splendid a victory, due in such a large measure to English arms; and as with most official poetry, the result is tame and uninspired. But *The Poet's Pilgrimage* is redeemed by its charming Proem, in which he describes his return home after the journey, the happiness of his children, the joy of unpacking the toys he had brought back for them from Belgium:

> Bring forth the treasures now,—a proud display,—
>   For rich as Eastern merchants we return!
> Behold the black Beguine, the Sister grey,
>   The Friars whose heads with sober motion turn,
> The Ark well-fill'd with all its numerous hives,
> Noah and Shem and Ham and Japhet, and their wives.[214]

It is not difficult to see where Southey's heart really lay. He was a man of strong and deep affections: the tragedy of his poetry is that he so seldom allowed them to appear.

But if his highest happiness was in his family life, there too he was most vulnerable. And only a few months after this joyous return, a blow fell upon him there that marked him for the rest of his life. We have seen how he adored his one son Herbert. Every one agrees that he was a remarkable child, with that so rare combination of precocity and charm which had distinguished his cousin Hartley Coleridge. Dorothy Wordsworth, who was inclined to be tart about other people's children, thought he was "delightful": "the perfection of a child loving books and learning, he is all a child at play and has all the simplicity of a child in all his attainments". While De Quincey, who first knew Herbert when he was in petticoats, described him as "very interesting even then, but annually putting forth fresh blossoms of unusual promise, that made even indifferent people fear for the safety of one so finely organised, so delicate in his sensibilities, and so prematurely accomplished".[215]

No one feared more for the boy's safety than his father. He had always had presentiments about the deaths of children—after all, such deaths had often touched him: he had himself lost three sisters, a brother, and two daughters in infancy, Coleridge had lost Berkeley, Wordsworth had lost his sweet Catharine and a little son in 1812. Over and over again in his letters we come upon this premonition, repeated to an almost morbid degree. Thus when he writes to Cottle, asking him to come and stay at Greta Hall and promising to show him his library, he must add: "I would say my children too—if on this subject I were not far too sensible of the uncertainty of human life ever to look before me with confidence."[216] And in proportion to the intensity of his love for Herbert, so were his fears. De Quincey gives a touching instance of this: "the only rude thing I ever knew him to do, the only discourteous thing", was done on Herbert's account. They were landing on one of the islands of Derwentwater on a rather stormy day; the gentlemen were helping the ladies out of the boat; one of them picked Herbert up with great care and started to carry him, when Southey, "in a perfect frenzy of anxiety for his boy, . . . rushed forward, and tore him out of the arms of the stranger without one word of apology". It was not until some minutes afterwards that Southey realised how rude he had been: "fear for his boy quelled his very power of perception".

So when Herbert fell ill early in March, 1816, his father was at once deeply alarmed. For the only time on record in his mature years, he was quite unable to work: during the whole five weeks of Herbert's illness, he did nothing. The child suffered terribly (it is not clear what his disease was: it began with "an endemic cough and low fever" and it ended with what Dorothy Wordsworth calls "an inflammation on the heart"). Adequate medical help was not to be had in Cumberland. Dr. Southey offered to come down from London, but by that time it was too late: the boy died on 17th April.

His father never entirely recovered from this blow. Outwardly, things soon began to go on much as before, but his friends knew that he had changed. Dorothy Wordsworth put her finger on the spot: "All agree that he is an altered man. His buoyant spirits I fear will never return." In a sense they never did. His laughter became in time as noisy, as infectious as it had once been, but something of his resilience and his zest for life had been irretrievably lost. With Herbert, says De Quincey very truly, "died for ever the golden hopes, the radiant felicity, and the internal serenity, of the unhappy father. . . . For *him*, in this world, he said, happiness there could be none; for his tenderest affections, the very deepest by many degrees which he had ever known, were now buried in the grave with his youthful and too brilliant Herbert!"[217]

X

POLITICS AND CONTROVERSY

(*1816-1826*)

IT WAS perhaps as well that Southey could not afford to indulge his grief. As soon as Herbert was buried, he had to sit down doggedly at his desk and take up the threads of his work again. The second volume of the *History of Brazil* was on the point of completion; he had an official ode to write, a *Carmen Nuptiale* for the Princess Charlotte; and there was an article on La Vendée to be finished as soon as possible for the next *Quarterly*. The last of these was the most pressing, for it touched his immediate financial needs. He was afraid that he might now be too late to get the paper into the April number, in which case his payment for it must be delayed three months. But Murray acted with an unlooked-for generosity—had he perhaps heard through Bedford and Gifford of Southey's troubles? He sent £50 for the article, which relieved Southey of all anxiety as to when it appeared, and he proposed subjects for half a dozen future papers, offering the handsome sum of £100 for each of them. This seems to have become, from now onwards, the standard fee that Murray paid for all Southey's contributions to the *Quarterly*. He did not write for every number, but at this rate they must have brought him in an average of about £275 for the next twenty-three years.[218]

They had now come to reflect a change in the main direction of his political interests. Hitherto, as we have seen, he had been chiefly preoccupied with foreign affairs, with the French Revolution, Spain and Portugal, the war against Napoleon. But as that war drew to an end he began to turn his mind more seriously to home politics. In the years 1810 and 1811 he wrote three papers on reform: of Parliament, of the army and navy, of the public service. He followed them up in 1812 with a more elaborate discussion of the state of the poor, the doctrines of Malthus, and the manufacturing system. It was here, in the condition of the working classes, the means of bettering it and of checking revolutionary tendencies among them, that his real interest lay: in 1816-1818 he showed it in a series of five long essays; ten years later, in *Sir Thomas More: or, Colloquies on the Progress and Prospects of Society*—a work that was first planned in November, 1817.[219]

151

It would be misleading, and Southey himself would have thought it pretentious, to speak of his "political theory": he was not a man who cared for, or as a rule understood, theories of any kind. But as a collection of his plans and ideas for the government of England at this time, these essays and the *Colloquies* are worth studying. They represented the views of no party. If their character was predominantly Tory, they recommended too many measures of practical reform to be acceptable to the die-hards, while they were not "liberal" enough to please the coming young Tories of the school of Canning and Peel. "Liberalism" had indeed very little part in them. It was a conception Southey could not away with: he set his face steadfastly against the rising doctrines of *laissez-faire*.

He believed, and he consistently maintained, that it was the business of the State to provide what we now call "social services". Poverty was not to him, as it was to too many of the economists of his day, an act of God, deplorable but irremediable: it was an evil that could be greatly lessened, or even abolished altogether. Macaulay, in his famous essay on the *Colloquies*, poured great scorn on this notion: "He seems to be fully convinced that it is in the power of government to relieve all the distresses under which the lower orders labour." "Certainly I am", Southey would have replied. "I incline to think there will come a time", he told Rickman in 1816, "when public opinion will no more tolerate the extreme of poverty in a large class of the community, than it now tolerates slavery in Europe." A century later, the wheel has come full circle. Our sympathies lie with Southey rather than Macaulay.

The lines on which he proposed to tackle the problem of poverty, and all other social evils, were frankly authoritarian. Modern ideas of democracy, when they raised their heads, got short shrift from him. The franchise, even as it stood in his day, seemed to him too wide, in such constituencies as Westminster, for instance: he was in favour of "taking away votes from the ignorant, who cannot possibly know how to use them". As for universal suffrage, that "would be proclaiming anarchy at once".[220]

"Anarchy" and "mob-rule" were not mere bogies to people of that generation, who remembered with horror the years 1792-1794 in France, and saw in their own country the assassination of a Prime Minister, the Luddite disturbances, the Cato Street conspiracy, and the Bristol Reform Bill riots. The thought of revolution reduced sane and courageous men to panic. "You are quite right in apprehending a Jacquerie; the country is mined below our feet"—these are not the words of a nervous old woman: it is Scott writing to Southey in 1812. An even more remarkable instance comes from the other side, from the man who was to become the high priest of the Whig Reformers, Earl Grey: condemning the effect of irresponsible agitators in stirring up discontent, he wrote to a friend in 1819 that "if a convulsion follows their attempts to work upon the minds of the people, inflamed as they are by distress, . . . I shall not precede you many months on the scaffold".[221]

When such forebodings filled the minds of shrewd and sound observers, it is hardly to be wondered at that Southey, out of touch with the realities of politics, prone as he was to extremes and violent language, should have become an alarmist. His letters—especially those to Rickman, whose fears chimed with his own—sound a shrill crescendo from now onwards. He sees perdition staring England in the face, and he never hesitates to say so. Indeed as he gets into his stride, like Jeremiah and Carlyle he comes to take a ghastly pleasure in breathing forth his prophecies of doom. It is unattractive, on occasion absurd; but seen against the background of his time, it is not unintelligible.

That is the foolish side of Southey's activities as a political writer. But, as it has already been suggested, there is a fine and sensible side too. We may hold that his views on the future of democracy have been falsified in the event, and yet recognise that in some respects he saw further than the optimistic Liberals of his day, who so obviously had the angels with them. He was an early critic of the industrial system. He argued that it bred a greedy, selfish class of capitalists who, with their hangers-on, "would care nothing for the honour and independence of England, provided their manufactories went on, their *breweries* flourished [a hit at Whitbread, whom he loathed] and their salaries were paid".[222] It meant a steadily increasing pauperisation of the people. And worst of all, it involved "a new sort of slave-trade"; for "the London workhouses supplied children by waggon-loads to those manufactories which would take them off the hands of the parish; . . . a set of child-jobbers travelled the country, procuring children from parents whose poverty was such as would consent to the sacrifice, and undertaking to feed, clothe and lodge them for the profits of their labour".[223]

This last evil, which shocked him to the core, he never ceased to denounce.[224] And in time his exposure of the cruelties the children suffered was listened to and had its effect. His was not a lone voice. The elder Peel had initiated legislation on the subject in 1802: two other Tories, Oastler and Sadler, had opened a fresh attack on the system in 1830-1831, with Southey's cordial approval. His works had a considerable influence upon Shaftesbury, and helped to turn his mind in this direction. When Southey died, Shaftesbury described him in his diary as "essentially the friend of the poor, the young, and the defenceless—no one so true, so eloquent, and so powerful".[225]

That praise was not too high. For a man who had lived such a rigidly *bourgeois* life, Southey showed, in occasional flashes, an extraordinarily vivid perception of the miseries of poverty: "He who has ever seen the habitations of the city poor in the cellars and garrets of courts and alleys, will easily believe that the fireside of the pot-house holds out a stronger temptation than even the physical effect of the liquor." He was stirred to deep indignation by the injustice of the game laws, by the cruelties practised on climbing-boys, by "those shocking instances of persons dropping down in the streets, or crawling to brick-kilns, and dying from inanition, cases which make us shudder when we read of them, which can scarcely be regarded otherwise than as a national disgrace whenever they occur". And he put a bitter, memorable saying into the mouth of Sir Thomas More: "How large a part of your population are like the dogs at Lisbon and Constantinople, unowned, unbroken to any useful purpose, subsisting by chance or by prey, living in filth, mischief and wretchedness; a nuisance to the community while they live, and dying miserably at last!"[226] This is something we look for in vain in Macaulay, tender-hearted though he often was: Southey's mind was, in this field, the more imaginative and the less complacent.

He had hold too, though he hardly knew it himself, of the right end of the stick. For he was dimly aware that since the Industrial Revolution the greatest economic problem, instead of being one of production, was one of distribution; but as he did not fully understand the matter, he failed to put it with his usual trenchant clarity. To him the great capitalist was anathema— and not only the industrial capitalist, but the great landowner too, with "the command of whole counties", who could thus "sing ' We are seven ', like Wordsworth's little girl, into the ear of a minister, and demand for himself situations which he is unfit for".[227]

His remedy was consistent with the rest of his ideas: higher taxation and more power for the government of the country.

Over and over again he insists on the need for strong government, first of all for winning the war and then equally in time of peace. "The influence of government cannot be lessened without destroying government"; "order is the first thing needful in society".[228] Only by the action of a strong and enlightened government, rich through the yield of increased taxation, can the condition of the poor be radically improved. It can be done, he says, by a combination of measures: by undertaking a policy of great public works to lessen unemployment; by the establishment of savings banks and a system of national education; by improving the conditions of pay and service in the army and navy and so rendering them more attractive (he had long cried out for the abolition of flogging); by the assistance of emigration to the colonies. "It is time that Britain should become the hive of nations, and cast her swarms; and here are lands to receive them." He adds that the colonies, "when they may have ceased to depend upon the parent country, [might] remain connected with her by the union of reverential attachment on one side, and common interests on both"—an anticipation of the modern idea of Dominion Status.[229]

Such was the meaning of what Southey called "practical reform". It is true that along with it there went in his utterances much prejudice, much short-sightedness, much ignorance, and some absurdity. If he advocated national education, to take only one instance, it must be on Dr. Bell's system, which handed the whole superintendence over to the Church of England—a burden that the Church of that day was in no fit state to carry.[230] But it is none the less true that his political writings, of which Macaulay made such brilliant and imperishable fun, offered a serious contribution towards solving some of the problems of government that faced his contemporaries. They have a definite place in the development of progressive ideas in England, both on their own merits and for the influence they exercised over Young England and the Christian Socialists.[231]

They might easily have had a more immediate effect than they did if Southey had taken two opportunities that were offered to him in 1816 and 1817. In August, 1816, he heard from Bedford that J. C. Herries and Nicholas Vansittart, the Chancellor of the Exchequer, had been discussing his latest *Quarterly* article on the poor—that which stands as the fifth of the *Essays, Moral and Political*—and had agreed that the government ought to make fuller use of Southey's talents. Ten days later Bedford wrote to say that Vansittart had raised the question with Lord Liverpool, the Prime Minister, who had approved of the idea and had asked

Southey to come up to London and discuss it with him. Bedford thought he should make the journey. To any one else, he said, he would urge it as a matter of self-interest: to Southey he would plead that it was his duty to his country.

But he was not to be stampeded into a decision: coolly and carefully he weighed the project up in his mind. What it would come to, he foresaw, was that he should move to London and manage a newspaper—not necessarily a daily, perhaps a weekly— in the government interest. It might mean that his ideas would have a better chance of being carried into effect; it would give him another platform for expressing them, perhaps a more popular one than the *Quarterly*; and of course it would increase his income, and add greatly to his political influence. The last of these considerations can have weighed little with him, for he was genuinely without a desire for power. As to money, any addition to his income would be offset by the necessity of living in London—far more expensive than Keswick, and the place above all others he hated. He came to the conclusion that his acceptance would benefit nobody. "In any way that may be thought desirable I will do my best", he wrote; "but alas, Grosvenor, what *can* I do that I have not been doing?" It would be no gain, he argued, merely to transfer his work from the *Quarterly* to some new journal—and he could not carry on with both at once. All he could suggest was that he might write "a small book or large pamphlet upon the state of the nation". But if the Ministers still wished to discuss the matter with him, having heard this statement of his views, he would come up to London. After three days' further reflection, he definitely decided that it would be most unwise for him to become in any way "a salaried writer" for the government, "for whatever might come from me would be received with suspicion, which no means would be spared to excite". He accordingly turned the whole suggestion down. Its original author Herries did not at once abandon it altogether: he spoke of it again to Bedford at the end of December, but by then it was quite out of court.[232]

An even more interesting proposal was made to him in March, 1817. At the end of the previous year Dr. Stoddart had been dismissed from the editorship of *The Times* by its proprietor, John Walter II. Stoddart, a cantankerous and impracticable person, at once went off and founded a high Tory rival to his former paper, which he called by the not very original name of the *New Times*. (The Radicals, to whom he was a figure of fun, called him Dr. Slop: his new venture they happily dubbed the *Slop Pail*.) Southey had heard of the change, and had not approved of it. He thought it meant that Walter was abandoning his Tory principles, "believing that neither the Ministry nor the Opposition can stand, and that *Hunt* is about to be Lord of the Ascendant". He may therefore have been surprised when he was approached by Crabb Robinson (who was among Walter's personal friends) with a cautious and oblique invitation to become Stoddart's successor. It was indeed, characteristically, very cautious and oblique—one is almost tempted to describe it as Crabb-like. Southey was merely asked whether, "if an offer were made to him to superintend a lucrative literary establishment, in which he would have—if he desired it—a property, of which the emolument would be very considerable, and which would give him extensive influence over the whole kingdom", he would be prepared to consider the suggestion. All this circumspection was thrown away. Knowing of the situation on *The Times* and of his friendship with Walter, Southey at once understood the real nature of the proposal. This time he declined without hesitating. No financial consideration, he said, would induce him to give up his literary pursuits and a country life.

There was an end of the matter. But it is interesting to see what Walter had in mind when he started the idea; and this we now know more clearly than Southey did himself. He was apparently willing to offer Southey £300 a year to write two leading articles a week, or £2000 a year and a share in the paper's profits if he would contribute a daily leader and undertake part of its management. It had not been Walter's practice as a rule to leave the control of the paper to an omnipotent editor: he had preferred to have some part in the direction of its day-to-day policy himself. But he was now considering a change in this plan, and Crabb Robinson noted that he was "even desirous to sell all his property in the paper if he could put it in the hands of a man of reputation and talent, and I found [he] was disposed to offer a share in the paper to Southey and entrust the whole management to him". Walter evidently supposed, like a good many other people, that literature had made Southey rich. Perhaps he was taken aback when he received so decided a refusal. At all events he changed his mind, kept financial control of the paper in his own hands, and appointed as its editor Thomas Barnes, who had for some time been a member of the staff. It was a wise choice, for Barnes developed into a great journalist, and under him *The Times* shot to the head of English newspapers. In the course of the next thirty years, it was to play a vital part in moulding progressive opinion in England. Under Southey, it might only too easily have slipped into a backwater of reaction, lost its footing in the hectic race, and come to grief like its powerful evening rival the *Courier*.[233]

But what of Southey's interests? Were they wisely served by the discouraging refusals he gave to these two tempting offers? On the whole, he knew his own business best. He was ill fitted for the rough-and-tumble life of a political journalist: he had lived too little in the world, his mind was too set and his temper too short, he suffered too much from moral indignation. He did better to remain where he was, at Greta Hall, surrounded by his family and his cats, with Skiddaw and Derwentwater for his playground, busy with history and biography and his punctual *Quarterly* reviewing.

A month earlier, at the beginning of February, 1817, a notable recruit had been added to the vast army of seditious pamphlets already in circulation: the republican drama of Southey's youth, *Wat Tyler*. Its publication at this time, more than twenty years after it was written, was, it need hardly be said, unauthorised. The manuscript had apparently remained in the hands of a dissenting minister of Plymouth named Winterbottom, who had been present when Southey gave it to Ridgeway. Its discovery now was a godsend to the Radicals: here was an opportunity to discredit the Poet Laureate, that black reactionary, to convict him of apostasy out of his own mouth. The poor little drama had an instant *succès de scandale*. It was hawked about the streets of London as a threepenny pamphlet; Radical publishers like Sherwin and Hone issued edition after edition; the author was told first that 30,000, then that 60,000, copies had been sold.

He at once took the only possible counter-action: he attempted to reclaim his property at law and to secure an injunction against the publishers of these unauthorised editions. But here the Spirit of Irony took a hand. The case came before the Lord Chancellor, Eldon, the arch-reactionary of England. He might have been expected to support his fellow-Tory. Instead, he held, quoting good precedent, that "a person cannot recover in damages for a work which is in its nature calculated to do an injury to the public"; and since Southey had not established—and on this argument could not establish—his right to the property in *Wat Tyler*, the injunction must be refused. So its sale went on unchecked.[234]

The whole affair was an annoyance, no more, to Southey. It caused him a couple of disturbed nights, it greatly worried his wife, and the legal action involved him in a tiresome journey to London. But he did not take it to heart, and as for being ashamed of this product of his early years—"I have no objection to acknowledging old Uncle Wat," he told his brother Henry, "not being fool enough to be ashamed of what I was at the age of 20. My enemies might indeed triumph if I were." He would not sit on any stool of repentance for the republican sentiments of the play, its "opinions of universal equality, taken up as they were conscientiously in early youth, acted upon in disregard of all worldly considerations, and left behind me in the same straight-forward course as I advanced in years". He had held those opinions, he said, when they were bitterly unpopular—in the days when a Church and King mob sacked Dr. Priestley's house in Birmingham, "when a spirit of anti-Jacobinism prevailed, which I cannot characterise better than by saying that it was as blind and as intolerant as the Jacobinism of the present day". When he republished the piece in the collected edition of his poems in 1838, he summed up the whole matter by saying that he was no more "ashamed of having been a republican, than of having been a boy".[235]

But if Southey himself took it philosophically, the episode was none the less unfortunate for him, and it certainly damaged his public reputation. His Liberal enemies saw to that. Their press, as a matter of course, kept up a fire of abuse. *Wat Tyler* was noticed in a more august place too. On 14th March William Smith, one of the Members for Norwich, referred to it in a speech in the House of Commons. He had taken occasion to speak of "tergiversation of principle" among political writers. He did not condemn it as such, for he recognised that every one had a perfect right to change his opinions: what did disgust him, however, was "the settled, determined malignity of a renegade". And this he illustrated by contrasting a passage from a recent *Quarterly* article, said to have been written by Southey, with one from *Wat Tyler*: he went on to describe the play as "the most seditious book that ever was written" and to hint, rather amusingly, that the government should suppress it for its dangerous political tendency and punish its author.

In Parliament, this speech was promptly answered by Wynn.[236] Outside, Southey determined to take a hand himself. He justified his political principles in a letter published in the *Courier* of 17th March: there he was supported by Coleridge, who rushed to the defence of *Wat Tyler* (though in quality he thought it a "wretched mess of pig's meat") in two articles on that and the following day.

Now Southey began a more extended *apologia* in the form of a *Letter to William Smith, Esq., M.P.*[237] He took the same ground as he had taken to his friends: he neither regretted nor repented *Wat Tyler*, though in his mature years he had outgrown the opinions it maintained. As for "tergiversation", he retorted upon the Liberals their own charge, and with effect. They, who had begun by supporting the Revolution and its doctrines of freedom, had gone on to become sympathisers with Napoleon and his hateful tyranny, from which Europe had been delivered only by a Tory England. And he clinched the matter by quoting words he had written eight years earlier: "' They had turned their faces towards the east in the morning to worship the rising sun, and in the evening they were looking eastward still, obstinately affirming that still the sun was there.' I, on the contrary, altered my position as the world went round." It was a good rejoinder, and the whole *Letter* is a fine, manly piece of political pamphleteering, marred only by an unfortunate touch of complacency here and there.

Its reception was what might have been expected. Scott rejoiced that he had answered "that coarse-minded scoundrel William Smith"; Wordsworth thought it "completely triumphant", though he regretted that Southey had not taken the chance of rebutting more completely the charge that he had become "a Tool of Power. A most false and foul accusation, for a more disinterested and honourable man than Robert Southey does not breathe". On the other side, Hazlitt devoted three intensely savage articles in the *Examiner* to the *Letter*. The first of them contains one of the most superb pieces of invective in the language, where he says that Southey's "engagement to his first love, the Republic, was only upon liking; his marriage to Legitimacy is *for better, for worse*, and nothing but death shall part them". He goes on to describe that "detestable old hag" in a passage of magnificent complexity—for "why", he cries at the end of it, "why should not one make a sentence of a page long, out of the feelings of one's whole life?"[238]

Now it was indeed war to the death between Southey and the Radicals. Unfortunately for his subsequent reputation, his opponents were more skilful than he at polemics: he had lived too exclusively in their pages, embalmed like a fly in amber. And his opposition to them put him out of touch with the rising generation of young poets, who were on the Left as he himself had once been. Shelley thought him corrupt; Keats was under the spell of Leigh Hunt and Hazlitt—he applauded that great sentence, in a famous phrase, as "like a whale's back in the sea of prose".[239]   Byron's position was somewhat different from theirs: he was older than they were, more hard-bitten, less doctrinaire. But his view of the episode coincided with Smith's, and so he told John Murray: "It is no disgrace to Mr. Southey to have written *Wat Tyler*, and afterwards to have written his birthday or victory odes (I speak only of their *politics*), but it is something, for which I have no words, for this man to have endeavoured to bring to the stake (for such would he do) men who think as he thought, and for no reason but because they think so still, when he has found it convenient to think otherwise."[240]

This view was also held, more mildly, by some of Southey's friends. Wynn more than once remonstrated with him on the violence of his language; Crabb Robinson noted that "Southey vindicates his change of opinion successfully but does not plead to the charge of illiberality in abusing the present race of democrats."[241]   But this argument was really beside the point. Southey's position was that of all honest extremists, in politics or in religion. Holding the views he did with intense sincerity, it was a plain matter of duty for him to combat and destroy the pernicious doctrines of his opponents, whoever they might be. That he had once held those doctrines himself might be embarrassing, but it was irrelevant. The issues at stake were too important for any private consideration of that kind to weigh with him: it would have been dishonesty if they had. One may regret that in persecution he showed all the zeal and gusto of the convert; but that can be no more than a general comment on the corrupting effects of fanaticism.

Southey's indifference to the onslaught made upon him was real, not assumed. It is quite extraordinary how little he cared for his critics: extraordinary, and as one turns over their envenomed, malignant pages one almost finds it repulsive. How *could* he be so indifferent to such an assault? The answer is simple. He was a man who had nothing to conceal and nothing to be afraid of. *Wat Tyler* was the only skeleton his enemies ever found in his cupboard, and that was hardly a very discreditable one. It has often been remarked that he was self-righteous. That is true, as even a casual reader of his letters will agree; but it is important to understand in what his self-righteousness consisted. It was not in the least, as it generally is, pharisaical or canting or feigned: it was the excess of a genuine righteousness. And though it may have struck his contemporaries as unattractive—it certainly repels

S.   L us to-day—it added greatly to the strength of his position, giving him, as it were, an extra hide to protect him against the shafts of his opponents.

A week or two after the *Letter to William Smith* appeared, he started for another long Continental tour, mainly in order to take his thoughts off Herbert's death, which still preyed on his mind. His companions were a Cumberland friend, Mr. Senhouse of Netherhall, and Edward Nash. After five days in Paris, they travelled to Italy by way of the Grande Chartreuse and Mont Cenis, from which he found the descent into Piedmont "beyond description delightful". They then went on to the Italian Lakes, and at Como he had the pleasure of meeting Landor, who was then living there. They came back by way of Switzerland and down the Rhine through Germany. At Brussels, Southey re-visited Verbeyst, buying from him a complete set of the *Acta Sanctorum* in fifty-two volumes folio. The tour, which lasted altogether thirteen weeks, did much to improve his health and spirits: "the continual exercise, change of air, and excitement agreed admirably with me, to say nothing of the wine, which everywhere about the Rhine is the true Amreeta, and deserves to be called the ' Liquor of Life '".[242]

Lest any one should doubt whether he really minded being attacked, he quickly inserted his head into two more hornets' nests. Not content with going for the political heretics for all he was worth, he must needs prepare a frontal assault on religious heresy too. He was now hard at work on his *Life of Wesley*. This, the second greatest of his biographies (it was published in 1820), has never enjoyed the popularity of his *Nelson*, partly because it is a very much bigger book, partly because the subject has not the same splendour; but it has steadily kept its place nevertheless, and it is still alive. With a wider knowledge of eighteenth-century history, and with different points of view, later generations have rewritten Wesley's life for themselves, and they will go on doing so, for it is a fascinating and important study. But no one has yet succeeded in writing another biography as vivid and attractive as Southey's: it remains the standard life for the ordinary reader. Nor is it likely to be displaced, for two reasons. First, because of the time at which Southey wrote. Almost all biographical classics, from Cavendish's *Life of Wolsey* to Strachey's *Queen Victoria*, have been written by people who were con-temporaries, or nearly contemporaries, of their subjects. In the majority of cases they knew them personally. Now though Southey did not know Wesley—as a small boy he had, however, seen him at Bristol—the atmosphere of his childhood was the same as that of Wesley's old age: their lives overlapped by fourteen years. He knew less of the eighteenth century, perhaps, than a modern scholar; but he understood it from the inside, for he had lived in it.

And secondly, the book's continued vitality is due to its own merits. They were not for the most part new to Southey's readers, for they were the same as those of all his mature work: forthright vigour, independence of mind, lucidity, and a high power of narrative. But the *Life of Wesley* also shows one rather surprising virtue: a considerable measure of charity. It is as if Wesley had imparted something of his own spirit to his biographer, for it was a charity that went hand in hand with narrow-mindedness. He wished to do justice to the Methodists although he was not in sympathy with them. That might have been a bad foundation for biography, but in this case it was an excellent one: it meant that Southey was free from any tendency to worship his subject, to make the *Life* a piece of dead hagiography; and it gave the book that quality of cold, clear daylight which makes its portrayal of Wesley so convincing.

As Southey expected, the book was bitterly attacked on its appearance, especially in the Nonconformist press, by humbugs, by fools and ill-informed enthusiasts. But not by them alone. Dr. William Okely weighed in from Bristol with a temperate defence of the character of the Moravians, which he considered to have been unjustly impugned in the book.[243] The Rev. Richard Watson, a leading Methodist, produced some able, if laborious, *Observations on Southey's Life of Wesley*, pointing out some of the deficiencies in Southey's theological knowledge. The unctuous and patronising tone of the pamphlet may be gauged from its concluding sentence: "To the whole of Mr. Southey's attempt to delineate the character of the Founder of Methodism, we may apply a quotation aptly levelled at his incompetency for the task, by one of Mr. Wesley's biographers: ' Sir, thou hast nothing to draw with, and the well is deep '."[244]

But two more remarkable criticisms of the *Life of Wesley* were also passed. Alexander Knox, a theologian who had known Wesley personally, published some *Remarks* on the book in 1822, later amplified in a private letter in which he defended Wesley from the charge of ambition. Southey accepted this criticism, and promised to alter the text of the *Life* accordingly. Coleridge wrote, as was his custom, an illuminating commentary in the margins of his copy of the book, which was, he says, "more often

in my hands than any other in my ragged book-regiment; . . .
to this work, and to the life of R. Baxter, I was used to resort
whenever sickness and languor made me feel the want of an old
friend, of whose company I could never be tired. How many and
many an hour of self-oblivion do I owe to this Life of Wesley".[245]

This was not the only religious controversy in which Southey
engaged during these years. His dislike and mistrust of Nonconformity had not led him in any way to moderate his hatred of
Catholicism, which had burnt steadily in him ever since his first
visit to Portugal. He hit out both to left and right, so to speak,
in his *Book of the Church*, a popular ecclesiastical history of England
published in 1824. To Crabb Robinson, who had a strong taste
for theology, it was "a very entertaining book, even though it
succeeded the *Arabian Nights*".[246] Few readers would find so much
pleasure in it to-day, but it had a considerable success on its first
appearance, and this prompted Charles Butler to write a reply,
from the Catholic point of view, called *The Book of the Roman
Catholic Church*. Southey's answer was the *Vindiciae Ecclesiae
Anglicanae*—described by Mrs. Coleridge, who did not like such
controversies, as "a Tartar". Southey was never uncivil to Butler
personally; but his language on the whole subject was now
unmistakably shrill, for he saw Catholic Emancipation on the
way. Like many other Englishmen of all parties, both then and
since, he regarded the political power of Catholicism with the
gravest dread. He feared it in Ireland, in home affairs, and above
all with regard to the established Church. He fought valiantly
all along in the losing battle against Catholic Emancipation: it
was a particularly cruel blow to him that it should in the end
have been put through by a Tory government.[247]

These attacks both on Roman Catholics and Nonconformists
were completely sincere. Yet although he was a punctilious
churchman and a supporter of the Establishment through thick
and thin, doctrinally Southey was never wholly at ease in the
Church of England: in religion, as in politics, his was a cross-
bench mind. We have seen how his "Christian Stoicism" originated at Oxford. In his mature years he developed a close sympathy
with the Quakers, though not with their pacifism: "if it were
not for Buonaparte", he told Wynn in 1807, "I should have little
hesitation in declaring my conviction that it is the true system
of the Gospel". His controversies always centred on the *politics*
of religion: in matters of belief he displayed the widest charity
and very little of the dogmatic spirit. And here, as everywhere,
he showed his independence of mind, refusing for instance to

subscribe to the doctrine of eternal punishment: "I cannot believe in an Eternity of Hell", he wrote. "I hope God will forgive me if I err, but I cannot say *Lord, help my unbelief*." That was a remarkable sentiment, even for an Anglican, in the early nineteenth century; and it is characteristic of Southey's whole religious position—that of a true and deeply convinced Christian, whose faith constantly sustained him in the cruellest trials of his life.[248]

Meanwhile, he had become involved in yet another controversy, the most famous of them all: that with Shelley and Byron. His first had been primarily political, his second and third religious: the issues of the fourth were in the widest sense moral.

In March, 1816, Shelley sent Southey a copy of *Alastor*. In a charming little covering note, he referred with gratitude to Southey's hospitality, adding that he regarded Southey "with admiration as a poet and with respect as a man", that he hoped he would read the poem in a spirit of charity, forgetting how widely they differed from one another and not attributing their differences to unworthy causes.[249] Unfortunately, Southey's answer has not survived. We know that he received the poem, and we can therefore be sure that he acknowledged it, for he was punctilious in such matters.

At the end of 1818 Shelley wrote a letter to Leigh Hunt from Naples, in which he said he had heard that "Southey on one occasion said to a friend of his that he on his own knowledge knew me to be the *blackest of villains*"; and he felt sure that Southey, not Gifford, had been the author of a bitter review of Leigh Hunt's *Foliage* in the January *Quarterly*.[250] All this was mere gossip, of course: "the blackest of villains" is a very un-Southeyan phrase, and Southey did not in fact write the review in question.

A year later Shelley again discerned Southey's hand, this time in a *Quarterly* review of his own *Revolt of Islam*. Again he complained to Leigh Hunt of it;[251] and in the following summer he wrote to Southey himself from Pisa, directly challenging him as to the authorship of the article. His letter was, as always, most polite in tone: "I know nothing that would give me more sincere pleasure than to be able to affirm from your own assurance that you were not guilty of that writing."

On this occasion we have Southey's answer. He began by stating that the review was not his work. "I have never in any of my writings mentioned your name, or alluded to you even in the remotest hint, either as a man or as an author." He went on, however, to say that such specimens of Shelley's work as he had seen seemed to show that his poetic powers were "of a high order, but the manner in which those powers have been employed is such as to prevent me from feeling any desire to see more of productions so monstrous in their kind, and so pernicious in their tendency". He cannot think of Shelley, he says, "without the deepest compassion". "Opinions are to be judged by their effects—and what has been the fruit of yours? . . . Have they not brought immediate misery upon others, and guilt, which is all but irremediable, on yourself?" (This is a plain reference to Shelley's *liaison* with Mary Godwin and the suicide of Harriet Shelley in December, 1816.) He urges Shelley to reconsider his rejection of Christianity before it is too late. Truly, as Dowden remarked, this was a reply "kindly in purpose, but unrelenting in the cruelty of its kindness".[252]

Shelley answered quickly, expressing his "sincere pleasure" that Southey had not written the article, and going on to deal with his points in detail. He continues to reject Christianity as a corrupted and debased superstition, instancing Southey's own spirit. Instead, he says, "of refraining from 'judging that you be not judged', you not only judge but condemn, and that to a punishment which its victim must be either among the meanest or the loftiest not to regard as bitterer than death". "Merely because I regulated my domestic arrangements without deferring to the notions of the vulgar, although I might have done so quite as conveniently had I descended to their base thoughts— this you call *guilt*. . . . I am innocent of ill, either done or intended; the consequences you allude to flowed in no respect from me."

Once more Southey made up his mind to answer. His last letter only develops with inflexible sternness the points he has already made. The concluding passage sums it all up. "Here, sir, our correspondence must end. I never should have sought it; but having been led into it, it appeared to me a duty to take that opportunity of representing you to yourself as you appear to me, with little hope indeed of producing any good effect, and yet not altogether hopeless; for though you may go on with an unawakened mind, a seared conscience, and a hardened heart, there will be seasons of misgiving, when that most sacred faculty which you have laboured to destroy makes itself felt. At such times you may remember me as an earnest monitor whom you cannot suspect of ill-will, and whom it is not in your power to despise, however much you may wish to repel his admonitions with contempt. Believe me, sir, your sincere well-wisher, Robert Southey."

Two years later, when he heard of Shelley's death, Southey summed up what he thought of him in a slightly milder mood: "I knew that miserable man, and am well acquainted with his dreadful history. . . . His story taking it altogether is the most flagitious and the most tragic which I have known in real life. . . . Shelley was not, like Lord Byron, wicked by disposition. His natural feelings I believe to have been kind and generous. But he adopted the Devil's own philosophy that nothing ought to stand in the way of his own gratifications, and to this he acted up. . . . His writings were not bad enough in some respects to do much harm, and far too bad in others. What merit they had was of too high a kind to be attractive, and their obscurity and extravagance served in some degree to sheathe the poison which they contained."[253]

Meanwhile another adversary, glanced at in this letter, had intervened, bitter and without scruple where Shelley had been gentle and courteous. Like him, Byron had a high opinion of Southey's works: *Roderick* he thought "as near perfection as poetry can be—which considering how I dislike that school I wonder at. However, so it is".[254] But that did not reconcile him to the man, still less to the politician. In 1816, driven abroad by the ostracism of London society, he left England for ever. From then onwards his comments on his enemies became rapidly more and more venomous. We have seen what he thought of the *Wat Tyler* episode. He was made angrier by the *Quarterly Review* article on *Foliage*, containing what he called an "oblique and shabby" attack upon Shelley: as a matter of course he accepted the common report that it was Southey's work. Such was his mood when, in September, 1818, he wrote the dedication to *Don Juan*—a piece of savage banter addressed to the Poet Laureate.

All this, though fierce enough, was straightforward warfare of a kind quite ordinary in those days. But the controversy now took on a personal edge that turned it from a literary and political dispute into a duel of almost murderous intensity. A rumour reached Byron that Southey had said he and Shelley were "in a league of incest" together. "He is a burning liar", was Byron's furious comment. (It was a subject on which he was naturally sensitive. The rumour was quite untrue.) The first two cantos of *Don Juan* were published in July, 1819. Taking the advice of his friends, Byron withheld the dedication, though Southey knew of its existence.

The first public blow in the quarrel came from Southey in the Preface to *A Vision of Judgement*, published in 1821. This was a poem written in hexameters, describing the arrival of George III in heaven, and his reception there. Even his son thought this a regrettable subject: "it must be allowed", he remarks in his quaint Victorian manner, "that to speculate upon the condition of the departed, especially when under the influence of strong political feelings, is a bold, if not a presumptuous undertaking". In the preface Southey took occasion to deliver a frontal assault on the younger poets of the day, with Leigh Hunt, Shelley, and above all Byron in his mind. "The school which they have set up", he says, "may properly be called the Satanic school; for though their productions breathe the spirit of Belial in their lascivious parts, and the spirit of Moloch in those loathsome images of atrocities and horrors which they delight to represent, they are more especially characterised by a Satanic spirit of pride and audacious impiety, which still betrays the wretched feeling of hopelessness wherewith it is allied."[255]

It was inevitable that Byron should reply to this. His first move came in Canto III of *Don Juan*, which appeared that August; his second in the prose appendix to *The Two Foscari*. The latter was duly answered by Southey in a letter to the *Courier*, dated 5th January, 1822, in which he directly denied the accusation that he had "scattered abroad calumnies, knowing them to be such, against Lord Byron and others". He improved the occasion with some further remarks on the "Satanic school" and ended by advising Byron, if he wished to reply, to do so in verse, since "for one who has so little command of himself, it will be a great advantage that his temper should be obliged to *keep tune*".

This rejoinder put Byron beside himself with rage. "He looked perfectly awful", says Medwin, who was with him when he first received the letter: "his colour changed almost prismatically; his lips were as pale as death." After re-reading it, his first thought was to start for England at once and call Southey out. The challenge was sent, but by the discretion of his friend Douglas Kinnaird, who was charged with it, it was not delivered. He had a more effective answer up his sleeve: he made up his mind to take the advice Southey had so rashly offered him, to write an answer in verse.

It was *A Vision of Judgement* itself, and not the preface, that offered him his great opportunity. For it not only displayed what he thought bad politics: it was undeniably a very bad poem. And it was made still more absurd by being written in hexameters, a metre that greater poets than Southey—Spenser before him and Bridges after him—have failed to assimilate into English. Byron hit them off to a nicety when he called them "spavined dactyls": even Southey's admirers could find little to say in their favour.[256] Neither Dryden nor Pope ever had an opportunity quite as good as Byron's now: *A Vision of Judgement* afforded an almost unequalled opening for satire.[257]

Byron certainly took it. The poem that resulted, to which he gave almost the same title as Southey's, is slighter than *Don Juan*; and for all the venom that lay behind it, it lacks the almost tragic intensity, the close piling of epithet upon epithet, that distinguishes the *Dunciad*. But it is none the less a superb effort, and right from the very start:

> Saint Peter sat by the celestial gate:
> His keys were rusty, and the lock was dull.

It contains at least one passage of high poetry, the description of Junius. And with the arrival of Southey upon the scene, the fun gets better and better. In Stanzas 96-99, Southey is made to describe his own career:

> He said—(I only give the heads)—he said,
>   He meant no harm in scribbling; 't was his way
> Upon all topics; 't was, besides, his bread,
>   Of which he butter'd both sides; 't would delay
> Too long the assembly (he was pleased to dread),
>   And take up rather more time than a day,
> To name his works—he would but cite a few—
> "Wat Tyler"—"Rhymes on Blenheim"—"Waterloo".
>
> He had written praises of a regicide;
>   He had written praises of all kings whatever;
> He had written for republics far and wide,
>   And then against them bitterer than ever;
> For pantisocracy he once had cried
>   Aloud, a scheme less moral than 't was clever;
> Then grew a hearty anti-jacobin—
> Had turn'd his coat—and would have turn'd his skin.
>
> He had sung against all battles, and again
>   In their high praise and glory; he had call'd

Reviewing "the ungentle craft", and then
　　Become as base a critic as e'er crawled—
Fed, paid, and pamper'd by the very men
　　By whom his muse and morals had been maul'd:
He had written much blank verse, and blanker prose,
And more of both than anybody knows.

Then, to end up with, Southey pulls out his *Vision of Judgement*:

He ceased, and drew forth an MS; and no
　　Persuasion on the part of devils, saints,
Or angels, now could stop the torrent; so
　　He read the first three lines of the contents;
But at the fourth, the whole spiritual show
　　Had vanish'd, with variety of scents,
Ambrosial and sulphureous, as they sprang,
Like lightning, off from his "melodious twang".

Those grand heroics acted as a spell:
　　The angels stopp'd their ears and plied their pinions;
The devils ran howling, deafen'd, down to hell;
　　The ghosts fled, gibbering, for their own dominions—
(For 't is not yet decided where they dwell,
　　And I leave every man to his opinions);
Michael took refuge in his trump—but, lo!
His teeth were set on edge, he could not blow!

In the midst of this confusion, George III slips into heaven unnoticed:

And when the tumult dwindled to a calm,
I left him practising the hundredeth psalm.

Southey's letters contain very little reference to Byron's *Vision of Judgment*. He cannot have been greatly wounded by it: his self-esteem was too secure, his sense of humour, though it was real enough in some directions, did not run to the appreciation of satire. Nevertheless, it may be significant that he carried the controversy no further during Byron's life-time. Only on the appearance of Medwin's *Conversations of Lord Byron* did he feel it necessary to enter the ring again, which he did for the last time in a further letter to the *Courier* dated 7th December, 1824. Here he denied outright the charge that he had been the reviewer of *Foliage*. At the same time, though "papers in the *Quarterly Review* have been ascribed to me (those on Keats's Poems for example), which I have heartily condemned both for their spirit and manner", he expressed his agreement with the opinions set forth in the article in question, and went on to describe his intercourse with Shelley and their correspondence. Finally, he reverted to the old charge he had made in the preface to *A Vision of Judgement*, that Byron had "set up for pander-general to the youth of Great Britain as long as his writings should endure", and he concluded by saying that Medwin's book proved Byron to have been "as regardless of truth, as he was incapable of sustaining those feelings suited to his birth, station, and high endowments, which sometimes came across his better mind".

The last word lay perforce with Southey. But it was an empty advantage: his adversary had so clearly carried off the honours. Byron's *Vision of Judgment* was a retribution that he thoroughly deserved for writing a tawdry and boring poem on a subject in doubtful taste in a metre he could not handle. As to the merits of the argument, the moral and ethical issues that lay behind it, we may sympathise at once with Southey and with Byron, for each was honestly defending his own integrity and all he stood for. (That Byron cast his arguments in a comic, satirical vein does not detract in the least from the passionate sincerity with which he held them.) Something of this view was expressed by a judicious contemporary in *Blackwood's Magazine*: "Mr. Southey is, and always was, too much of a monk, to understand a man of the world like Byron; and Byron was too decidedly, or rather too exclusively, a man of the world to understand a monk like Southey. Hence this absurd exaggeration of each other's errors and defects. In Southey, one of the most learned and accomplished scholars, and pure and virtuous men, that the modern world has produced, Byron could see nothing but the Tory partizan, and the author of certain articles in the *Quarterly Review*. In Byron, on the other hand, in one of the greatest of the great Poets of England, . . . Southey could see nothing else but a ' pander-general to youthful vice ', and the founder of ' a Satanic school '. This nonsense on both sides excites a universal smile—nothing more."[258]

To these contentious years of Southey's life belongs one further disagreement—milder than the others, but also more painful in a personal sense. The *Essays of Elia* appeared in January, 1823, and Southey, as one of Lamb's oldest friends, took the opportunity to mention them in the *Quarterly Review*. But the occasion he chose was unfortunate, and the compliment he paid them, though sincerely meant, was worse than left-handed. In the course of an article on "The Progress of Infidelity", he remarked that the book "only wanted a sounder religious feeling to be as delightful as it was original." He had at first written "saner". Then, realising that was a tactless adjective to apply to a work of Lamb's, he altered it to "sounder", the first word that occurred to him, intending to revise the whole sentence in proof at his leisure; but no proof was sent to him, and the unlucky word stood.[259]

It was not the first time Lamb had been, as he thought, shabbily treated by the *Quarterly*—it was in fact the fourth; and he determined on a public reply. This took the form of a "Letter from Elia to Robert Southey", which appeared in the *London Magazine* of October. He came straight to the point. "Sir", he began, "you have done me an unfriendly office. You have given an ill name to my poor Lucubrations. . . . There stands your reproof, in the very front of your notice, in ugly characters, like some bugbear, to frighten all good Christians from purchasing." Not only so: the attack is retorted upon Southey's own religious intolerance. "You have never ridiculed, I believe, what you thought to be religion, but you are always girding at what some pious, but perhaps mistaken folks, think to be so." But characteristically, Lamb's main effort in this *Letter* was given, not to the defence of his own book, but to that of his friends. Southey had attacked Leigh Hunt as an infidel: Lamb rushed to his defence, and took the opportunity, in a most charming passage, to describe with loving care the characters of all his own circle.

Southey's reaction now was also typical. When he read the *Letter* he was genuinely astonished. "So little was I conscious of having done anything to offend him," he wrote afterwards, "that . . . I expected a letter of friendly pleasantry." He quickly wrote to Lamb to tell him that he had not had the smallest intention of "any way offending or injuring a man concerning whom I have never spoken, thought, or felt otherwise than with affection, esteem, and admiration". But he refused to begin a dispute with him "to make sport for the Philistines". Instead, if Lamb would forgive the article as he gladly forgave the *Letter*, he would take the first opportunity of calling on him to make it up. Mr. Lucas has justly praised Southey's letter for its "fine temper": the reply shows one even finer. Indeed, it is the quintessence of Lamb all through, from its beginning—"The kindness of your note has melted away the mist which was upon me. I have been fighting against a shadow"—to its touching little postcript: "I do not

think your handwriting at all like Hunt's. I do not think many
things I did think."

This difference at least was now over. Seven years later,
Southey made some amends for his share in it with a poem in
praise of Lamb that appeared in *The Times*, and when Lamb died
in 1834 Southey paid him a strong tribute: "When his sad story
may be told there is no writer whose works will be perused with
deeper sympathy. Never was there a kinder, a more generous, or a
more feeling heart than his." In the eyes of posterity this episode,
like most of the controversies in which he engaged, has injured
Southey far more than his opponent. The Elians have never
forgiven him that unfortunate sentence: only a few years ago
Mr. Blunden dismissed him with asperity as "that biped Rectitude". But a more detached view would perhaps see Southey as a
man who suffered—that is the proper word, for it was a disease—
from what Coleridge had long ago diagnosed as "too high a state
of health" in moral matters: his moral judgment was over-
developed to an almost morbid extent. It is not surprising that
he should sooner or later have fallen out with Lamb, that gentle
apostle of tolerance, over an affair of this kind.[260]

Large though these quarrels loom in Southey's biography,
they occupied but a small proportion of his time and thoughts.
Nor, with the exception of the *Life of Wesley*, do his controversial
works rank high among the books he produced in these years. He
himself would have given first place to the *History of Brazil*, the
second volume of which appeared in 1817, the third and last in
1819. It is the largest of his works in size, and the most important
contribution he made to historical studies. In a letter to Henry
Koster he summed up his own thoughts on the book: "I am far
from regretting that so much time and labour has been bestowed
upon a subject for which few English readers (such as readers now
are) can be expected to feel much interest. . . . What I have done
is in many parts imperfect; it is nevertheless even now a great
achievement. As long as I live I shall carefully correct and enlarge
it from whatever documents, written or printed, may come to my
hands, and centuries hence, when Brazil shall have become the
great and prosperous country which one day it must be, I shall be
regarded there as the first person who ever attempted to give a
consistent form to its crude, unconnected and neglected history."[261]

This estimate of his own achievement was accurate. It is true
that the book has not in all respects taken the high place he
anticipated for it: it is not to Brazil "what the work of Herodotus
is to Europe". He used no important documents to which later

historians have not had access, and with the opening of the
Portuguese and other archives a great deal of information has
become available that was unknown to him. But it is still, over
120 years later, the standard history of the subject in English;[262]
and he has been faithfully remembered in Brazil. The centenary
of his death in 1943 was gracefully commemorated there, in the
Revista do Instituto Histórico e Geográfico Brasiliero and—what would
have particularly pleased him—in the undertaking of a new
translation of his *History*, to replace that of Fernandes Pinheiro,
which appeared in 1862.[263]

The *History of Brazil* formed part of a much vaster design.
Unhappily, it is the only part we have, for the *History of Portugal*
was never completed. We know that much of the book was
actually written, but, for the present at least, the manuscript has
disappeared.[264]

Two other works, projected in this period, were never even
begun. More than once he threw out the idea of writing *The Age
of George III*, a history of his own times. And in 1820 Mrs. Warren
Hastings inquired if he would undertake a biography of her
husband, who had died two years earlier. He jumped at the idea.
"I have no fear of the labour," he told Wynn, "and none of any
difficulty in writing with perfect integrity. . . . It is a noble
subject, and admits in perfection of that ornamental relief which
it is always delightful to meet with, and which I delight in
introducing." Indeed, it would have been an almost ideal subject
for him, and it is a matter for great regret that he never carried
it through. Apparently the plan split on the old rock of official
biographers: there was a Mr. Baber who was to select the papers
to be put into Southey's hands, and "this Mr. Baber appears to
have some very injudicious notions about keeping back whatever
relates to Hastings' private history and character". On these
terms Southey very properly declined to act. As a result, the work
was not done for another twenty years, when the Rev. G. R. Gleig
produced those "three big bad volumes" that were treated in such
cavalier fashion by Macaulay in the *Edinburgh Review*.[265]

In these years Southey embarked upon his other major history,
that of the Peninsular War. We have seen that it grew out of
his work for the *Edinburgh Annual Register*. Like the *History of
Brazil*, it eventually ran to three quartos, which appeared slowly,
in 1823, 1827, and 1832. Meanwhile, in 1828 another history of
the war had begun to appear: Napier's, which at once outshone
Southey's and before long killed it stone dead. It was a better
history, not merely in the military sense—that was to be expected,

for Napier was a soldier and Southey a civilian; it was far better documented, for Southey had unwisely refused to ask the Duke of Wellington for information, while Napier had the Duke's papers at his disposal; and it represented after all a fairer and more balanced view of the war, particularly in the case of Sir John Moore, of whose capacity Southey always maintained a low opinion. Napier's book is one of the classics of English historical writing. But it would be wrong to suppose that it is better written than its rival; for even Napier could not surpass Southey in ease and clearness of narrative.[266]

Long ago Southey had remarked that his mind was turning to history, away from verse. Almost as soon as he was appointed Poet Laureate, he gave up writing large-scale poetry altogether: *Roderick*, published in 1814, was the last of his epics. In a financial sense, it was the most successful. It put his account with Longmans on the right side for the first time; a second edition was called for early in 1815, a third before that year was out and a fourth in 1816; two years later he said it had brought him in £700. Not until 1825 did he produce another long poem, and then it was the *Tale of Paraguay*, a small affair beside *Roderick*. The rest of his verse output in these years consisted mainly of his official work as Poet Laureate. He certainly earned his £90 salary. The Prince Regent had not after all seen fit to dispense with the birthday and New Year odes, and Southey went on contributing them punctually: many remained in manuscript. Of those that were published, only two are of interest: *The Poet's Pilgrimage*, which was unique in that it made money (£215 by the first edition alone, so he told his doctor brother); and the "Funeral Song for the Princess Charlotte of Wales", written at the end of 1817. This piece is a fine achievement in the difficult, unrewarding *genre* of official poetry, and it is Southey's masterpiece as Laureate. Oddly enough, he thought meanly of it himself for once, telling Bedford that it was "precisely one of those compositions which are not bad—only good-for-nothing".[267] But an authentic solemn majesty rings through it like the tolling of a bell: it recalls, even though it cannot rival, the *Installation Ode* of Gray.

In the background of all this work, life at Greta Hall went on its old course. Herbert's death had been an irreparable loss, but as the years passed his father began to feel it less acutely, and in February, 1819, the gap was filled, as far as it ever could be, by the birth of another son, Charles Cuthbert. This was an unexpected event, for Edith had borne no child since 1812. The boy grew up very much to his father's liking, if he had none of the brilliance of the brother who had preceded him: he went up to Queen's College, Oxford, and even ually took Holy Orders. He was the editor of his father's *Life and Correspondence*.

After his return from Italy and Switzerland in 1817, Southey made no more expeditions to the Continent for eight years. Instead, he took trips into various parts of England and Scotland, often combined with the inevitable, wearying visits to London. In the course of one of these tours he visited Oxford to receive an honorary D.C.L. at the Encaenia of 1820. He wrote a full account of the ceremony to his three younger daughters, concluding in a charming vein of mock-gravity: "Little girls, you know it might be proper for me now to wear a large wig, and to be called Doctor Southey, and to become very severe, and leave off being a comical papa. And if you should find that ell-ell-deeing has made this difference in me you will not be surprised. However, I shall not come down in a wig, neither shall I wear my robes at home." After the ceremony, at which he was well received by the undergraduates, he went out to walk alone in the Meadows. He found only one of his contemporaries in Oxford: Joseph Phillimore, one of the protagonists in that famous Westminster fight of 1791 and now the Regius Professor of Civil Law.

At Greta Hall visitors came and went. In 1822, for instance, there arrived a Frenchman, Amédée Pichot, who was on a literary tour of the country, which he afterwards described at length. His account of Southey is rather jejune in character, but in criticising his poetry he made one acute remark: "on le soupçonne d'avoir plus souvent recours à sa mémoire d'érudit qu'à son imagination de poète".[268] In August, 1825, Scott came. It was twelve years since they had met, and Southey "found him, as might be expected, much aged and altered. He looks older than he is. I should take him, by his appearance, for three score". (He was to age much more quickly that autumn, when financial disaster overtook him.) This visit was followed by a brief one from Canning, whom Southey knew only slightly. It made him think that if he had been three years older and had gone to Eton instead of Westminster, Canning would have been one of his friends. As it was, they met no more.

With the passing years, the friends of his youth began to die off. Robert Allen, who had introduced him to Coleridge, died in 1805, George Burnett in 1811. He suffered a great blow by the death of Charles Danvers early in 1814: Danvers had been his closest Bristol friend, he had corresponded with him constantly, and it was at his lodgings that he had met Landor in 1808. For

SOUTHEY · IN 1812

*From a drawing by John Downman in the possession of
Miss H. Read*

a time this loss made him think he never wanted to see Bristol again: it left him, he told Wynn, "in that state in which dreams are more distressing than waking thoughts, and when time has scarred over the wound there will always remain a gloom over what used to be some of the happiest recollections of my life".[269]

On 1st March, 1821 his formidable aunt Miss Tyler died.[270] He expressed no hypocritical grief—"my affection for her had been long and justly cancelled", was his sensible comment; but her death removed one of the few remaining landmarks of his childhood. He was often turning back to those early years at this time: in the previous July he had begun his series of autobiographical letters to John May, one of the most delightful things he ever wrote. He went on with them at irregular intervals as far as his schooldays at Westminster: there, to our great loss, they were abandoned.

But if, in the course of nature, the number of his old acquaintance was lessening, and if as time went by he no longer kept up with some of them—his correspondence with William Taylor of Norwich, for instance, had almost completely lapsed, though without unkindness on either side—he did form in these years three new friendships, two of which at least were to count a great deal to him.

At the end of May, 1818, he received a letter from an unknown young woman named Caroline Bowles. Her father had been a sea-captain in the service of the East India Company who had settled on the Hampshire coast near Lymington, but both her parents were now dead: she was a little over thirty years old, delicate in health, straitened in means, and very lonely. She had long been in the habit of writing verse, and it now occurred to her that a metrical tale, which she had completed some time before, might possibly be worth a little money. But how was she, a provincial spinster, to gain an *entrée* into the world of publishers? Recollecting Southey's kindness to Kirke White, she made up her mind to write to him, sending the tale and asking his advice as to its publication.

His response was in character. He took great care not to raise her hopes: "booksellers will not purchase poetry", he said, "unless from some writer who is in vogue". As for the poem itself, a lugubrious tale entitled *Ellen Fitzarthur*, Southey found in it much gentle, feminine beauty, while confessing that he disliked its subject—death—because he was "old enough to avoid all unnecessary pain. Real griefs do not lessen the susceptibility for fictitious ones, but they take away all desire for them." He

S.   M shrewdly observed that it would have found a ready market if it had been written as a prose novel. However, he undertook to recommend it to Murray, and in a series of further letters he proposed various improvements that his own greater experience suggested. These careful, detailed letters to a completely insignificant stranger are a most striking tribute to his generosity of heart, for, as Crabb Robinson once remarked, his time was his wealth.[271] He was always ready to write to any young author who asked for his advice and seemed to him worth helping. Kirke White had been one example, Ebenezer Elliott the "Corn Law Rhymer" was another, Charlotte Brontë was to be a third.

In the case of Caroline Bowles, he reaped a great reward for his kindness, for it was the foundation of his friendship with her. They did not see one another until the summer of 1820, when they met in London, but their correspondence was uninterrupted from the outset, and as time went on it became more frequent. *Ellen Fitzarthur* eventually found a publisher in Longman, and it was followed by a succession of other volumes with typically mournful titles—*The Widow's Tale* (1822), *Solitary Hours* (1826), *Chapters on Churchyards* (1829), *Tales of the Factories* (1833). Like Kirke White and her contemporary Mrs. Hemans, Caroline Bowles had a slender vein of true poetry in her, thickly overlaid though it was by her didactic purpose and her sentimentality. The exact antithesis of her poetry is Crabbe's, which was one of her models; for while hers is weak and imprecise, his is powerful, sombre, accurately observed, and therefore moving. But whatever were her deficiencies as a poet, as a friend she was invaluable. She was a woman of great charm—that is evident enough in her face, with its frail, slender features, and it stands out plainly from her letters. She was also, as she was to prove later on, a woman of character. She came to mean more and more to Southey in the last twenty years of his life.[272]

In addition to his secretaryship to the Speaker, John Rickman held a number of miscellaneous appointments, including, from 1803 onwards, the joint secretaryship to two Commissions, for the Caledonian Canal and for the building of roads and bridges in the Highlands of Scotland. This work brought him into constant touch with Telford, who was engineer to both bodies: the two men had many qualities in common, and they became fast friends. In the summer of 1819, Rickman suggested to Southey that they should accompany Telford on one of his tours of inspection of the Highlands. The idea appealed to Southey—it was a change from another Continental tour, and it promised to be an unusual experience. He reached Edinburgh on the first stage of his journey on 17th August.

That afternoon Telford arrived from Glasgow. Southey liked him immediately: "I was upon cordial terms with him in five minutes", he noted. Three days later they set off. Their route lay through Aberdeen and Inverness: thence, after a detour as far north as Fleet Mound, they went along the Caledonian Canal and so down the west coast by Ballachulish, Inveraray, and Loch Lomond to Glasgow. They ended up with a visit to Robert Owen's model factory and village at New Lanark—a project in which Southey always took a close interest. As usual, he kept a journal all the time. It is perhaps even more placid and uneventful than the diaries of his Continental expeditions. But it is worth reading as a quiet picture of Scotland drawn by a detached and observant southerner; it contains a good deal of characteristic and interesting comment on the state of the Scottish poor; it pays a high tribute to the work the government was doing for the country in reclamation and improvement ("practical reform", in fact); and it displays Telford more vividly than the rather arid reports that are otherwise our main authority for his work. Southey was genuinely sorry when the seven weeks' trip came to an end, and he said so in his journal: "This parting company, after the thorough intimacy which a long journey produces between fellow travellers who like each other, is a melancholy thing. A man more heartily to be liked, more worthy to be esteemed and admired, I have never fallen in with; and therefore it is painful to think how little likely it is that I shall ever see much of him again—how certain that I shall never see *so* much."[273] But they did not forget one another, and when Telford died in 1834 he remembered Southey in his will.

The last and the most interesting of these late friendships was formed four years afterwards. In the autumn of 1823 a young man in his early twenties called at Greta Hall. This was Henry Taylor, the son of a melancholy and eccentric gentleman farmer of County Durham. He had never been sent to school: all his education had come from his father and from his own voracious reading. He had spent a year in the navy as a midshipman, and four more in a small post at the Treasury. In 1822 Gifford had accepted an article from him for the *Quarterly*, and he soon began to contribute to the *London Magazine*. At the beginning of 1824 he entered the Colonial Office, to which he devoted the main energies of his life. He became one of the architects of the modern Colonial Empire, and he ranks among the most important of

Victorian civil servants. Like some other members of that distinguished body, he was also well known as a man of letters, particularly by his plays *Philip Van Artevelde* and *Edwin the Fair*.

But all that lay well in the future. At this time he was no more than a bookish and rather awkward young man, anxious to meet one of the contemporary authors he most admired. They took to each other at once, and it was not long before he was enrolled in the number of Southey's intimate friends and became one of his most frequent correspondents. This close and easy relationship does Southey much credit: Taylor was less than half his age; in politics he was almost a Benthamite, one of Southey's peculiar aversions; while in religion he was for many years something between a Deist and an agnostic—he once made the illuminating remark that he could understand religious experience only "as a man can apprehend the objects of sense who has been born without the organs". Yet Southey allowed none of this to make the least difference to him, and their friendship was one of the things that did most to brighten the sad closing years of his life.[274]

Among its first fruits were two tours in the Low Countries, on both of which Taylor was among his companions, in the summers of 1825 and 1826. In the course of the first he revisited Brussels (making further large purchases from Verbeyst) and the field of Waterloo. This of course called up sad recollections of the tour of 1815, when Herbert was still alive and Nash, now dead too, was of the company. But on the whole the trip was a cheerful affair. From a letter of Henry Taylor's we catch sight of Southey, in high good humour, speaking French "without shame and without remorse",[275] and all went well until they reached Leyden. Here Southey was struck down with a septic foot, which compelled him to rest. Even this accident, however, turned out happily, for it proved the means of introducing him to the poet Bilderdijk. With him Southey found much in common— especially in politics, for they were both strong conservatives; and his wife had published a Dutch translation of *Roderick* a year or two earlier. They insisted on his moving over into their house and looked after him most kindly until he was able to travel on again three weeks later.

His tour in the following year, with Rickman and Taylor, covered much the same ground; it included a second visit to the Bilderdijks, this time in good health.[276] At Brussels he received the startling news that he had been returned M.P. for Downton in Wiltshire, never having heard anything of the matter before.

When he got back to England, he found a letter from the Earl of Radnor waiting for him. It seemed that the Earl had so much admired *The Book of the Church* that he had decided to offer its author this nomination borough, which was under his control. It was out of the question for Southey to accept it, even if he wished to, for two reasons: he held a Crown pension during pleasure, and he had not the necessary qualification of an estate worth £300 a year. He at once turned the proposal down. In December another suggestion was made by the high Tory Sir Robert Inglis. Would Southey accept the seat if a qualification were purchased for him and if the Earl of Radnor could be induced to keep his offer open meanwhile? A present of £300 a year on the condition of sitting in Parliament might seem a tempting offer, but he declined it: he was too old, he said, he was unsuited to political life, and he "would not give up future utility for present effect". In any case, it soon appeared that the Earl had taken Southey's refusal as final and that his offer was no longer open. There the matter ended. It is interesting to see how highly some of the die-hard Tories thought of his work; as for Southey's decision itself, it was obviously right.

The news of his election to Parliament reached Keswick before he did. The sensation in the little town may be imagined. The wildest rumours flew about. "One story is that I am to have six thousand a year upon this occasion", he told his brother Henry. "Another was that I had written from Holland and predicted the end of the world for Thursday last."[277] When he arrived in the mail-coach on 7th July, he found that the town band was awaiting him and that "the whole posse of the place had assembled to see what alteration dignity had produced in my stature and appearance".

But such celebrations, however well intended, were sadly out of place, for as he approached Greta Hall he was met by his family with the news that his youngest daughter Isabel was seriously ill. Little more than a week afterwards she was dead. She was not fourteen. This was a blow only less severe than the loss of Herbert, and Edith never wholly recovered from the shock. "Its effect", Southey wrote a few weeks later, "has been as if a sudden weight of years had been laid upon her, and something of the same kind I feel in myself. Were it not for those who are left, how earnestly I should desire to depart and be at rest, for these trials are worse than death."

XI

IN LABORE QUIES

(1826-1843)

MORE THAN twenty years earlier, Southey had adopted a motto: *In Labore Quies*. It was borrowed, so he told a friend, from the sixteenth-century Spanish historian Esteban de Garibay. About 1810 he had a charming little book-plate designed for him by Bewick, on which appears his family's coat of arms, with this motto underneath.[278] Nothing more appropriate could have occurred to him; for those three words are the hallmark of his life, and above all of its closing chapter.

Isabel's death hit him a hard blow, ageing him in spirit, taking away more of his *joie de vivre*. As in 1816, so now he allowed his grief little indulgence, quickly going back to the *History of the Peninsular War* and his other labours. But it is significant that one of the first tasks he turned to was the melancholy business of sorting and setting in order all his past correspondence, as if he felt that his own death had now approached a step nearer. He was suffering physically, too, from a distressing rectal complaint that threatened to prevent him from taking the long walks in which he had always delighted. However, early in 1828 he was delivered from this infirmity by an operation in London.[279]

He was only in his early fifties, but his mind had in many ways grown prematurely old. As he looked out on the world around him, he saw little enough to praise, and a very great deal to damn: he had become out of touch with his own age. The years 1828-1832 saw the rise of Liberalism in England, the rapid unfreezing of the country from the iron frost of Toryism in which it had been gripped for twenty years and more. We have already noted what Southey thought of Catholic Emancipation. He said he could never forgive Wellington and Peel for betraying their principles on this question: "they have broken the staff of their strength, and I suspect they have an evil eye upon Church pro-perty". But worse soon befell: the Whigs came into power in November, 1830; Catholic Emancipation was followed by Parliamentary Reform.

As the struggle over the Reform Bill developed, his language became more and more frantic, until at times one begins to wonder if his mind is not becoming unhinged. He was encouraged in this violence by Rickman, whose political judgment, such as it was, had been wholly overturned by the crisis: Southey was staying with him in Palace Yard at the time of the change of government. In October, 1831, while the agitation was at its height (it was the very month of the Bristol Riots), the great epidemic of cholera that had been ravaging the Continent spread to England. Its coming had been watched at the Lakes with gloomy foreboding. "Wordsworth has invested all the money he could command in the American funds", wrote Southey in the previous June. "I am staked down by my books and my employments; but if I were free I would take my family to Denmark or Sweden, as the likeliest places for safety. Yet there is the cholera in the Baltic, and not improbably on its way here, perhaps as a dispensation of mercy." When it arrived, he maintained that it had been sent by God as "one means of awakening the nation to a sense of its madness and its wickedness".[280]

As a comment on the Reform Bill this is absurd enough; but he had something else in his mind too. "One good I confidently hope for from this visitation", he wrote in February, 1832, to a young friend, the parson of a slum parish in Manchester. "The preparatory measures of precaution have made the squalid misery of the lower orders matter of public notoriety. What you and I have so long known, and what was always known to those whose business or duty leads them among the poor, is now brought publicly to the knowledge of those who, if not ignorant of it, might at least excuse their gross inattention to this great and crying evil, by affecting to be so. They who are insensible to the moral evils of such poverty, and even to its political dangers, may be roused by the physical consequences, when they see it acting as a recipient and conductor not only for sedition and rebellion, but for pestilence also." Here he was on strong ground: the cholera epidemic did act in precisely this way, revealing the horrors of slum life to many who had known nothing of them before. Improvement in sanitary conditions was slow in coming until Chadwick took it up with his vigour and administrative drive in the forties; but there is no doubt that it was stimulated by the epidemic of 1832.[281]

Here is another instance—possibly the most striking of all—of the peculiar nature of Southey's ideas on social and political questions. Side by side with an extreme ultra-Toryism and a morbid tendency to panic there goes a perception of the wretchedness of the poor such as few of his contemporaries possessed—none, perhaps, who had acquired it wholly by imagination, at second hand, as he had. Nothing could be clearer than his vision on that point; few things more foolish and shortsighted than his comments on wide political questions.

But though he might be ageing rapidly and his Toryism becoming more and more violent and narrow, he had a considerable faculty for getting on well with the younger generation, even when he entirely disagreed with their politics: personally, there is no doubt that he mellowed as he grew into old age. In this respect Henry Taylor was a great help to him; for he was a man of wide sympathies, sociable by nature, tactful as well as affectionate in handling his distinguished but at times somewhat difficult friend. So, for instance, when Charles Greville met him at a breakfast-party given by Taylor in November, 1830, he found the Laureate "remarkably pleasing in his manner and appearance, unaffected, unassuming and agreeable".[282] One of the party on that occasion was John Stuart Mill, who called on Southey at Greta Hall in the course of a tour in the Lake District a year later. Southey always expressed the highest disapproval of Utilitarianism and all its works, but his reception of Mill was characteristically kind, and it led the young man, describing the meeting to John Sterling, to make a shrewd point about Southey's character. He thought him "a remarkably pleasing and likeable man. . . . He seems to me to be a man of gentle feelings and bitter opinions. His opinions make him think a great many things abominable which are not so; . . . now when he knows an individual and feels disposed to like him, although that individual may be placed in one of the condemned categories, he feels . . . no principle of repugnance, nor excites any. No one can hold a greater number of the opinions, and few have more of the qualities he condemns, than some whom he has known intimately and befriended for many years".[283]

This last remark was very true. When he made it, Mill probably had in mind their common friend Henry Taylor, but there were other cases equally outstanding: Wynn, for instance, actually consented to become Secretary at War in Grey's Reform ministry in 1830-1831; William Taylor of Norwich was an avowed free-thinker. Once he had met a man and liked him personally, Southey hardly ever allowed differences of opinion, even on subjects of the last importance, to come between them. Here lay one of the secrets of his remarkable capacity for friendship.

Henry Taylor was also the means of introducing another man of genius to Southey: in February, 1835, he invited Carlyle to meet him. Carlyle's previous impression had been adverse. As a young man he had taken the popular side in the *Wat Tyler* controversy (upon insufficient and partisan evidence, as he afterwards admitted), calling the Laureate "a most unblushing character" and in 1820 referring to his political articles in the *Quarterly Review* as "delirious speculations".[284] But when he met Southey face to face, his own early Radical opinions having very greatly altered in the meantime, he was not unfavourably impressed. "A lean grey-white-headed man, of dusky complexion [so he described Southey in his journal]; unexpectedly tall when he rises, and still *leaner* then. The shallowest chin; prominent snubbed-Roman nose; small care-lined brow, huge brush of grey-white hair, on high crown, and projecting on all sides; the most *vehement* pair of faint-hazel eyes I have ever seen. . . . A well-read, honest, limited (strait-laced even), kindly-hearted, most irritable man."

There was certainly no doubt about the irriatbility. Before the evening was over, Carlyle was unwise enough to ask Southey if he knew De Quincey, whom he had himself met in Edinburgh seven years earlier. It was a tactless question. De Quincey had just been publishing in *Tait's Magazine* his reminiscences of Coleridge; and the revelations they contained of Coleridge's weaknesses, especially in the matter of opium, had given the deepest offence to the poet's relatives and friends, Southey among them. The effect of the question now was violent. "'Yes I do know him', answered Southey, 'and know him to be a great rascal: and if you have opportunity, I will thank you to tell him so ': his brown-dun face was overspread suddenly almost with black." The obnoxious subject quickly dropped, but Carlyle's interest was now aroused, and in the subsequent conversation he noted the rapid changes of colour on Southey's face—the red blush when he was pleased, the "serpent-like flash of *blue* or black blush" when, much more rarely, something annoyed him. His final comment showed deep insight. "I said to myself, ' How has this man contrived, with such a nervous-system, to keep alive for near sixty years? Now blushing, under his grey hairs, rosy like a maiden of fifteen; now *slaty* almost, like a rattle-snake, or fiery serpent? How has he not been torn to pieces long since, under such furious pulling this way and that? He must have somewhere a great deal of methodic virtue in him; I suppose, too, his heart is thoroughly honest, which helps considerably! '" For once the tortured language has achieved precision: "methodic virtue" is an admirable summary of Southey's character.[285]

It was natural that, at his age, Southey's old friends should now be dying off. He suffered a distressing series of such losses in the years following Isabel's death. In 1828 his uncle Mr. Hill died. This was hardly unexpected, for he had reached the ripe age of seventy-nine, but his nephew felt it deeply none the less. It removed from the world a wise, understanding relative who had steadily befriended him for forty years, and in the intellectual sphere the person who shared most closely his Portuguese and Brazilian interests. Something of this he expressed the following year in the verse dedication of the *Colloquies* to his uncle's memory. On this occasion the accent of personal emotion gave his verse a body and fullness it too often lacks, and the concluding lines have a truly noble ring in them:

> . . . Meantime, with dutiful and patient hope,
> I labour that our names conjoin'd may long
> Survive, in honour one day to be held
> Where old Lisboa from her hills o'erlooks
> Expanded Tagus, with its populous shores
> And pine woods, to Palmella's crested height:
> Nor there alone; but in those rising realms
> Where now the offsets of the Lusian tree
> Push forth their vigorous shoots,—from central plains,
> Whence rivers flow divergent, to the gulph
> Southward where wild Parana disembogues
> A sea-like stream; and northward in a world
> Of forests, where huge Orellana clips
> His thousand islands with his thousand arms.

The next of his friends to go was Scott. They met for the last time in London on 26th May, 1828. Less than two years later, Scott had his first paralytic stroke, followed by the second in April, 1831. He knew he had not long now to live. That summer he sent a message to Southey, saying that he must come and see him soon, or it would be too late. All the time he went on with his work, the dogged, heroic grind so movingly described in his *Journal*. He consented to go abroad for that winter, spent it in Malta and Naples, returned to England in June, 1832, and died at Abbotsford on 21st September.

Southey and he had met little in later life, and in some respects they moved apart. Scott, for instance, did not approve of the violence of Southey's political opinions, Tory though he was himself. "I like his person," he told Lockhart, "admire his genius and respect his [stock] of immense erudition, but *non omnia*—in point of reasoning and political judgment he is a perfect Harpado —nothing better than a wild bull." But their friendship, always cordial though never intimate, lasted unbroken until the end of Scott's life.[286]

The year 1834 brought the deaths of two of his most intimate early friends—Coleridge on 25th July and Lamb on 27th December. Coleridge had been living at Highgate, in the kind care of the Gillmans, since 1816, and he had seen little of his brother-in-law. He had taken a hand in the *Wat Tyler* affair, defending Southey in his own way in two articles in the *Courier*. They met at a dinner-party in London in 1825, and Southey may have visited him—he certainly intended to—in the summer of 1828. A year before his death, Coleridge complained of Southey's "unkind neglect". And so, when he heard that Coleridge had died, Southey could only remark that "he had long been dead to me, but his decease has naturally wakened up old recollections. . . . All who were of his blood were in the highest degree proud of his reputation, but this was their only feeling concerning him". "Living wholly to himself as he had so long done," he remarked to W. L. Bowles, "his death has brought with it little grief and no loss to any of them." Southey, as usual, made no pretence of expressing a sorrow he did not feel; but it cut one more of the now slender ties that bound him to his early life.[287]

It was otherwise with Lamb, for excepting the unhappy episode of 1823 no shadow had ever come between them, and Southey spoke of him with real tenderness. Of the first Romantic generation, Landor, Wordsworth and he were now the sole great figures still surviving: Blake had died in 1827, Hazlitt in 1830, Crabbe in 1832. But while Southey met Landor only twice in these years, and then for short periods, his intercourse with Wordsworth, living no more than fifteen miles away, was constant. They drew very much closer together in old age, through similarity of opinions, through isolation from the rest of the world, through family friendships and increasing personal sympathies. Wordsworth proclaimed it by dedicating *Peter Bell* to Southey in 1819 "as a public testimony of affectionate admiration from one with whose name yours has been often coupled (to use your own words) for evil and for good". That was very true. Ever since Jeffrey had denounced Wordsworth and Southey as members of a new "sect of poets" in 1802, they had been joined together in public estimation. For his part, Southey was glad enough to have it so: "if my name be found in such company hereafter," he wrote (even more wisely than he knew), "it will be enough".[288]

Southey was not, in general, very forward to praise his contemporaries. "I think little of Campbell's poetry", he remarked in 1804. "His *Pleasures of Hope* are neither sense nor English. Something there is in him, but not much. . . . The best poet *in season* at present is that lump of lasciviousness Little Moore."[289] We have seen what he thought of the work of Byron and Shelley. But for Wordsworth he showed a loyal appreciation that never wavered. He was among the first people to recognise Wordsworth for a great poet, and he stuck to his opinion through thick and thin until, in old age, he saw it become fashionable to agree with him.[290] It is only fair to recall this generous recognition of his friend's greatness as an offset to his own rather irritating self-satisfaction.

Wordsworth's opinion of Southey was not equally favourable. He carefully made no pretence to speak of him as a poet on a level with Coleridge or himself. In 1812 he told Crabb Robinson that he considered Southey "one of the cleverest men that is now living. At the same time he justly denied him ideality in his works. He never inquires, says Wordsworth, on what idea his poem is to be wrought, what feeling or passion is to be excited; but he determines on a subject, and then reads a great deal and combines and connects industriously, but he does not give anything which impresses the mind strongly and is recollected in solitude". Again, writing to Miss Fenwick after Southey's death, more than thirty years later, he says: "Observe the difference of execution in the poems of Coleridge and Southey, how masterly is the workmanship of the former compared with the latter; the one persevered in labour unremittingly, the other could lay down his work at pleasure and turn to anything else. But what was the result? Southey's poems, notwithstanding the care and forethought with which most of them were planned after the material had been diligently collected, are read once, but how rarely they are recurred to! how seldom quoted, and how few passages, notwithstanding the great merits of the works in many respects, are gotten by heart."[291]

Such opinions as these got him into trouble with Landor, gossip having misrepresented him as saying that he would not give five shillings for all Southey's poetry. We can be sure that Wordsworth used no such phrase as that, and he indignantly denied it himself. But it may well have originated in some (probably quite just) criticism of his friend's poetry, for he never attempted to conceal his views. Indeed, on one occasion at least he expressed them pretty clearly to Southey himself, when he wrote him a letter laying down, in his *ex cathedra* manner, what were the requirements of epic poetry, and going on to illustrate them from the examples of Tasso, Spenser, Homer, Virgil and Milton—but without a word on Southey himself, who was after all an epic poet, whatever his quality, where Wordsworth was not.[292]

On the other hand, he fully recognised the merits of Southey's prose. "I need scarcely say", he wrote in 1829, "that Mr. Southey ranks very highly, in my opinion, as a prose writer. His style is eminently clear, lively, and unencumbered, and his information unbounded; and there is a moral ardour about his compositions, which nobly distinguishes them from the trading and factious authorship of the present day."[293]

Whatever their differences on literary matters might be, personally they were now near friends. The ties between the two poets' families were very strong too: there was a continual going to and fro between Rydal Mount and Greta Hall and many picnics by Thirlmere, the two parties meeting half-way. Speaking of Wordsworth's family, Southey told Caroline Bowles that "no man was ever more fortunate in wife, sister, or sister-in-law, than he has been. There is no woman out of my own house (except one whom I shall not name to you) with whom I am so intimate as Miss Hutchinson, or whom I love altogether so well". And when Dorothy Wordsworth's mind failed and she appeared to be dying in June, 1835, Southey remarked to his son-in-law that "there are few persons whom I should miss more, or regret so much".[294] This friendship extended to the next generation. Edith May Southey was one of Dora Wordsworth's best friends: Wordsworth himself paid his tribute to the pair, together with Sara Coleridge, in "The Triad", written in 1828.

Wordsworth on his side was strongly attached to Southey. At Rydal Mount there were five portraits over the dining-room fireplace—of Chaucer, Spenser, Bacon, Shakespeare, and Milton. The only other ornaments on that wall were a bust and a portrait of Southey. At the beginning of 1839 Wordsworth "spoke of him with great feeling and affection" to Crabb Robinson; and during Southey's long last illness he behaved with all the solicitude and kindness of an intimate family friend.[295]

Meanwhile, the household at Greta Hall was beginning to

break up, Sara Coleridge was married at Crosthwaite to her cousin Henry Nelson Coleridge in September, 1829. They went to live in London, taking her mother with them. In January, 1834, came another wedding—of Edith May Southey to the Rev. J. W. Warter, whom the Archbishop of Canterbury presented to a living in Sussex for his father-in-law's sake.[296]

The house now became a quieter place: its best days were over, as its master himself said. At the end of September that quietness and peace were suddenly turned to tragedy. The story is graphically told by a visitor who chanced to arrive at the very moment it happened. "On passing the drawing-room he noticed several ladies apparently in a very cheerful mood; on giving his name, after waiting about five minutes, Southey came to him, the very image of distraction, took his hand and led him into his study. For a long time he remained silent—at length told him he believed he must dismiss him; in fine he disclosed to him that within the last five minutes, since he rang the bell at the lawn gate, Mrs. Southey had, without previous indication or symptom, gone raving mad, and to that hopeless degree that within an hour he must take her to an asylum."[297] For a few months she was in a Retreat for Lunatics near York. She then became well enough to be brought home, but she never recovered her sanity.

Edith Southey had always been a listless woman of low vitality. Ever since 1815 she had suffered from a variety of complaints, chiefly nervous, and the successive losses of Herbert and Isabel had been terrible blows to her, from which she never completely rallied. But there were other causes of her mental collapse as well. At Crosthwaite they suffered from a hysterical revivalist curate, Mr. Whiteside, whose "pestilent preaching" had preyed on her mind. Worse still, it seems that she was continually in secret anxiety about money, fearing that they were overspending their income or that her husband would die leaving his family unprovided for.[298]

This last cause appears to have been the most potent of all. Yet it is ironical that it should have been so; for no man was ever more careful of his family's interests than her husband, and now at length he was getting to the top of the tree, his works were commanding fairly high prices from the publishers, and he seemed to be on the verge of affluence in old age. For the *History of the Peninsular War* he had £1000 from Murray. Far better than that (because the *History* eventually extended to three big quartos), in 1830 he was offered £750 by Longmans for a single volume of naval history in their *Cabinet Cyclopædia*; and when Murray learnt of his rivals' *coup*—Southey always published with both houses, playing off one against the other with some skill—he agreed to pay at the same rate for six volumes in his "Family Library". The next year he contracted with a third firm, Messrs. Baldwin and Cradock, to prepare an edition of Cowper, with a life of the poet prefixed, for a thousand guineas. When the disaster of his wife's illness fell upon him, he told Bedford that for the first time in his life he had means in hand for the whole of the following year: "I can meet this additional expenditure, considerable in itself, without any difficulty. As I can do this, it is not worth a thought; but it must have cost me much anxiety had my affairs been in their former state."

It may perhaps seem surprising that an author of Southey's eminence should have achieved such a modest measure of financial stability as that only when he was past the age of sixty. He had a family to provide for, it is true, including a son of fifteen and two unmarried daughters ("Southey has a little world dependent upon his industry", said Wordsworth some years earlier). He was besides of a most generous disposition, always prepared to send money—sometimes large amounts—to his relatives or friends when they were in distress. He assisted all his brothers in turn and, as we have seen, made himself largely responsible for the family of his brother-in-law Coleridge. His letters reveal numerous other instances of private charity, which he was often able to afford only at the cost of real sacrifice. The most remarkable instance occurred in 1821, when, hearing that his friend John May had lost his fortune through the mismanagement of a brother in Brazil, Southey instantly arranged to transfer to him his entire savings—£625 in 3 per cent Consols.[299] Yet his life had been an extremely frugal one of unremitting hard work: books had been his only extravagance, and they after all were his tools. That such a man as he should feel at his age that, whatever happened, it was necessary for him to go on working as long as he had the strength surely reflects small credit on the state of literature in England at the time.[300]

As it happened, there was a change of government that winter, and it brought Peel into power as Prime Minister. For all his *bourgeois*, Lancashire manufacturing origins, at which his contemporaries so freely sneered, Peel was a man of genuine culture. He showed it now in a striking way. The position of his government was precarious: it lasted only four months, and even for that short time it was kept together and in control of the House of Commons with the greatest difficulty. Yet he found oppor-

tunity, quite soon after he took office, to consider the duties of
the State towards literature, and on 1st February, 1835, he wrote
to Southey to offer him a baronetcy. This was magnanimous of
him, for he knew what Southey thought of his conduct over
Catholic Emancipation, and he was an acutely sensitive man in
such personal matters. He went further than that. Together with
his official letter making the offer, he sent another marked
"private", asking this question: "Will you tell me, without
reserve, whether the possession of power puts within my reach the
means of doing anything which can be serviceable or acceptable
to you; and whether you will allow me to find some compensation
for the many heavy sacrifices which office imposes upon me in the
opportunity of marking my gratitude as a public man, for the
eminent services you have rendered, not only to literature, but to
the higher interests of virtue and religion?"

Southey replied expressing his astonishment and gratification
at the offer, but declining it outright because he could not afford
to support the honour. He went on to answer Peel's further
question with perfect frankness. If he were to die at once, he
thought his life insurance, the sale of his property, the proceeds
of his books and of a possible posthumous edition might reasonably be expected to bring in £12,000-£15,000—not an inadequate
provision for his family. But, he continued, "broken sleep, and
anxious thoughts, from which there is no escape in the night
season, have made me feel how more than possible it is that a
sudden stroke may deprive me of those faculties, by the exercise
of which this poor family has hitherto been supported. . . . If I
were rendered helpless, all our available means would procure
only a respite from actual distress." At this point he suppressed
a touching phrase. "I had said in my letter that I could afford to
die, but not to be disabled", he remarked to Wynn afterwards;
"the words came naturally from my pen, but I struck them out,
lest they should look as if I were endeavouring to trick out a
plain statement." In these circumstances, he told Peel that what
he would most have appreciated would have been an increase in
the amount of his pension; but he understood that lay sinecures,
from which such grants usually came, had been abolished—one
of the fruits of the recent reforming zeal—and that therefore this
was probably impossible.

Peel seems all the time to have had in mind another measure
as well. The government still disposed of a small Civil List
pension fund of £1200 a year, and he intended to use it all for the
encouragement of letters. Probably through Aberdeen, the

SOUTHEY IN 1828

From an engraving after the painting by Sir Thomas Lawrence

Secretary of State for War and the Colonies, Henry Taylor was asked to suggest some names of possible beneficiaries. Naturally, he put Southey's down first. But there was a difficulty in the way: it was felt that a further grant to Southey, who had held a government pension since 1807, would be opposed on political grounds. And so Peel waited until his ministry was visibly tottering, and when nothing could save it he wrote to Southey announcing that his pension from then on would be increased by £300 a year.[301] His fellow-pensioners were to be four: one other poet, James Montgomery, the historian Sharon Turner, Mary Somerville the scientist, Airy the Astronomer Royal.

As Peel had anticipated, the new grant to Southey did not pass without criticism. Nothing was said in Parliament, but the Liberal press had its comments to make. The *Sunday Herald* of 26th April, 1835, for instance, carried a leader on "Literary Pensions". Having stated that the Laureateship was worth £300 (in fact, £90), and computing Southey's total income from the State as £750, the writer returned to the old attack on his change of opinions, adding some more original observations on the quality and nature of his books: "His writings are all of a kind very easy of execution, and have been most abundantly rewarded in the enormous prices which he is known to have obtained for his works. . . . Every part of his labours have had the acquisition of money exclusively in view." The King should be petitioned to withhold his consent to "so scandalous a reward of everything that is disgraceful in the public character of literary men".

Such remarks worried Southey little: he must have been used to them by now, and they can have weighed nothing in the balance against the security and ease that had fallen to him in his old age. No longer need he feel anxiety over his current expenditure: he could concentrate entirely on works that would bring in considerable capital sums for the benefit of his family. When all taxes were deducted, he had a clear income of £375 a year from his pension, which sufficed for the expenses of his household.[302] It was a great relief.

He had now three large-scale undertakings on hand at once. Five years earlier he had contracted with Longman to write a volume on the naval history of England for the *Cabinet Cyclopædia.* The book grew larger, its plan altered while he was working on it, and it ended up, not as a formal naval history, but as (to quote its title) *Lives of the British Admirals, with an Introductory View of the Naval History of England.* The "Introductory View" runs from Cæsar's invasions to the death of Elizabeth, occupying the whole

S.   N

of the first volume and three-quarters of the second (both published in 1833). Then come the "Lives of the Admirals": Howard
of Effingham (vol. ii): the Earl of Cumberland, Sir John Hawkins
and Drake, Cavendish, Sir Richard Hawkins, Grenville (vol. iii,
1834); Essex, Raleigh (vol. iv, 1837); Frobisher, Sir Robert
Mansel, Sir William Monson (vol. v, 1840). This was all that
Southey was able to complete: the fifth volume was rounded off
with a life of the Earl of Sandwich by Robert Bell, and there the
series stopped. It seems strange that so experienced an author as
Southey should have made such a wrong estimate of the size of
the work, but it was a fault to which he was prone: the *History
of Brazil* and the *History of Portugal* provide an even more remarkable example. The *Lives of the Admirals* can hardly be called a
satisfactory book, viewed as a whole, and naturally they have all
been superseded now by more modern works, based on the results
of fresh research and a more complete examination of the docu-
mentary evidence. But they were not a mere popularisation, based
solely upon the familiar authorities. Here, as usual, Southey had
something of his own to contribute: he was the first writer on
the Elizabethan seamen to have a wide knowledge of the history
of sixteenth-century Spain, and he quoted freely from Spanish
works, with their different view of the Englishmen's activities.
The narrative and descriptive passages are written, it need hardly
be said, with his habitual skill.[303]

But if prolixity and an excessive love of detail injured the
Lives of the Admirals, they were essential qualities in another
of the books he was engaged upon at this time, *The Doctor*. This
work had a thirty years' history. "Were I with you," he wrote
to Wynn on 8th January, 1805, "you should have the story of
Dr. Daniel Dove of Doncaster and his horse Nobbs—a tale which
like the mysteries of the Druids must never be committed to
writing." Three months later he was urging Bedford to compose
"a grotesque satire *à la Garagantua*" (for "in my conscience I do
not think any man living has more of Rabelais in his nature
than you have"), and that summer the two friends began to discuss
a mythical character known as the Butler, who was " to be
biographised in a style compounded of those of Rabelais, Swift,
Sterne, and Baron Munchausen".[304] It was out of a union of
these two things—the Dr. Dove theme and the Rabelais-Sterne
manner—that *The Doctor* was eventually born.

It was taken a stage further in 1813, when he was challenged
to write up the story of Dr. Dove, which he had been relating to
his wife, his sisters-in-law, and his next-door-neighbour Miss

Barker (the "Bhow Begum" of *The Doctor*). The tale did not originate with him. It was said to have been a hawker's book, and Coleridge used to tell it: the essential point was that it should be made as long-winded as possible, and of course it afforded endless opportunities for embellishment. As he came to write the story, Southey realised that he could make of it a vast, rambling miscellany, of a type exactly suited to his mind, at once a novel, a book of anecdotes, and a commentary on life and literature, seasoned with every imaginable sort of quotation that his memory or his books could provide. For twenty years he worked at it intermittently in odd hours, whenever he felt inclined.

Presently a third idea occurred to him. The book should be published anonymously, and he would take the greatest trouble to keep the secret of his authorship. When the first two volumes were eventually sent to the printer, the manuscript was in an unknown hand: the greater part of it had been transcribed by Sara Hutchinson, Wordsworth's sister-in-law. Grosvenor Bedford and Henry Taylor were in the secret, but it was kept from some at least of Southey's own family. When the first two volumes appeared at Greta Hall early in 1834, he put them aside, remarking "Some novel, I suppose"; and he amused himself by watching his son's reactions to the book as he read it.[305]

The Doctor made some stir at first—a very faint echo of the excitement caused by the anonymity of the Waverley Novels. Among those who were thought likely candidates for the authorship were Isaac D'Israeli, Sir Egerton Brydges, Hartley Coleridge, and Theodore Hook. But the secret was no better kept than most others of the same sort: before long every one knew Southey to be the author. The third volume appeared the next year, the fourth in 1837 and the fifth in 1838: two more were published posthumously in 1847, and the whole work appeared in one thick, large volume in 1848.

For all its touches of Rabelais and *Tristram Shandy*, the book is quite *sui generis*, without competitors or successors. It has been highly praised by some good critics, and scornfully damned by others: the reader must make up his own mind, for it is genuinely a matter of taste whether he likes it or not. Nothing could be more rambling, tangential, diffuse—exasperating to those of a tidy habit of mind. Yet there are passages of irresistible charm. The fourth and sixth chapters, for example, give an exquisite description of an eighteenth-century yeoman's household; there is a charming account of a company of puppets in chapter 23; chapter 129 contains the immortal Story of the Three Bears; while the Memoir of Cats' Eden and the chapter on the Statues at the close are wholly delightful. *The Doctor* is a very good bedside book, to be read discontinuously, dipped into and skimmed; and for those who are intimidated by its bulk, there is an admirable modern abridgement by Canon FitzGerald.[306]

The third work at which Southey was now labouring was his edition of Cowper, a careful and solid piece of work. He compared the published letters with the original manuscripts wherever he was able to. It was his custom to read them aloud every evening, while one of his daughters sat by, checking over what he read with the existing printed copies: a great deal of suppressed and mishandled material was thus brought to light. It was not his fault that the edition was not more complete than it is; but a rival edition, Grimshawe's, was also in progress in which some material appeared that he was debarred from using. None the less, his edition is even to-day the standard general collection of Cowper's works, though some parts—especially the poems—have been re-edited since on more modern lines. The text is preceded by a substantial and attractive biography, occupying the best part of three of the original fifteen volumes. It is a pity that it was not reprinted by itself, when it would have shown to better advantage. The publication of the edition was completed in 1837, but Southey never received the full payment for his work on it, as Messrs. Baldwin and Cradock went bankrupt in the financial crisis of that year.

At the same time he was also engaged in editing his own poems. Longmans proposed to issue a new edition of them, in a number of small volumes to appear one by one at monthly intervals. Their main object was to provide a complete collection that should check the sales of the pirated edition published by Galignani in Paris in 1829; but Southey took it as an opportunity to revise the whole of his poetical works with the greatest care, incorporating all his last thoughts and establishing what he intended should be a definitive text. He also supplied short prefaces to the volumes, setting forth the circumstances in which each of the long poems and the groups of shorter pieces were composed. Some of these prefaces contain autobiographical details of considerable interest. The edition appeared in 1837-1838.

For nearly eighteen months after his wife's return from the asylum, he never left Greta Hall, watching over her continually with the most devoted care. "Time passes with her as in a dream, or a succession of incoherent dreams", he told Lightfoot; "no fancy keeps possession of her mind long, but none are of a cheerful kind. She likes however to have us present, and if any one does not return from a walk as soon as she expected, she becomes uneasy and would fain send in search of the absentee. . . . We receive no guests and, except very rarely in an evening, see no company—our first object being (of course) to keep her as contented as we can. For the same reason, a morning's walk is my longest absence from home; and as my presence is evidently of as much comfort to her as anything can now be, and as it contributes mainly to keep up my daughters' spirits, I know not when circumstances will permit me to leave home, even for a short time."[307]

His health and spirits naturally suffered from this close confinement. As it happened, he received a subpœna to attend a trial at Lancaster in September, 1836, and so he was able to see what effect his absence for a day or two would have upon her. She showed no undue anxiety while he was away. He felt much better for the change—ending up by walking home from Rydal Mount, to Wordsworth's admiration and astonishment—and he determined now to venture on a longer holiday, killing several birds with one stone. He wanted to examine some of Cowper's letters he had not seen, at Edgbaston near Birmingham and in London, and to stay with his daughter and son-in-law in Sussex. Moreover, he longed to revisit once more the scenes of his childhood and his remaining friends in the West Country. And so he made up his mind to go on a great circuit, taking Cuthbert with him.

They went first into the West Midlands, and thence to Bristol, where they stayed with Cottle. On Sunday at Bedminster church they were "placed in the churchwardens' pew, immediately opposite the spot where my grandmother's stood, when I had been last in that church, five and fifty years ago. The church had been repaired and newly pewed since that time; but I remembered some of the monuments, and there was the old view from the windows which I once knew so well". He revisited his grandmother's house, where he had been so happy as a small child, and Corston, where he had been less happy at school. His son noted that "he had forgotten nothing—no short cut—no by-way; and he would surprise me often by darting down some alley, or threading some narrow lane—the same which in his schoolboy days he traversed". During this brief visit he also saw a good deal of Landor, who was then living at Clifton. An observant small girl met the two poets out in the street together, and she remembered it long afterwards: "I was one day bowling my hoop up and down the Royal Crescent, when Mr. Landor appeared walking with his friend Southey. Southey was in an old-fashioned spencer, his hair tied behind in *queue* style, with a black ribbon. I remember quite well his eagle eye and aquiline nose, and the excitement of meeting the author of the *Curse of Kehama* in real life."[308] Southey's final comment on the place was affectionate: "Landor . . . agrees with me that no city in England is to be compared with Bristol for singularity and beauty. Of this I am sure, that no one ever more dearly loved his native place than I do, though I expect and hope to end my days where I shall be gathered to my children —not to my fathers."

From Bristol they went on to visit W. L. Bowles the poet at his Wiltshire parsonage of Bremhill. Southey was charmed with the house and the garden, so typical of its period, with the "jet-fountain, something like a hermitage", and its pond with two swans, Snowdrop and Lily, who marched up to the breakfast-room window to demand their food if it was not forthcoming at the proper time. As for the vicar himself, he was a delightful old gentleman: "his oddity, his untidyness, his simplicity, his benevolence, his fears, and his good nature, make him one of the most entertaining and extraordinary characters I ever met with".

Next, calling at Taunton upon Miss Mary Southey, the poet's aged aunt, they went on to Nether Stowey to stay with Thomas Poole. What recollections that must have stirred in Southey's mind, going back to the first visit he ever paid there, forty-two years before, when he and Coleridge had preached Pantisocracy— Coleridge long since estranged and now dead! From Poole's they passed on to visit several of the great houses of Somerset and Devon—Holnicote and Killerton, the seats of Sir Thomas Acland, Mamhead, Powderham—to Lightfoot at Crediton, then back to the north coast at Barnstaple and so westward into Cornwall (again full of memories, of Nanswhyden and that dismal first journey to Portugal in 1795). They were making for Helston, where they stayed with Derwent Coleridge, now master of its grammar school. While they were there, Southey saw for the first time the scenes of two of his ballads, St. Michael's Mount and St. Keyne with its well. Caroline Fox the diarist records an amusing episode of this visit. Southey took down a book from a shelf in the house at Helston, "when Derwent Coleridge, who must have been in a deliciously dreamy state, murmured apologetically, 'I got that book cheap—it is one of Southey's'. It was quietly replaced by the poet; Mary Coleridge exclaimed 'Derwent!' and all enjoyed the joke except the immediate sufferers".[309]

They spent Christmas at Tavistock, whence after another visit to Lightfoot they went on to see Caroline Bowles in Hampshire and so at last reached their ultimate objective, Warter's parsonage near Worthing. Leaving Cuthbert behind there (the boy was now preparing for the university, under his brother-in-law's tuition), Southey returned to Keswick, arriving in the third week of February "to the joy of all who were capable of feeling and expressing it, and as much to the contentment of my poor Edith as anything can be in her condition".[310]

While he was with Caroline Bowles at Buckland he had received a striking letter—the last and the most interesting of the long series addressed to him by young authors asking for his advice. It was signed "C. Brontë", an odd name that he mistook for a pseudonym, and with it were enclosed some verses for his inspection and judgment. Unluckily, the letter seems now to have disappeared, but we have Southey's reply, written after mature deliberation at home in March. Its tone is kindly but discouraging: "You evidently possess, in no inconsiderable degree, what Wordsworth calls the 'faculty of verse'. I am not depreciating it when I say that in these times it is not rare. Many volumes of poems are now published every year without attracting public attention, any one of which, if it appeared half a century ago, would have obtained a high reputation for its author. Whoever, therefore, is ambitious of distinction in this way ought to be prepared for disappointment." He goes on to give her, "with all kindness and all earnestness", a serious warning—prompted, one may surmise, as much by the tone of her letter as by the verses themselves: "The day dreams in which you habitually indulge are likely to induce a distempered state of mind; and, in proportion as all the ordinary uses of the world seem to you flat and unprofitable, you will be unfitted for them without becoming fitted for anything else. Literature cannot be the business of a woman's life, and it ought not to be." He then develops the familiar argument that domesticity and marriage are a woman's proper career; but at the end of the letter his austerity relaxes a little as he remarks "Farewell, madam. It is not because I have forgotten that I was once young myself, that I write to you in this strain; but because I remember it. . . . Though I may be an ungracious adviser, you will allow me, therefore, to subscribe myself, with the best wishes for your happiness here and hereafter, your true friend, Robert Southey."

When this letter turned up in the sale room seventy years afterwards, it was found to have been endorsed by Charlotte

Brontë with these words: "Southey's advice to be kept for ever. My twenty-first birthday. Roe Head, April 21, 1837." And to her biographer Mrs. Gaskell she described it as "kind and admirable; a little stringent, but it did me good". She determined at once to write a second time, in reply. This letter is extant. In it, after thanking Southey for his answer to what she now considers to have been a "crude rhapsody", she goes on to tell him who she is and what her circumstances are, adding that she will treasure his letter and follow his advice. It is a most moving document, at once spirited and pathetic; and it elicited a further reply from Southey, inviting her to visit him if ever she should be in the Lake District: "You would then think of me afterwards with the more good-will, because you would perceive that there is neither severity nor moroseness in the state of mind to which years and observation have brought me." Some time later Charlotte Brontë told Mrs. Gaskell of this invitation. "'But there was no money to spare,' said she, 'nor any prospect of my ever earning money enough to have the chance of so great a pleasure, so I gave up thinking of it.' At the time we conversed together on the subject we were at the Lakes. But Southey was dead."[311]

In the autumn of 1837 his long vigil over his wife at last came to an end. She died, after a period of great weakness but little apparent suffering, on 16th November. In writing to a friend just before her death, he paid her a touching tribute: "No infant was ever more void of offence towards God and man. I never knew her to do an unkind act, nor say an unkind word."

Four months later he lost his brother Tom. As they had grown older, their relations had unhappily become much less close: the strong affection they showed for one another in their early years had given place to irritation, almost at times to dislike. Money lay at the root of it. Tom was a happy-go-lucky, somewhat feckless person: he had married a woman without means, and attempted to bring up a large family on his commander's half-pay. As early as 1815 he was in difficulties and asking for help, like so many other people, from his brother Robert. Only very shameless characters applied in that quarter in vain: he was then promised "something within three months, when that which is now impossible will only be inconvenient". Three years later Robert reckoned that he had sent him a total of £130, out of his own exiguous income, in the course of the previous eighteen months, and by then he had begun to apply to his younger brother Henry too. It might not have been so bad if Tom's children had been more attractive, but Robert ruefully remarked that "the eldest has nothing winning, and the two next act upon my affections as the repulsive end of the magnet upon the needle".

Not long afterwards Tom moved his family up to a house in Newlands, only four or five miles from Greta Hall. He then began to talk of emigrating, but abandoned the idea after a brief prospecting visit to Canada in 1823. Next, under Robert's persuasion, he sat down to a solid job of work: the writing of his *Chronological History of the West Indies*, which was published in 1827 and is still of some value to-day. He was, it is clear, one of those people who are commonly said to be their own worst enemies. According to his elder brother, he had an "unlucky propensity for writing tart letters"; "some imprudence or other his letters seldom fail to announce", is his wry comment on another occasion; while in October, 1830, "Tom writes to me in such a strain that I shall not trust myself at present to answer him." He was by now deeply in debt, from which both his brothers were trying to extricate him. The end of the story is obscure: what is plain is that for the last half of his life he was a constant financial burden upon Robert, where previously they had been devoted friends. It was a sad change.[312]

Southey was in London in the spring of 1838 for a short time, and saw Carlyle again. Since they last met, *The French Revolution* had been published. It had had no more than a *succès d'estime* until the praise of the best-qualified critics, led by John Stuart Mill, turned the tide of public opinion in its favour. Among the earliest warm admirers of the book was Southey, who had read it as soon as it came out. He recommended it to Wynn at once, and now, meeting the author again, he had the satisfaction of telling him in person how much he liked it. "Fancy my surprise", wrote Carlyle in 1867, "at finding Southey full of sympathy, assent, and recognition of the amplest kind, for my poor new Book! We talked largely of the huge Event itself, which he had dwelt with openly or privately ever since his youth, and tended to interpret exactly as I,—the suicidal explosion of an old wicked world, too wicked, too false and impious for living longer;—and seemed gratified, and as if grateful, that a strong voice had at last expressed that meaning. My poor *French Revolution* evidently appeared to him a Good Deed, a salutary bit of 'scriptural' exposition for the public and for mankind. . . . Southey was the only man of eminence that had ever taken such a view of me, and especially of this my first considerable Book." Or, as he put it more simply in a letter to his old mother: "The Poet Southey,

one of the chief men of England, was here last week; and left
word among his friends that he meant to read the F. R. *six times*."

Carlyle's second picture of Southey is as vivid as the first. He
saw him as a considerably older man, "strangely care-worn,
anxious, though he seemed to like talking, and both talked and
listened well; his eyes especially were as if full of gloomy
bewilderment and incurable sorrow". Shelley was mentioned,
and "at some point of the dialogue I said to Southey, ' A haggard
existence that of his '. I remember Southey's pause, and the tone
and air with which he answered, ' It *is* a haggard existence! '"[313]

That low cry came from the heart. For all the distress his
wife's last illness had caused him, and the relief he must have felt
when at length she died, the misery of his life without her was
intense. "Whether Hope and I shall ever become intimate again
in this world, except on the pilgrimage to the next, is very
doubtful", he remarked to Henry Taylor.[314] "I am haunted in
dreams more distressingly than can be described. At times the
burden of loneliness seems to weigh me down. And yet the fear
of dreams destroys all the satisfaction that I should otherwise feel
at night in thinking that another day was gone." Those words
were written to Caroline Bowles, to whom he instinctively turned
for comfort. He felt that he could not bear to go on living alone,
and in the course of this spring he asked her to become his second
wife. At first she gently refused. She was in delicate health
herself, she was twelve years younger than he was, and he was an
old man for his age. But he went on begging her to consent, and
at last in July she yielded to him.[315]

It would perhaps have been happier for them both if they had
been married at once, but the engagement was kept secret for the
time being: he did not announce it even to his own family for
three months, and the wedding was fixed for the following
summer. Meanwhile, some of his friends—his neighbour Senhouse and the ever-kind Crabb Robinson among them—had
arranged to take him off for one more trip on the Continent.

This time the tour was a short one, through Normandy,
Brittany, and Touraine, ending up at Paris. As a travelling companion, Southey showed the same pleasant disposition as ever, but
it was evident to the other members of the party that he was
failing in body and mind. He was always losing his way, even
in the hotels where they stayed, and for long periods he was shut
up in silence. His interest in the curiosities of the country, so
lively in former days, seemed almost to have vanished, except
when, at his special request, they turned aside to see the battlefield

of Crécy, or Chinon and the other places especially associated with Joan of Arc. In Paris he enjoyed the bookshops, and nothing else.[316]

Back in England, after a stay of some weeks with Caroline Bowles and his first and last journey in a railway train (an experience he disliked), he returned to Keswick with the intention of settling down to work once more. He had just written a *Quarterly* paper on Telford's *Life*, had another in hand, and had agreed with the young publisher Moxon to edit a "General Collection of Old Ballads, Songs and Carols". As to the future, his mind seems to have been easy. His second daughter Bertha was about to marry her cousin Herbert Hill; and he felt satisfied that by remarrying he was providing for the comfort of his son, his unmarried daughter Kate, and his sister-in-law Mrs. Lovell, as well as for his own.

The wedding took place on 4th June. Only a few weeks afterwards a marked change began to come over him. He had lately suffered from a series of attacks of influenza, which had reduced him to a state of great physical exhaustion: now it became apparent that his mind was permanently weakened too. His friends were puzzled at receiving no answers to their letters—he had always been such a punctilious correspondent. Poor Bedford, who was dying, was deeply hurt that Southey neither wrote nor called: "I should have gone hundreds of miles to see him", he said. And Southey, when he passed through London with his bride in August on the way to Keswick, confessed to Henry Taylor that he could not find his way about the streets, and that he caught himself staring vacantly at his watch without thinking of the time it told.[317]

He arrived home determined to resume work on three unfinished books: a second series of *Colloquies*, the *History of Portugal*, and the *History of the Monastic Orders*. "I am in good heart, with a reasonable prospect of getting through all that I have projected in prose and verse", he told Wynn at the beginning of September. But the handwriting of that letter belied such hopes. It is a note of only a single page, written obviously with great care, but crookedly, the ends of the lines tailing away—very different from his usual neat, clear manner. And on the blank page is a report from his wife: "I am inexpressibly anxious to keep from general knowledge, that with a visible sinking of the physical frame there has been for some time past a weakening of the mental powers—not in the slightest degree pertaining to *irrationality*, but causing a degree of confusion and bewilderment which makes it difficult, at times impossible, for him to arrange his ideas on paper, and for the present absolutely precludes all literary labour. . . . In the mean time my only comfort is, and it will comfort you to hear it, that he is *perfectly happy*, except when making fruitless efforts to employ himself with his pen."[318]

By November it was common knowledge that Southey's mind had failed. For a time he still enjoyed reading, but when Wordsworth called on him in July, 1840, he found him "past taking pleasure in the presence of any of his friends. He did not recognise me till he was told. Then his eyes flashed for a moment with their former brightness, but he sank into the state in which I had found him, patting with both hands his books affectionately, like a child". Dr. Arnold, who went over from Fox How to see him at the end of the year, reported that "his faculties seem gently to have sunk asleep, his body having outlived them, but in such a state of weakness as to give signs that it will soon follow them". However, in May, 1841, he was still going out for walks. He was in no pain, but occasionally, as time went on, he became irritable and even violent. His memory rarely returned to him, though once, in December, 1841, his wife heard him saying softly to himself "Landor, ay, Landor". Those are his last recorded words. Early in February, 1843, he had an apoplectic seizure, and a little more than a month later he died, on the morning of 21st March.[319]

It was well that he should have been in such a state of insensibility during his last illness; for the members of his family were quarrelling violently with one another. The main cause of the trouble seems to have been a common one: Kate Southey was jealous of her stepmother. Caroline may not have been very tactful: she was no weakling, but a woman of character and spirit, and perhaps she handled Kate wrongly. No doubt, too, her nerves and Kate's were both overstrained. At all events, from the hostility between them a rift developed that involved the whole family, and even their friends took sides as well. Mrs. Southey was supported by the Warters, by her brother-in-law Henry, by Landor, and by the Rev. F. Myers, the vicar of St. John's, Keswick, a sensible and unprejudiced witness: Kate's part was taken by her brother, the Hills, and the Wordsworths.[320]

Nor were these dissensions stilled by death. Wordsworth was not invited to the funeral, which took place at Crosthwaite on 23rd March. It is characteristic of him that he should have made up his mind to attend it all the same, and he was driven over by his son-in-law Edward Quillinan. Hartley Coleridge, who was too late to be present, records that the two factions among the relatives and friends remained sternly divided, refusing to speak to each other. Quillinan, however, preserves a more cheerful detail. As the bearers approached the grave on that dismal morning, two robins suddenly burst into song from a blackthorn hedge near by:

> Heedless of the driving rain,
> Fearless of the mourning train,
> Perch'd upon a trembling stem
> They sing the poet's requiem.[321]

Greta Hall was soon given up by the family, and Southey's beloved library—it comprised 14,000 volumes at his death—was sold: a large number of the Portuguese and Spanish books were bought for the British Museum and are there to-day. Amédée Pichot chanced to revisit Keswick at the time of the sale. He felt the full melancholy of the scene and described it vividly and with charm: "On sait ce que c'est, dans un palais même, que le lendemain d'une vente publique, volontaire ou involontaire; il ne restait plus à Greta Hall que les quatre murailles, dans la bibliothèque comme dans les autres pièces. C'était la saison des fleurs et le jardin n'en semblait plus triste, après avoir été piétiné par la foule des curieux ou des brocanteurs, qui n'avaient respecté ni la pelouse ni les plates-bandes; par un gazouillement sous l'ombrage, les oiseaux sans doute ayant été chassés par le tumulte des enchères. Je cueillis un pavot, pour faire sécher et conserver ses larges pétales entre les pages du volume où Southey a fait entrer mon nom dans un des vers de l'épître sur son portrait, adressé à Allan Cunningham".[322]

Southey had long intended that a selection from his letters should be published and his biography written, and with that end in view he had appointed Henry Taylor as his literary executor. But when Taylor came to the task he found the obstacles in the way too great: the family quarrel made things most difficult, the mass of material was enormous, and he was a busy man, holding a very responsible position in the Colonial Office. He devolved the task on to Cuthbert. It is our loss. For if Taylor had been able to undertake the book it would have been something different from what it is—a mere undigested and imperfectly edited collection of letters, strung on the slenderest biographical thread. All the same, one must feel grateful to Cuthbert: he worked under great difficulties, in the intervals of an active life as a parish priest; and inadequate though the *Life and Corres-*

pondence may be as a biography, it yet presents a vivid and attractive picture of Southey himself, through the medium of his own delightful letters.

The question of erecting some memorial to him was raised almost as soon as he died. Like everything else in the family at that time, it became a subject of controversy. Landor was asked to write an epitaph by one party, Wordsworth by the other. In the end, there were three memorials. A bust was put up in Poets' Corner, and another in Bristol cathedral. Crosthwaite church was (deplorably) restored in the poet's memory, and an elaborate marble monument, surmounted by his figure at full length, placed in the south aisle. On it there appear the grave, fitting lines written by Wordsworth as his last tribute to the memory of his friend, with their noble conclusion:

> . . . Wide were his aims, yet in no human breast
> Could private feelings meet for holier rest.
> His joys, his griefs, have vanished like a cloud
> From Skiddaw's top; but he to heaven was vowed
> Through his industrious life, and Christian faith
> Calmed in his soul the fear of change and death.

XII

THE WRITER

True ease in writing comes from art, not chance,
As those move easiest who have learn'd to dance.
                              POPE, *Essay on Criticism*.

FEW LIVES have ever been devoted to literature more completely than Southey's. As a child, brought up largely in isolation and compelled to amuse himself, he very early discovered the pleasures of reading and writing verse. At Westminster and Balliol, in the formative years of his career, he could put his heart into nothing else. And when he attempted to turn his mind to some profession—to medicine or the law—he found it was useless: he only wanted to be a writer. Authorship was his true vocation. He was well apprenticed to the trade, enduring many years' drudgery as a journalist and reviewer, to which he submitted very cheerfully, as the price he had necessarily to pay for following his own bent. The making and reading of books was always his highest pleasure, and so it continued to the end. His very last letters speak of the works he intended to complete: when his mind had quite failed he would still walk round his library, looking at his books and taking them down from the shelves one by one.

During his long and industrious life he wrote some forty-five books, together with hundreds of short poems and a multitude of articles in the *Quarterly* and elsewhere. We have now examined the conditions of his life and seen something of the circumstances in which his principal works were produced. What are their characteristics, their qualities and limitations? What value or interest have they for us to-day?

In his own time he was thought of primarily as a poet. Wordsworth and some other discerning judges might consider that his prose had higher and rarer merits: for the general public his reputation was founded by *Joan of Arc*, established by the four succeeding epics, and crowned by his appointment as Poet Laureate. Nowadays, those long poems are condemned out of hand, and they are seldom read; but they were none the less the corner-stone of his fame.

There is little to be said for *Joan of Arc*, except from a historical point of view: the poem is mainly interesting as an early manifesto of the Romantic Movement. It has none of the tender beauty of Wordsworth's *Evening Walk* (published in 1793); nor can it match the *Lyrical Ballads*, which followed it by two years, in arresting power. But it was a portent in 1796 all the same, from the political views it expressed. It was startling, as Anna Seward remarked, to find Henry V branded as a wicked tyrant. The epic poem had never been used before to preach the doctrines of pacifism—

> What are Crécy, Poitiers, Azincour,
> But noisy echoes in the ear of pride?—

or democracy:

> But little cause to love the mighty ones
> Has the low cottager! for with its shade
> Does POWER, a barren death-dew-dropping tree,
> Blast ev'ry herb beneath its baleful boughs!

In a literary sense, however, *Joan of Arc* is a conservative piece of work, strongly marked with the character of the late eighteenth century. Book IX (the Maid's Vision) is a pure Gothic tale of horror, such as Mrs. Radcliffe or "Monk" Lewis might have conceived; while there are occasional descriptive passages after—but a very long way after—the manner of Thomson and Gray:

> 'Twas now the hour
> When o'er the plain the pensive hues of eve
> Shed their meek radiance, when the lowing herd,
> Slow as they stalk to shelter, draw behind
> The lengthening shades; and seeking his high nest,
> As heavily he flaps the dewy air,
> The hoarse rook pours his not unpleasing note.

As we should expect in the work of a man of twenty-one, the poem is full of echoes, particularly of Milton and Spenser. Its only artistic merit consists in the forthright vigour with which the story is told, wishy-washy though the language and sentiment often are; and the bland, *naïve* tone of the whole thing is disarming and sometimes attractive.[323]

The next of the epics to be written, though not to be published, was *Madoc*, the longest, the least successful, the most tedious of the five. It need not detain us. The story is highly involved, and it is impossible to feel the smallest interest in the cardboard characters with their outlandish names—Yuhidthiton, Tlalala, Tezozomoc and the rest of them. The poem is unlikely to find readers now, except among specialist students of Romantic literature, and perhaps Welsh or Mexican nationalists.

Its successor, *Thalaba*, is a great deal more attractive and interesting. The poem was written in almost exactly a year (1799-1800), much of it in very pleasant circumstances, at Danvers's house in Bristol, at Burton and in Portugal. Something of this happiness seems to be reflected in *Thalaba*, which is sunny and gracious in tone. Coleridge referred, in a beautiful phrase, to its "pastoral charms and wild streaming lights": there are its merits exactly.[324] The tale has a Moslem setting, and it relates the destruction of the Domdaniel ("a seminary for evil magicians, under the roots of the sea") by the hero, Thalaba. As in all Southey's mythological pieces, the episodes fail to convince the reader because they are at once incredible in a human sense and uninteresting as miracles. They happen with too much ease: thousand-mile journeys through ice-bound passes and burning deserts occur almost casually—we are not made to feel their difficulty at all. Southey himself sensed this defect, for he wrote to Bedford at the time of the poem's publication to ask "if enough interest was excited, or if miracles, like pantomime-tricks, were so rapid as to weary and satiate".[325]

But though the plot may be uninteresting, *Thalaba* has many incidental quiet beauties. Occasionally there is a flash of close observation:

> One Flame alone was left,
> A pale blue Flame that trembled on the floor,
> A hovering light, upon whose shrinking edge
> The darkness seem'd to press.
>
> A yellow light, as when the autumnal Sun,
> Through travelling rain and mist
> Shines on the evening hills.

And there are some charming descriptive passages. In the fourth book, for instance, during his journey over the desert to Bagdad, Thalaba sees a mirage:

s.   o

> But oh the joy! the blessed sight!
> When in that burning waste the Travellers
> Saw a green meadow, fair with flowers besprent,
> Azure and yellow, like the beautiful fields
> Of England, when amid the growing grass
> The blue-bell bends, the golden king-cup shines,
> And the sweet cowslip scents the genial air,
> In the merry month of May!

If only Southey had written more of England, which he knew and loved devotedly, instead of dealing with remote subjects for which neither he nor we can really feel any deep sympathy, he might have been a major poet.

Technically, *Thalaba* is of interest as an experiment in unrhymed irregular stanzas. To be successful, a poem in such a form must pulsate with a strong rhythm. Unhappily, rhythmical drive was not among Southey's qualities. He tried to supply the deficiency by the frequent repetition of phrases, which becomes an irritating trick; and too often the verse of *Thalaba* lapses into prose in consequence. In language, the poem shows a great advance on *Joan*. There are still some passages of an artificial eighteenth-century character, such as that at the beginning of Book V about the pelican and the tiger (incorrectly described as "the spotted prowler of the wild"); but altogether the language of *Thalaba* is far purer, simpler, less derivative.[326]

With *The Curse of Kehama* we reach the finest of the epics, a poem of real distinction and even splendour. Like *Thalaba*, it is written in irregular stanzas; but they are rhymed, and that makes all the difference. It is a Hindu fable this time, hardly more interesting in detail than its predecessor, but incomparably grander in execution and scope. The poem opens with a gorgeous and imaginative description of the funeral of Arvalan, the tyrant Kehama's son. He has been killed by Ladurlad, whose daughter he had attempted to seize. The funeral over, Kehama turns to Ladurlad and pronounces upon him the famous Curse, which has the ring of true horror:

> I charm thy life
> From the weapons of strife,
> From stone and from wood,
> From fire and from flood,
> From the serpent's tooth,
> And the beasts of blood:

From Sickness I charm thee,
And Time shall not harm thee;
   But Earth which is mine,
   Its fruits shall deny thee;
   And Water shall hear me,
And know thee and fly thee;
And the Winds shall not touch thee
   When they pass by thee,
And the Dews shall not wet thee,
   When they fall nigh thee:
And thou shalt seek Death
   To release thee, in vain;
   Thou shalt live in thy pain,
   While Kehama shall reign,
   With a fire in thy heart,
   And a fire in thy brain;
   And Sleep shall obey me,
   And visit thee never,
And the Curse shall be on thee
   For ever and ever.[327]

The rest of the poem is concerned with the operation of the Curse
and the ultimate overthrow of Kehama. It works up to an
impressive climax at the end, and there is a very fine passage in
Book XIX, where Ereenia, one of the Glendoveers ("the most
beautiful of the Good Spirits") and the real hero of the story,
flies to the top of Mount Calasay. This is the Heaven of Heavens,
where Siva lives, with its Silver Bell, its great jewelled Table,
and the celestial Rose. Here he prays Siva to put an end to the
oppression of Kehama, and then

   So saying, up he sprung,
And struck the Bell, which self-suspended hung
   Before the mystic Rose.
   From side to side the silver tongue
   Melodious swung, and far and wide
Soul-thrilling tones of heavenly music rung.
   Abash'd, confounded,
It left the Glendoveer;—yea all astounded
   In overpowering fear and deep dismay;
   For when that Bell had sounded,
The Rose, with all the mysteries it surrounded,
   The Bell, the Table, and Mount Calasay,

The holy Hill itself with all thereon,
    Even as a morning dream before the day
Dissolves away, they faded and were gone.[328]

Thalaba was written in a year: *Kehama* took shape very much
more slowly. It was begun in Portugal, laid aside for long spells
at a time because Southey was dissatisfied with it, and completed
only at Landor's instigation. That may be why it is a better
poem. With Southey, difficulties and hesitation are usually a
sign of good work (this is often true of his prose as well: the
Life of Nelson cost him immense trouble in its details). The things
he wrote fluently seldom have any power. *The Curse of
Kehama*—there can be no doubt of it—stands with *Gebir* at
the head of English oriental poems of the Romantic period,
a very much more distinguished work than *Lalla Rookh* or *The
Giaour.*

. Its successor, the fifth of the series, was *Roderick, the Last of
the Goths.* Some good judges, such as Coleridge and Lamb, have
given it the highest place among Southey's long poems.[329] It is
true that it boasts much the most interesting plot; the central
theme, Roderick's penitence and expiation, is a noble one; and
the King himself comes near to being a real character. But the
poem is not very easy reading all the same. It is written in
blank verse, in some respects admirably handled; but the metre
has not the charm of the light irregular rhythms of *Kehama*,
thickly interspersed with rhymes. The modern reader who wishes
to sample Southey's epic poetry at its most attractive will do best
to begin with *Kehama* or *Thalaba* rather than *Roderick.*
    In the collected edition of Southey's poems, each of the five
epics occupies one volume. The other five volumes contain the
shorter pieces, by which he is usually remembered to-day. First
place among them must go to the ballads and metrical tales: he
had in him a true vein of the grotesque, which finds its best
expression here. "The Old Woman of Berkeley", "The Inchcape
Rock", and the story of Bishop Hatto were familiar to most of us
as children, and they do not lose their charm. The same is true
of the subtler "Battle of Blenheim". Nor are these the only good
ones: "Queen Orraca and the Five Martyrs of Morocco", for
instance, is a fine story. In these pieces Southey is in his element:
nobody has ever equalled him in the peculiar *genre* of the comic-
grotesque, except Barham in the *Ingoldsby Legends*—and they are
an altogether more elaborate affair. His pure comic pieces are
also very entertaining. The best of them show extraordinary

metrical dexterity: that indeed is the main point of "The Cataract of Lodore" and "The March to Moscow".

The historical poems are of less interest. They include a group of some fifty inscriptions and epitaphs, modelled on those of Akenside and the Italian poet Chiabrera, both of whom were favourites with Southey. One might have expected this form to suit him, for the very defects of his verse—a certain stiffness and impersonality—can become virtues in an inscription. Yet on the whole these pieces are disappointing. They are diffuse, they lack pith; and, as Saintsbury said, "they too frequently have the elevation on stilts, the monumental effort in plaster, the slightly flatulent rhetoric, so incomparably parodied and ridiculed in the *Anti-Jacobin* by means of the immortal lines on Mrs. Brown-rigg".[330] The best of them are those referring to episodes in the Peninsular War. Among the other historical pieces, only one is remarkable: the "Funeral Song for the Princess Charlotte of Wales", which has already been discussed.

There still remains a handful of small lyrical poems, and these comprise Southey's most charming contribution to English verse. They all have one feature in common: they describe the peace and pleasure of domestic life. That is what he most deeply loved: it is not surprising that it should have called forth his best poetry. Two of these pieces are famous, and have often appeared in anthologies: "The Holly Tree" and "My Days Among the Dead are Passed".[331] But there are other poems in the same spirit too, and at least one of the same calibre—the sonnet on Winter:

> A wrinkled, crabbed man they picture thee,
> Old Winter, with a rugged beard as grey
> As the long moss upon the apple-tree;
> Blue-lipt, an ice-drop at thy sharp blue nose,
> Close muffled up, and on thy dreary way,
> Plodding alone through sleet and drifting snows.
> They should have drawn thee by the high-heapt hearth,
> Old Winter! seated in thy great arm'd chair,
> Watching the children at their Christmas mirth;
> Or circled by them as thy lips declare
> Some merry jest or tale of murder dire,
> Or troubled spirit that disturbs the night,
> Pausing at times to rouse the mouldering fire,
> Or taste the old October brown and bright.[332]

Or again, the gentle ballad "Brough Bells", and the graceful inscription for his daughter's album, "Little Book, in Green and Gold".[333] A few lines of this character will now and then appear in his long poems, and sometimes they freshen the dullest wastes: the Poem to *The Poet's Pilgrimage to Waterloo* provides one example, the opening of *A Vision of Judgement* another.[334] He wrote such pieces occasionally at all times of his life: the sonnet and "The Holly Tree" date from 1798, one of the other poems from as late as 1831.

The central defects of Southey's poetry are two. In the first place it has no magic: it does not *sing*.[335] The second defect is even more important than the first: indeed, it is probably responsible for it. We have seen how Southey found that poetical composition excited him too much, upsetting the delicate balance of his mind and breaking into his sleep. (It was linked, one cannot doubt, with his weird, astonishing dreams, of which he has left a fascinating record that a modern psychiatrist might with advantage explore.)[336] His first thought had always to be of his family and of the bread and butter he must earn for them. It was well enough for Wordsworth to devote himself wholly to poetry so early—he had private means and only his sister to think of; or for Coleridge—he could comfortably put his responsibilities on to other people: for Southey it was different. The disturbance of composing poetry with concentration—the difficult, and some-times agonising, process described in Dorothy Wordsworth's *Journals*—was a luxury he could not afford. He chose rather to write tales in verse and light pieces, which he threw off with a fatal facility. Presently he found even that too exciting, and he turned over almost completely to prose.

This does not imply a claim that he was a potential Words-worth or Coleridge: it only means that he did not let himself go, or give his poetical talent full scope. Of set purpose, he kept it within constricting limits, never allowing it the time or the concentrated energy that great poetry demands. Instead, verse took turn and turn about with history, politics, and reviewing: the four last epics were almost entirely written before breakfast. Whether one considers that he did his duty best by bringing up a family and providing for them at the expense of his poetry, or that in doing so he sinned against the light, failing to use the talent committed to him, must depend upon one's point of view.

One might feel more inclined to judge him harshly on this issue if he had not left us something besides his verse: the huge, delightful legacy of his prose. Here he is a master beyond dispute, an artist of a high order.

To understand his achievement fully, it must be looked at in a historical as well as an aesthetic light. In poetry, it is a commonplace to say that the *Lyrical Ballads* marked a revolutionary departure from eighteenth-century practice. Wordsworth and Coleridge set out to free English poetry from "gaudiness and inane phraseology": they tried to describe "incidents and situations from common life" in "the language of conversation in the middle and lower classes of society".[337] But this revolution was not confined to poetry alone: an exactly parallel development took place in English prose at the same time, in which an important part was played by Southey.

We are accustomed to speak of the "clarity" of eighteenth-century prose. The Romantics would have thought that an odd and mistaken judgment, at best no more than a half-truth. They were for ever decrying the style of the second half of the century, of Johnson and Gibbon, with its periods and regular rhythms. "The essence of this style", said Coleridge, "consisted in a mock antithesis, that is, an opposition of mere sounds, in a rage for personification, the abstract made animate, far-fetched metaphors, strange phrases, metrical scraps, in every thing, in short, but genuine prose."[338] In other words, such impression of lucidity as it gave was specious, they considered, not genuine, serving only to disguise the poverty of the thought.

The Romantic prose-writers reacted from the Johnsonian style in two ways. Wordsworth, Coleridge, and Lamb turned to the seventeenth century for their models. The *Tract on the Convention of Cintra* is impregnated with the style and spirit of Milton, Coleridge's prose was deeply influenced by the great Caroline divines, Lamb's by Fuller and Sir Thomas Browne. All of them have one thing in common: they are essentially poetical styles, intensively evocative and musical. Southey did not hark back so far. His closest affinities are with Swift, and still more with Defoe. This was quite natural, for the problems that faced them were the same: they were all three voluminous authors, writing constantly for the press. And it is significant that each of them wrote a children's classic: Defoe in *Robinson Crusoe*, Swift in *Gulliver's Travels*, Southey in "The Story of the Three Bears".[339] That is a difficult feat, which few great writers have achieved, for a single false note is fatal—nothing will do short of complete simplicity, sincerity, and truth.

But whereas the terse style of Swift and Defoe was in harmony with the spirit of their age (it developed from the masters of the preceding generation, from Dryden and pamphleteers like

Halifax), Southey was an almost unique practitioner of the art in the early nineteenth century. The nearest parallel to him among the writers of his own time is to be found in Cobbett; but admirable though Cobbett's work is, it cannot compare with Southey's in variety or poetic feeling. Contrast him, on the other hand, with Hazlitt, another prolific writer. Hazlitt's style is far more elaborate and highly wrought, enriched with every kind of device of quotation and inversion. It is an instrument of greater power than Southey's, perhaps of greater range; but on the other hand it has less clarity and ease. Above all, it is an obviously self-conscious style, whereas Southey's is completely self-effacing.

Yet the art is there all the same. Coleridge observed that "in the very best styles, as Southey's, you read page after page, understanding the author perfectly, without once taking notice of the medium of communication; it is as if he had been speaking to you all the while"; and more recently it has been well said that "we look through it as through pure gently-flowing water".[340] But nothing could be more incorrect than to suppose that because his style is so quiet and unassuming it was easily achieved or can easily be imitated. He was in fact, in his own way, as self-conscious an artist as Hazlitt, only his was the *ars celare artem*.

During the course of his life he forced himself out of the debased eighteenth-century manner in which he began to write into a crisp, nervous style of his own.[341] In his prose he pursued a lonely path, of a piece with the stubborn independence of his career. The Romantic tendency was in general towards ornament: the object he set before himself was above all to be plain and brief. He was thus at variance with Coleridge and Lamb and Hazlitt; but also, in writing as much as in politics, with the *Edinburgh Review*. Jeffrey and his young disciple Macaulay still looked back to the late eighteenth century for their models. Their rotundity, the regular rise and fall of their sentences, has little parallel in Southey, whose style is altogether lighter and more pliant. But those are the very qualities that give it special value for us to-day; for it stands nearer to our ideals and needs than that of any other of his contemporaries.

Southey himself attributed his development as a prose-writer to his early work in verse. "To write poetry is the best preparation for writing prose", he said. "The versemaker gets the habit of weighing the meanings and qualities of words, until he comes to know, as if by intuition, what particular word will best fit into the sentence." But he never trusted to his intuition as infallible, or presumed upon it too far. At the age of sixty he remarked that "it is long since I have been a rapid writer, and the pains which I take in collecting materials and making myself fully acquainted with the subject before me, render it impossible that I should be so. It is only by being never idle, when I can possibly be employed, that I am enabled to do much".[342]

His methods of work were strictly ordered to this end. He conformed to a regular time-table, which changed little during the whole of his life at Greta Hall. Here is a description of his routine given to Wynn in 1833: "Candle-light is the time upon which I reckon for getting through my needful labours, whatever they may be. Some little I do before breakfast. Immediately afterwards come Cuthbert's lessons; and the post generally brings me enough for the remainder of the morning. By the time my despatches are made up, the hour for exercise arrives, and out I go for a walk of from one to two hours, with a book in my hand, if the weather will permit; but be the weather what it may (snow excepted), out I go. We dine at four; I never remain at table after dinner, but retire to my room, and read till I am disposed to sleep: that sleep is perhaps the soundest and most refreshing that I get. Tea is ready at six, and from then till half-past nine I am close at my desk. When I can call those three hours my own, sufficient for the day is the work thereof."[343]

Within these hours, he always took the greatest care to vary his occupations, to leave whatever he was doing as soon as he felt himself becoming stale or tired and turn to something else. This he found necessary in order to quieten the excitement he always dreaded. "It has been by never over-working," he told his eldest daughter, "never carrying on any employment, however intent I might be upon it, till it produced anything like a sense of exhaustment, that I have with God's blessing preserved my health and spirits unbroken to the very threshold of old age."[344] Again, we can see that this method deliberately deprived him of the concentration essential for producing great poetry; but it must have helped to give him just the quickness and buoyancy that distinguish his prose.

Nor did he consider that his work was done when he had written the last line of a book or essay. The proof stage was of great importance to him. "I read all my proof-sheets twice, aloud, once on the day when they arrive and a second time on the morrow—except the proofs for the Q.R., which require more breath than I can afford. I weigh every sentence upon the ear, and take especial care as far as possible to avoid all ambiguity of

language, which our pronouns sometimes render very difficult."[345]
The labour was well expended. As a result, one can read page
after page of Southey's works without having to pause to re-read
a single sentence: it is all crystal clear. Of how many other
English writers is that true?

He was often asked what was the secret of his style—a foolish
question, which he never treated seriously. To him it was nine-
tenths a matter of common sense and practice. "The notion of
writing everything *exquisitely* is nonsense", he once remarked to
Henry Taylor. "It is by writing much that a man learns to write
well; and if he lives by writing he must publish all that he can
get paid for. Ultimately every one's reputation rests upon his
best productions, and not upon the average of them."[346]

Southey was not, then, a happy-go-lucky author, blessed by a
kind Providence with a talent for writing quickly: he was a
conscientious and laborious artist who achieved mastery in his
craft by hard work as much as by talent and inspiration. In the
course of this narrative of his life, enough passages have already
been quoted, from his letters and his published works, to make
clear something of the compass and capacity of his prose. We
have seen instances of his charming tone in writing to children,[347]
and of his gentle, sometimes dry, humour[348]—a very different
thing from the rather noisy nonsense he delighted to exchange
with Bedford, the fun of which seems now to have evaporated.
The quiet sketch of his uncle Thomas has shown how well he can
describe an odd character: his amusing account of Wilberforce
provides another example of the same power.[349]

His prose is often shot with poetry, as we have seen from the
letters he wrote during his second visit to Portugal in 1800-1801,
and from his descriptions of Oxford in the early morning, of the
Black Country, of the Waterloo bonfire on Skiddaw: many more
could be added to the list.[350] The concluding chapter of the *Life of
Nelson* is poetic all through, but let us take something less familiar:
the paragraph in which Southey recounts the end of the French
flagship at the battle of the Nile—a fine example of that use of
memorable detail in which the book excels:

It was soon after nine that the fire on board the *Orient* broke
out. Brueys was dead: he had received three wounds, yet
would not leave his post: a fourth cut him almost in two. He
desired not to be carried below, but to be left to die upon deck.
The flames soon mastered his ship. Her sides had just been
painted; and the oil-jars, and paint-buckets, were lying on the

poop. By the prodigious light of this conflagration, the situation of the two fleets could now be perceived, the colours of both being clearly distinguishable. About ten o'clock the ship blew up. This tremendous explosion was followed by a silence not less awful: the firing immediately ceased on both sides; and the first sound which broke the silence, was the dash of her shattered masts and yards, falling into the water from the vast height to which they had been exploded. It is upon record, that a battle between two armies was once broken off by an earthquake:—such an event would be felt like a miracle; but no incident in war, produced by human means, has ever equalled the sublimity of this coinstantaneous pause, and all its circumstances.[351]

Such passages must necessarily be rare, for it is not often that events like that have to be described. But Southey's histories and biographies are not just big, dull books, relieved only by a few purple patches. Their most remarkable quality is the general level of narrative skill they display. This is particularly true of the battle-pieces, which are described in a clear, classical manner—"classical" in both senses of the word, for at their finest they have a true hint of Thucydides about them.[352]

Nor is Southey a master of narrative only: he can excel also in description, and it is this that makes the *Colloquies* and *The Doctor* such delightful reading. Only a more extended example can do him justice here. Take this passage from the opening of the sixth Colloquy, where he describes the mellow beauty of an autumn morning at the Lakes:

... A fine day affects children alike at all seasons as it does the barometer. They live in the present, seldom saddened with any retrospective thoughts, and troubled with no foresight. Three or four days of dull sunless weather had been succeeded by a delicious morning. My young ones were clamorous for a morning's excursion. The glass had risen to a little above change, but their spirits had mounted to the point of settled fair. All things, indeed, animate and inanimate, seemed to partake of the exhilarating influence. The blackbirds, who lose so little of their shyness even where they are most secure, made their appearance on the green, where the worms had thrown up little circles of mould during the night. The smaller birds were twittering, hopping from spray to spray, and pluming themselves; and as the temperature had given them a

vernal sense of joy, there was something of a vernal cheerful-
ness in their song.   The very flies had come out from their
winter quarters, where, to their own danger and my annoyance, they establish themselves behind the books, in the folds
of the curtains, and the crevices of these loose window-frames.
They were crawling up the sunny panes, bearing in their
altered appearance the marks of uncomfortable age;   their
bodies enlarged, and of a greyer brown;   their wings no longer
open, clean, and transparent, but closed upon the back, and as
it were encrusted with neglect.   Some few were beginning to
brush themselves, but their motions were slow and feeble: the
greater number had fallen upon their backs, and lay unable to
recover themselves.   Not a breath of air was stirring;   the
smoke ascended straight into the sky, till it diffused itself
equally on all sides and was lost.   The lake lay like a mirror,
smooth and dark.   The tops of the mountains, which had not
been visible for many days, were clear and free from snow: a
few light clouds, which hovered upon their sides, were slowly
rising and melting in the sunshine.

On such a day, a holyday having been voted by acclamation,
an ordinary walk would not satisfy the children :—it must be
a scramble among the mountains, and I must accompany
them;—it would do me good, they knew it would;—they
knew I did not take sufficient exercise, for they had heard me
sometimes say so.   One was for Skiddaw Dod, another for
Causey Pike, a third proposed Watenlath; and I, who perhaps
would more willingly have sate at home, was yet in a mood
to suffer violence, and making a sort of compromise between
their exuberant activity and my own inclination for the chair
and the fireside, fixed upon Walla Crag.   Never was any
determination of sovereign authority more willingly received:
it united all suffrages: Oh yes! yes! Walla Crag! was the
unanimous reply.   Away they went to put on coats and clogs,
and presently were ready each with her little basket to carry
out the luncheon, and bring home such treasures of mosses
and lichens as they were sure to find.   Off we set;   and when I
beheld their happiness, and thought how many enjoyments
they would have been deprived of, if their lot had fallen in a
great city, I blest God who had enabled me to fulfil my heart's
desire and live in a country such as Cumberland.[353]

Southey's language will always take wing when he is speaking
of something that really touches his heart—whether it is family

happiness or gratitude for kindness or the sense of achievement at reaching the end of a long literary task.[354]

But why is it that a writer who commands a style of such remarkable range and flexibility is so little thought of to-day? There is a simple answer to that question: the intimidating bulk of his work. Nothing but a general selection from the entire range of his books can establish him in the high place he deserves to hold.[355] Such a selection, competently made, would show him for a great master of English narrative and descriptive prose. As it is, his large works are seldom read, and their merits are underestimated in consequence.

One modern critic, it is true, has spoken up for him boldly. In discussing English prose style not long ago, Mr. Herbert Read maintained that "of very few authors can it be said that they had no insidious faults", and he went on to name the only six for whom he thought that claim could be made. Among them was Southey, "whose style is a model of consistent ' workmanlike' qualities—the style of a man who writes swiftly and voluminously, and who has discovered the true economy of a clear mind and a clean pen".[356]

But such discriminating appreciation of his achievement has been rare, for his reputation has worn badly. In his life-time he was not admired, as we have seen, without reserve even by his fellow Lake Poets, or his friend Scott. On the other hand, the greatest of his enemies were willing to concede his merits as a writer. Byron thought his prose "perfect".[357] Hazlitt declared in *The Spirit of the Age* that his style could "scarcely be too much praised. It is plain, clear, pointed, familiar, perfectly modern in its texture, but with a grave and sparkling admixture of *archaisms* in its ornaments and occasional phraseology. He is the best and most natural prose-writer of any poet of the day". And even in respect of his personal character, one of Hazlitt's friends noted that "he never once, to the best of my recollection, either in print or otherwise, treated Southey as a dishonest man, but only as a weak, a vain, a self-willed, and a mistaken one. . . . If pressed (though not otherwise I confess) he admitted a saving clause in favour of his sincerity and love of truth".[358] A bitter opponent Hazlitt might be, but he was a just man too.

Southey had many friends among the younger men, but few disciples. Those he had were mostly drawn to him by the moral qualities of his works and teaching. R. H. Barham seems to have left no formal acknowledgment of the obvious debt the *Ingoldsby Legends* owed to Southey's ballads and grotesque pieces; but he spoke of Southey as "one to whom I am indebted for more comfort and resignation under calamity than to any other source save one".[359] The young Newman was an ardent admirer of his poems, again for their ethical content. "In his use of the doctrine of a future life," he wrote in an early essay, "Southey is admirable. Other writers are content to conduct their heroes to temporal happiness;—Southey refuses present comfort to his Ladurlad, Thalaba, and Roderick, but carries them on through suffering to another world." He thought *Thalaba* "the most sublime of English poems (I don't know Spenser)—I mean morally sublime"; and looking back over his life in the *Apologia* he connected the same poem intimately with the development of his mind: "Now it was, I think [i.e. in Italy early in 1833], that I repeated to myself the words, which had ever been dear to me from my school days, ' Exoriare aliquis! '—now too, that Southey's beautiful poem of Thalaba, for which I had an immense liking, came forcibly to my mind. I began to think that I had a mission."[360]

Even during his life-time, however, Southey's public reputation began to decline, and it quickly fell into the trough that is the common fate of most authors in the years immediately following their death.   When the *Life and Correspondence* appeared it had a tepid reception in the *Quarterly* as well as in the *Edinburgh* and the rest of the Liberal press. To Macaulay it only confirmed his low opinion of Southey's powers: it provoked Bagehot to speak of him with a most unusual touch of contempt.[361] Nathaniel Hawthorne, visiting Keswick in 1855, remarked that "few better or more blameless men have ever lived, than he; but he seems to lack colour, passion, warmth, or something that should enable me to bring him into close relation with myself".[362] In the same year Thackeray paid him a noble tribute in *The Four Georges*, but again it was to his private character and his letters rather than to his books.[363] And after that, increasing neglect settled upon him for the rest of the century: he did not emerge from the trough, as most good writers have done. He made little appeal to later generations. Gerard Manley Hopkins, though he enjoyed *The Doctor*, thought Southey "the writer who had the smallest notion of style and the least knowledge of the secrets of poetry, considering the magnitude of the works which he attempted";[364] Edmund Gosse recalls how his father presented him as a child with "the entire bulk of Southey's stony verse, which I found it impossible to penetrate";[365] while in 1909 there came from Arthur Symons the most scathing attack ever made upon Southey's poetry.[366] Only a few critics, most of whom were primarily concerned with the art of English prose, retained their admiration for him: Matthew Arnold, Morley, Dowden, Leslie Stephen, Saintsbury.[367]

Southey, then, had no direct successors: he founded no school. The most important contribution he made to English literature was not in the realm of poetry, though his poems are by no means without value and interest: it was in prose. There he played a great part in loosening up the muscles of the language, in releasing it from the artificiality into which at the end of the eighteenth century it had been debased by the imitators of Johnson and Gibbon and Burke. In Southey's hands, English prose became an altogether more supple instrument, something sparer, plainer, more precise: again and again, casting about for a single word to describe it, one returns to the adjective "easy". He cannot rival Swift, for he has no wit and he lacks passion; but for narrative and descriptive purposes his style is a perfect model, unsurpassed in modern English.

And for all the high merits of his more formal works, it is displayed to greatest advantage in his letters. Beyond dispute and without any qualification, he belongs to the great English letter-writers. When he sat down to write to a friend, he put himself wholeheartedly into the task, and his letters show all his powers in turn at their highest. In them he has drawn the most delightful and unstudied of all his portraits: his portrait of himself. There he stands to the life: independent, irritable, generous, tender, kind-hearted, loyal—above all, intensely human. There is not a nobler portrait in our literature.

NOTE ON THE SOUTHEY FAMILY

THE MOST important features of Southey's ancestry, as far as I have been able to trace them, are shown in the accompanying genealogical table. The information it contains has been drawn almost entirely from two sources: the beginning of Southey's own autobiographical fragment (L.C. i. 1-23) and an unpublished history of the family by Captain R. G. Southey, based on a full and careful examination of wills, parish registers, and other documents. Perhaps I may add the names of two other distinguished members of the family: Sir Richard Southey, K.C.M.G. (1808-1901), Colonial Secretary of Cape Colony and from 1873 to 1875 Lieutenant-Governor of Griqualand West; and Thomas Southey, wool broker, author of *The Rise, Progress and Present State of Colonial Wools* (1848) and other works on the same subject.

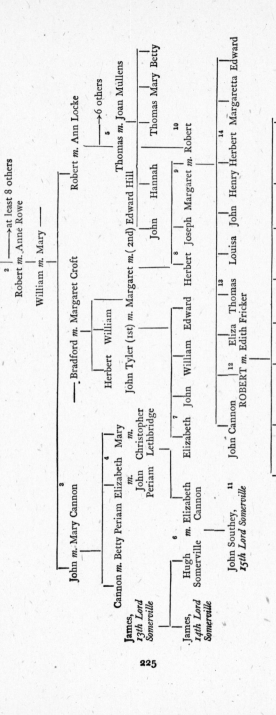

LIST OF SOUTHEY'S WORKS

(This list is based on those given in L.C. vi. 397-8, in Haller, 313-26, and in the *Cambridge Bibliography of English Literature* (1941), iii. 180-3, but it includes some corrections and a few additional items. Reprints issued after Southey's death have as a rule been excluded, with the exception of recent editions and reprints that appear to be obtainable to-day. American issues have been entirely omitted. Works published anonymously are indicated with an asterisk.)

1. *The Flagellant.* 1792. For Southey's share in this, see pp. 26-8 above.
2. *The Fall of Robespierre.* 1794. Issued under Coleridge's name: see p. 45 above.
3. *Poems . . . by Robert Lovell and Robert Southey.* 1794 (i.e. 1795: see note 66).
4. *Joan of Arc.* 1796+1798, 1806, 1812, 1817.
5. *Letters Written During a Short Residence in Spain and Portugal.* 1797+1799, 1808.
6. *Poems by Robert Southey.* 1797+1800, 1801, 1808. This was described on the title-page as the second edition: it included some poems reprinted from the volume of 1795, together with some new ones.
7. *On the French Revolution, by Mr. Necker.* 1797. Vol. ii translated from the French by Southey.
8. *Poems by Robert Southey. The Second Volume.* 1799+1800, 1801, 1806.
9. *The Annual Anthology*, vols. i and ii. 1799 and 1800. Edited by Southey : see page 80 above.
10. *Thalaba the Destroyer.* 1801+1809, 1814, 1821.
11. *The Works of Thomas Chatterton.* 1803. Edited by Southey and Joseph Cottle: see p. 68 above.
12. *Amadis of Gaul.* 1803. Translated from the Spanish by Southey.
13. *Madoc.* 1805+1807, 1812, 1815, 1825.
14. *Metrical Tales and Other Poems.* 1805. Reprinted from *The Annual Anthology.*
15. *Palmerin of England.* 1807. Translation from the Portuguese edited by Southey.
16. *Specimens of the Later English Poets.* 1807. Edited by Southey and Grosvenor Bedford: see pp. 112-3 above.
17. *Letters from England by Don Manuel Alvarez Espriella.* 1807+1808, 1814. Translated into French 1817, into German 1818.
18. *The Remains of Henry Kirke White.* 1807 (vols. i and ii)+1816 (ed. 7), 1819, 1821, 1823; 1822 (vol. ii). Edited by Southey.
19. *The Chronicle of the Cid.* 1808. Translated from the Spanish by Southey.

20. *The Curse of Kehama.* 1810+1811, 1812, 1818.

21. *The History of Brazil.* Vol. i, 1810 (ed. 2, 1822); vol. ii, 1817; vol. iii, 1819.

22. *Omniana, or Horae Otiosiores.* 1812. By Southey and Coleridge jointly: see p. 126 above.

23. *Revised and enlarged reprint of article "Bell and Lancaster's Systems of Education" (*Quarterly Review*, August, 1811). 1813. I have not seen a copy of this pamphlet and so cannot give its exact title.

24. *The Life of Nelson.* 1813+1814, 1825, 1827, 1830, 1831, 1840. Abridged ed., 1822. Reprinted 1906 ("Everyman's Library"), 1922 (edited by Sir Geoffrey Callender), 1940 ("Nelson's Classics").

25. *Roderick, the Last of the Goths.* 1814+1815, 1816, 1818, 1826. Translated into French 1820, into Dutch 1823-4.

26. *Carmen Triumphale, for the Commencement of the Year 1814.* 1814+ 1821 (together with No. 27).

27. *Odes to His Royal Highness the Prince Regent, His Imperial Majesty the Emperor of Russia, and His Majesty the King of Prussia.* 1814+ 1821 (under the title *Carmina Aulica*, and with No. 26).

28. *The Minor Poems of Robert Southey.* 1815+1823. A reprint of Nos. 6, 8 and 14.

29. *The Poet's Pilgrimage to Waterloo.* 1816+1816.

30. *The Lay of the Laureate. Carmen Nuptiale.* 1816.

31. *Wat Tyler.* 1817. Numerous other editions in that year and later, usually undated : see pp. 42, 158-61 above.

32. *A Letter to William Smith, Esq., M.P.* 1817+1817, 1817, 1817.

33. *The Byrth, Lyf and Actes of King Arthur.* 1817. Introduction and notes by Southey.

34. *The Life of Wesley and the Rise and Progress of Methodism.* 1820+ 1820, 1846 (ed. C. C. Southey). Translated into German 1828: reprinted 1925 (ed. M. H. FitzGerald).

35. *The Expedition of Orsua; and the Crimes of Aguirre.* 1821. Reprinted from the *Edinburgh Annual Register*, vol. iii.

36. *A Vision of Judgement.* 1821+1822, 1824 (both these editions with Byron's *Vision of Judgment*). Reprinted 1929 (ed. E. M. Earl), with Byron's *Vision of Judgment*.

37. *History of the Peninsular War.* Vol. i, 1823; vol. ii, 1827; vol. iii, 1832. (Octavo edition 1828-37.)

38. *The Book of the Church.* 1824+1824, 1825, 1837, 1841.

39. *A Tale of Paraguay.* 1825.

40. *Vindiciae Ecclesiae Anglicanae.* 1826.

41. *All for Love; and The Pilgrim to Compostella.* 1829.

42. *Sir Thomas More : or, Colloquies on the Progress and Prospects of Society.* 1829+1831.

43. *The Poetical Works of Robert Southey, complete in one Volume.* Paris. 1829.

44. *The Devil's Walk.* 1830. Originally "The Devil's Thoughts", written by Southey and Coleridge jointly at Nether Stowey and published anonymously in the *Morning Post* of 6th September, 1799. Attributed to Porson, the Greek scholar, and republished under his name 1830. Second edition, enlarged by Southey, with his name and Coleridge's on the title-page, 1830. (See Haller, 199-200; S.L. iv. 51; Historical MSS. Commission, 3rd Report, Appendix, 292.)

45. *The Pilgrim's Progress. With a Life of John Bunyan.* 1830+1839. For a later reprint of the *Life,* see No. 58.

46. *Attempts in Verse, by John Jones, an old Servant: with . . . an introductory Essay on the Lives and Works of our Uneducated Poets.* 1831+1836. The *Essay* was reprinted in 1925, ed. J. S. Childers.

47. *Select Works of the British Poets, from Chaucer to Jonson, with Biographical Sketches.* 1831.

48. *Selections from the Poems of Robert Southey.* 1831.

49. *Selections from the Prose Works of Robert Southey.* 1832.

50. *Essays, Moral and Political.* 1832.

51. *Lives of the British Admirals.* Vols. i and ii, 1833 (vol. i reprinted 1839); vol. iii, 1834; vol. iv, 1837; vol. v (continued by Robert Bell), 1840.

52. **Letter to John Murray, Esq., "touching" Lord Nugent.* 1833.

53. **The Doctor, &c.* Vols. i and ii, 1834 (ed. 3, 1839); vol. iii, 1835; vol. iv, 1837; vol. v, 1838; vols. vi and vii (ed. J. W. Warter), 1847. Reprinted in one volume, ed. J. W. Warter, 1848. Abridged edition, ed. M. H. FitzGerald, 1930.

54. *Horae Lyricae . . . by Isaac Watts . . . With a Memoir of the Author.* 1834+1837.

55. *The Works of Cowper. . . . With a Life of the Author.* Vol. i, 1835; vols. ii-ix, 1836; vols. x-xv, 1837.

56. *The Poetical Works of Robert Southey, Collected by Himself.* 1837-8. The engraved title-pages of vols. i-iii are dated 1837, of vols. iv-x, 1838: all the printed title-pages are dated 1838. The *Poetical Works* were reprinted in one volume in 1845.

57. *The Life of the Rev. Andrew Bell.* 1844. Vol. i is by Southey, ed. Caroline Southey; vols. ii and iii by C. C. Southey.

58. *Select Biographies. Cromwell and Bunyan.* 1844. The *Cromwell* is reprinted from the *Quarterly Review,* vol. xxv, the *Bunyan* from No. 45 above.

59. *Oliver Newman: a New-England Tale (unfinished): with other Poetical Remains.* 1845.

60. *Robin Hood: a Fragment.* 1847. By Southey and Caroline Southey jointly.

61. *Southey's Common-place Book.* Vol. i, 1849+1850; vol. ii, 1849+1851; vol. iii, 1850; vol. iv, 1851. Ed. J. W. Warter.

62. *Review of Churchill's Poems.* 1852. Reprinted from the *Annual Review* for 1804.

63. *Journal of a Tour in the Netherlands in the Autumn of 1815.* 1903 (?1902). With an Introduction by W. Robertson Nicoll.

64. *Poems of Robert Southey.* 1909. Ed. M. H. FitzGerald. Contains *Thalaba, Madoc, The Curse of Kehama, Roderick,* and a large selection of the minor poems.

65. *Letters of Robert Southey: a Selection.* 1912. Ed. M. H. FitzGerald. ("World's Classics.")

66. *Journal of a Tour in Scotland in 1819.* 1929. Ed. C. H. Herford.

NOTES

[1] For further details of Southey's ancestry, see the genealogical table on p. 225.

[2] *Bristol Journal*, 8th April, 1772; Bedminster parish register.

[3] He was buried on 22nd October, 1773 (Long Ashton parish register).

[4] Written in the form of letters to his friend John May in the years 1820-1825 and printed at the beginning of L.C. Except where it is stated to the contrary, the material for the rest of this chapter has been taken from this source. See also the early recollections of Bristol he set down in a letter to Grosvenor Bedford of 6th March, 1806 (L.C. iii. 32-6) and Haller, 7-31.

[5] B.L. c. 23, fol. 21.

[6] ibid.

[7] S.L. iv. 473.

[8] B.L. c. 23, fol. 22.

[9] There is a pretty engraving of the house on the title-page to the second volume of P.W.

[10] *Poems by Robert Lovell and Robert Southey* (1795), 11-12.

[11] Southey speaks of the "heronry" at Abbotsbury (L.C. i. 82): he clearly means to refer to the swannery.

[12] P.W. vol. i, pp. vii-viii.

[13] Southey states (L.C. i. 134) that he was admitted "upon the first of April (of all ominous days that could be chosen)", but the date is given in the admission book as 2nd April (G. F. R. Barker and A. H. Stenning, *The Record of Old Westminsters*, 870).

[14] In this description of the school I have made no reference to the severe damage suffered by its buildings during the air-raids of 1941 (for which see *The Times* of 14th and 15th May, 1941). My account of Westminster, and Southey's career there, is chiefly based on L.C. i. 135-62 (of which pp. 135-57 form the concluding part of his auto-biographical sketch); Haller, 31-52; George Colman, *Random Records* (1830), i. 67-9; J. Sargeaunt, *Annals of Westminster School* (1898); L. E. Tanner, *Westminster School: its Buildings and their Associations* (1923), and *Westminster School: a History* (1934); J. D. Carleton, *Westminster* (1938). The last four of these contain pictures of the buildings mentioned in the text. Biographical details of Southey's contemporaries will be found in Barker and Stenning, op. cit.: for particulars of the masters and dames referred to in this chapter, see Appendix IX to the same work.

[15] Verse letter to Wynn: Bodleian MS. Eng. poet. e. 27, fol. 1. The letter is undated, but it is clear from internal evidence that Southey

was still at school when he wrote it, while Wynn had already left. It can therefore be put between July, 1791 and April, 1792.

[16] See, for example, S.L. iii. 248, 327, iv. 158; *Colloquies*, ii. 96; *Cowper*, i. 6.

[17] S.L. ii. 290, iv. 411. For their quarrel, see B.L. c. 22, fol. 31. It was almost certainly to him that Southey wrote, in 1798, the sonnet "Fair be thy fortunes in the distant land" (P.W. ii. 97).

[18] S.L. iii. 303.

[19] ibid., ii. 355, 416.

[20] See p. 85.

[21] S.L. iii. 91.

[22] L.C. i. 80-1, 134, 139.

[23] Barker and Stenning, op. cit., 870; S.L. iii. 303; *Cowper*, i. 11n, 453. The manuscript of *Harold* is Bodleian MS. Eng. misc. e. 114. For a good description of the Challenge as it was then conducted, see the diary of that of 1809 kept by William Fox-Strangeways and printed in F. H. Forshall, *Westminster School, past and present* (1884), 575-84.

[24] *Vindiciae Ecclesiae Anglicanae* (1826), 6-7; L.C. iv. 86; *Diary and letters of Madame D'Arblay*, ed. A. Dobson, vi. 413; Southey's edition of *The Byrth, Lyf, and Actes of King Arthur* (1817), vol. i, p. xxviii.

[25] *Public Advertiser*, 26th and 29th November, 1791, quoted in Carleton, op. cit., 34-5; L.C. iv. 318-9; S.L. i. 203, iv. 362-3.

[26] See his guarded statement to Caroline Bowles on the subject (C.B. 40). He refers to the episode in *Espriella*, i. 274.

[27] C.B. 52.

[28] Haller, 34-5; S.L. i. 203.

[29] I owe these extracts from *The Flagellant* to the kindness of Mr. Lawrence E. Tanner.

[30] B.L. c. 22, ff. 5, 6. MS. note by Reed himself, dated 1793, in his copy of *The Flagellant*: see *The Elizabethan* (Westminster School magazine), October, 1894.

[31] B.L. c. 22, fol. 1. The date of this letter is uncertain: its postmark appears to be 3rd May, 1792. There is another allusion to Southey's letter of apology to Vincent in S.L. i. 6.

[32] B.L. c. 22, ff. 9, 7.

[33] ibid., ff. 7, 11, 13, 15, 17. This refutes Cuthbert Southey's statement (L.C. i. 162) that his father spent the spring of 1792 with Miss Tyler at Bristol. The autograph manuscript of *An Improbable Tale* is in the Bodleian (MS. Eng. misc. e. 22).

[34] L.C. i. 22-3, 163-4. B.L. c. 22, fol. 82. His letter of 21st June is dated from Duke Street.

[35] ibid., ff. 21, 23, 37; S.L. i. 5-6; L.C. i. 164. See also the verse letter, written from Bristol on 23rd November, 1792, and printed in *Reminiscences of Oxford* (Oxford Historical Society, 1892), 403-8.

[36] B.L. c. 22, fol. 27.

[37] ibid., fol. 49. The reference is to his younger brother Thomas, who had just entered the navy as a midshipman.

[38] *The Prelude*, x. 283-99.

[39] General references for Balliol and Southey's career there: L.C. i. 169-216; S.L. i. 15-20; Haller, 53-130; Sir C. Mallet, *A History of the University of Oxford* (1924-7), ch. xxiii; H. W. C. Davis, *Balliol College* (1899), 168-202. An engraving showing the front of Balliol as it appeared in Southey's time is reproduced in Mallet, iii. 282.

[40] B.L. c. 22, ff. 45-6; R.S. to Lightfoot, 5th February, 1810 (Lightfoot MSS.).

[41] *Victoria History of the County of Worcester*, iv. 329.

[42] S.L. i. 400.

[43] C.B. 27.

[44] For a detailed analysis of this reading, and its relation to Southey's early poetry, see Haller, 72-95.

[45] B.L. c. 22, fol. 61.

[46] ibid., ff. 56, 57, 82.

[47] ibid., fol. 82.

[48] ibid., fol. 106.

[49] ibid., fol. 110.

[50] Wynn to Bedford, 22nd June [1794]: B.L. c. 27, fol. 34.

[51] B.L. c. 22, fol. 48.

[52] The exact date of the meeting of Southey and Coleridge cannot be established, but the evidence points to 11th June. On the 8th Coleridge was still at Cambridge, intending to leave early the following morning (C.U.L. i. 20): he is unlikely to have reached Oxford before the 11th. The wording of Southey's letter, quoted in the text, does not suggest that he had met Coleridge only on the day he wrote. Unfortunately, we have nothing but the extract given in L.C. to go upon, as the original has been mislaid in the Bodleian Library.

[53] For a good sketch of the contrasting characters and powers of Southey and Coleridge see H. I'A. Fausset, *Samuel Taylor Coleridge* (1926), 72-7.

[54] J. Hucks, *A Pedestrian Tour in North Wales* (1795), 157.

[55] Cottle, 404.

[56] Among the Lightfoot MSS. there is, however, an interesting letter from George Burnett to Nicholas Lightfoot, written from Manchester on 22nd October, 1796, in which he gives his recollections of the plan formulated two years earlier. According to him it was first proposed in the rooms of Matthew Bloxam, an undergraduate of Worcester College.

[57] *Biographia Literaria*, ed. J. Shawcross (1907), i. 49n.

[58] L.C. iv. 194. *Espriella*, ii. 79, 288, 291, 295-6, 298-9. The universities are also attacked in L.C. vi. 190-1; S.L. iii. 510, iv. 533; in *Colloquies*, ii. 140; and in letters to J. W. Warter of 20th June, 1832, and 14th and 27th October, 1837 (Boult MSS.).

[59] The chief authorities for this chapter are L.C. i. 213-61; Haller, 130-68; Chambers, 27-45; Hanson, 46-89; C.L. i. 81-151; C.U.L. i. 21-32; Cottle, 2-35, 104-7, 404-7.

[60] P.W. ii. 22; L.C. iv. 241.

[61] I owe this information to Canon FitzGerald, who received it from the late Mr. E. H. Coleridge.

[62] B.L. c. 22, ff. 124-5.

[63] Mrs. H. Sandford, *Tom Poole and his Friends* (1888), i. 96-9.

[64] B.L. c. 22, fol. 127.

[65] Chambers (p. 30) says that Coleridge left Bristol on 21st August, but Southey's statement is quite explicit: on 3rd September he writes "Coleridge left me yesterday" (B.L. c. 22, fol. 126). *The Fall of Robespierre* is printed in Coleridge's *Poetical Works*, ed. E. H. Coleridge (1912), 495-517.

[66] R.S. to Thomas Marriott, 10th September, 1836 (Rawnsley MSS.). *Poems by Robert Lovell and Robert Southey* is dated 1795 on its title-page, but Southey states definitely that it appeared in the autumn of 1794 (P.W. vol. ii, p. xi).

[67] Seward to Lightfoot, 3rd October, 1794 (Lightfoot MSS.).

[68] L.L. i. 60.

[69] Chambers, 39n; Hanson, 440.

[70] P.W. vol. i, p. xix.

[71] It is printed, not very accurately, in L.C. i. 234-5. A perfect copy, giving the dates on which the lectures were to be delivered, is in Bodleian MS. Autog. b. 7, fol. 9.

[72] *The Observer, Part 1st. Being a transient glance at about Forty Youths of Bristol* (n.d.), quoted in T.L.S., 18th October, 1928, 759.

[73] B.L. c. 22, fol. 142.

[74] e.g. in his letters of 21st October, 1797 (Lightfoot MSS.) and 16th November, 1818 (L.C. iv. 320), and in the poem "The Dead Friend", written at Westbury in 1799 (P.W. ii. 202-3).

[75] B.L. c. 22, fol. 160.

[76] A list of the books borrowed from the Bristol Library by Southey and Coleridge, based on the Library register, has been printed by Mr. P. Kaufman in *Modern Philology*, xxi. 317-20. The record of Southey's borrowing runs from October, 1793 to November, 1795, and of Coleridge's from March, 1795 to June, 1798.

[77] B.L. c. 22, fol. 163.

[78] For Coleridge's contributions to *Joan of Arc*, see his *Poetical Works*, 131-48, 983-6, and *North British Review*, xl. 79-84 (which includes some of his tart and amusing *marginalia* on Southey's part of the poem). A book and a half of *Madoc* were written in 1794 (note in MS. of *Madoc* in Mrs. Boult's possession): Book I was apparently being revised in May, 1795 (B.L. c. 22, fol. 149; L.C. i. 238).

[79] 1 W.L. 155; 3 W.L. 1263, 1333-4.

[80] B.L. c. 22, fol. 169.

[81] ibid., fol. 171 (cf. L.C. i. 255). For Hoblyn, see Lysons, *Magna Britannia: Cornwall* (1814), cvii; Foster, *Alumni Oxonienses, 1715-1886* (1887-8), 669.

[82] Southey's journey, and his stay in Portugal, are described in his *Letters Written during a Short Residence in Spain and Portugal* (1797): see also L.C. i. 262-76; S.L. i. 20-29; Cottle, 191-9; Haller, 173-80. A full account of the influence of Spain and Portugal on his work is given in L.Pfandl, " Robert Southey und Spanien", *Revue hispanique*, xxviii. 1-315. See also E. Allison Peers, *The Romantic Movement in Spain* (1940), ii. 392, and his references to papers by Professor Buceta (ii. 394).

[83] See also his " Lines Written after Visiting the Convent of Arrabida", P.W. ii. 226-8.

[84] B.L. c. 22, fol. 176.

[85] N.L.W. MS. 4811, No. 3: Southey's depreciatory reference to Lovell was cut out by Warter, who printed the rest of the letter in S.L. i. 29-30. This collection of Lovell's poems does not appear to have been published. The chief authorities for the remainder of this chapter are L.C. i. 272—ii. 56; S.L. i. 29-104; Robberds, i. 211-347; C.L. i. 303-32; L.L. i. 125-62; Cottle, 106-7, 199-206, 209-221; *Fragmentary Remains of Sir Humphry Davy*, ed. J. Davy (1858), 32-43; Haller, 180-232.

[86] A. Seward, *Letters* (1811), iv. 290, 294, 302.

[87] 1 W.L. 155; L.L. i. 13, 15.

[88] L.C. iii. 136; S.L. i. 30, 42.

[89] C.L. i. 210-11.

[90] J. Foster, *Register of Admissions to Gray's Inn* (1889), 401. Two typical instances of Cuthbert Southey's inaccurate editing occur here. The letter printed in L.C. i. 295-7 was written on 1st, not 21st, November, 1796 (B.L. c. 22, fol. 211): the *Letters* were completed on 2nd, not 1st, January, 1797 (ibid. c. 23, fol. 1; L.C. i. 299). On the other hand, he is almost certainly right in assigning the letter printed in L.C. i. 303-4 to February, 1797, where Cottle (199-200) dates it November, 1796.

[91] C.L. i. 223; R.S. to Lightfoot, 21st October, 1797 (Lightfoot MSS.). The second edition of the *Poems* was advertised in the October number of the *Monthly Magazine* (iv. 304).

[92] C.B. 52.

[93] B.L. c. 23, fol. 5.

[94] Verses to Amos Cottle, printed in Cottle's *Icelandic Poetry* (1797), xxxii-xxxiii.

[95] Southey gave an excellent description of Rickman in a letter to Landor of 9th February, 1809 (L.C. iii. 216-7).

[96] E. H. W. Meyerstein, *Life of Thomas Chatterton* (1930), 491-7.

[97] B.L. c. 23, fol. 15; L.L. i. 114; *Common-place Book*, iv. 52; De Quincey, ii. 389.

[98] R.S. to Danvers, 5th September, 1797 (Boult MSS.); N.L.W. MS. 4811, No. 15; C.L. i. 231n.

[99] *The Anti-Jacobin*, 7, 15, 39, 46. "The Soldier's Wife" and "The Widow" appear in P.W. ii. 140-2: the Inscription was, perhaps significantly, omitted. It is fair to Southey to point out that the capitals, which add so much to the ludicrous effect, are not his but the parodist's.

[100] R.S. to Lightfoot, 21st October, 1797 (Lightfoot MSS.), and to H. C. Standert, 14th December, 1809 (Boult MSS.).

[101] 1 W.L. 196; E. de Selincourt, *Dorothy Wordsworth* (1933), 83.

[102] I am speaking of Norwich, as I spoke of Westminster, in its pre-war condition, making no allowance for damage by air-raids.

[103] Robberds, i. 367.

[104] A brief account of his life and work at Westbury is given in P.W. vol. iv, pp. ix-xi.

[105] *The Anti-Jacobin*, 286; E. V. Lucas, *Life of Charles Lamb* (1921 ed.), 165, 166, 525.

[106] B.L. c. 23, fol. 51.

[107] P.W. vol. vi, p. xiii.

[108] *Critical Review*, xxiv. 197-204.

[109] N.L.W. MS. 4811, No. 30. The italics are mine.

[110] 1 W.L. 229-30.

[111] C.L. i. 319; S.L. i. 89; Bodleian MS. Don. d. 3, fol. 4; C. J. Longman, *The House of Longman, 1724-1800* (1936), 487. For a full discussion of the question, see T. Hutchinson's edition of the *Lyrical Ballads* (1898), xiii-xix, liii-liv.

[112] L.C. iii. 313.

[113] B.L. c. 23, fol. 57.

[114] Southey's own copies of the first two issues of the *Annual Anthology* are in the Dyce Collection at the Victoria and Albert Museum. A list of the contributors was drawn up by J. Dykes Campbell and kindly communicated to me by Canon FitzGerald.

[115] R.S. to his wife, 16th May, 1799 (Boult MSS.). The sonnets referred to appeared in the volumes Lamb published jointly with Coleridge in 1796 and 1797: *Works of Charles and Mary Lamb*, ed. Lucas (1912 ed.), iv. 4, 5, 8, 210. Cf. also Lucas, *Life of Lamb* (1921 ed.), 98, 101.

[116] Between 28th June, 1799 and 18th April, 1800, he kept an intermittent diary of his journeys, which is printed in the *Common-place Book*, iv. 517-26.

[117] In L.C. ii. 20, writing to Tom, Southey states that he completed *Madoc* on the 11th. But writing to Wynn on 13th July, he says "Yesterday I finished *Madoc*" (N.L.W. MS. 4811, No. 42); and in his own copy of the manuscript of *Thalaba*, now in Mrs. Boult's possession, he states that he began the poem on 13th July. It is not unlikely that Cuthbert Southey misdated the letter to Tom.

[118] M.T. i.

[119] *Espriella*, iii. 384.

[120] ibid., i. 24-9.

[121] R.S. to Wynn, 9th December, 1799 (N.L.W. MS. 4811, No. 48). There is a puzzling little contradiction here. In his next letter to Wynn (ibid. No. 49), he says he has not consulted Beddoes, partly because he has had the advice of Davy, "the superior man infinitely", and partly because he thought that Beddoes would refuse to take a fee from him.

[122] C.U.L. i. 130.

[123] B.L. c. 23, fol. 88.

[124] The main sources for this chapter are L.C. ii. 58-226; S.L. i. 104-229; C.L. i. 354-430; C.U.L. i. 179-272; Robberds, i. 348-472; Haller, 233-310; Pfandl, op. cit.; Rickman, 44-91.

[125] B.L. c. 23, fol. 93.

[126] Some extracts from Southey's letters to Miss Seton were given by Mr. I. K. Fletcher in T.L.S., 20th November, 1937, 896. For Koster, see the *Modern Language Review*, xxxviii. 182, 185.

[127] R.S. to Miss Seton, 7th September, 1801: T.L.S., loc. cit.

[128] Davy, *Fragmentary Remains*, 46.

[129] N.L.W. MS. 4811, No. 74.

[130] ibid., No. 27.

[131] ibid., No. 77.

[132] Bodleian MS. Don. d. 3, fol. 13.

[133] N.L.W. MS. 4811, No. 83.

[134] R.S. to Danvers, February, 1802 (Boult MSS.). Southey says that Margaret was born in September, but the exact date is given in R.S. to Bedford, 1st September, 1802 (B.L. c. 23, fol. 125).

[135] ibid.

[136] The story of Edward Southey would make a good picaresque novel. There is unfortunately not space to deal with it here, but it should be remembered that he was always among his brother's liabilities, apt to ask for assistance at any time. Eventually Robert hardened his heart, but he continued to send him money when he was ill. After three careers in the army and one in the navy, he was in the Portuguese army for a short time: he then turned travelling actor. He seems to have been a not altogether graceless rascal, and Robert never wholly lost his brotherly feeling for him. Some details of his career may be pieced together from B.L. c. 23, fol. 159; Bodleian MS. Don. d. 3, ff. 9, 12, 30, 32, 46, 74, 75; d. 4, ff. 138, 198, 202, 216, 226, 232; d. 5, fol. 341; R.S.'s letters to Danvers of 9th December, 1803, 11th October, 1804, 14th October, 1806 and 30th January, 1807 (Boult MSS.), and letters to Lightfoot of 18th May, 1807 and 5th February, 1810 (Lightfoot MSS.); Hartley Coleridge, *Letters*, ed. G. E. and E. L. Griggs (1937), 272.

[137] Robberds, i. 485.

[138] L.C. ii. 214.

[139] S.L. iii. 320. Cf. Coleridge's comment: "The peace of Amiens deserved the name of peace, for it gave us unanimity at home, and reconciled Englishmen with each other." (*The Friend*, 1844 ed., ii. 33.)

[140] Jeffrey's review of *Thalaba* is one of the classic protests of the eighteenth century against the new Romantic Movement. A similar view was expressed by Mrs. Piozzi in 1808: "The fashionable poetry of Southey and Scott will fall into decay—it will never be classical. It leaves too little behind it. Handel and Milton must be for ever felt; Bach's Lessons and Pope's Moral Essays must be for ever *recollected*; Madoc and Thalaba, Teviot Dale and Marmion depend too much on their *colouring*. In a hundred years people will wonder why they were so much admired" (*Thraliana*, ed. K. C. Balderston, 1942, 1096: cf. also 1056n).

[141] B.L. c. 23, fol. 139; L.C. ii. 134.

[142] R.S. to Danvers, 5th April, 1804 (Boult MSS.); R.S. to Landor, 14th July, 1810 (Forster MSS., Victoria and Albert Museum). Cf. Professor Harper's remarks on Wordsworth : *William Wordsworth* (ed. 3, 1929), 571-2.

[143] Robberds, i. 502-3.

[144] Hartley Coleridge, *Letters* (1937), 219 (I have substantially altered the punctuation of the last two sentences, to make clearer what I think is their meaning); C.U.L. i. 407; Hawthorne, *English Notebooks*, ed. R. Stewart (1941), 179.

[145] M.T. 48, 118.

[146] C.U.L. i. 149; L.L. i. 315; C.L. 391-2. In addition to these, the best contemporary descriptions of Greta Hall and the household are in C.U.L. i. 159-61, 203-5, 251-2; M.T. 62-5; *Memoir of Sara Coleridge* (ed. 3, 1873), i. 12-17; Hartley Coleridge, *Letters*, 226-9; H.C.R. 189-90; De Quincey, ii. 311, 317-8, 336-9. Pictures of the house and the view from it appear as frontispieces to P.W. iii. and x., *Poetical Works* (one-volume edition, 1845), *The Doctor* (one-volume edition, 1848), L.C. vi, and in *Colloquies*, ii. 343, C.L. 336.

An historical account of the house, including a plan of the rooms as they were in Southey's time, is given in Mr. H. W. Howe's charming monograph *Greta Hall* (1943).

[147] C.L. 394; L.C. iii. 250; R.S. to H.H.S., 31st March and 6th April, 1817, 17th April, 1830 (Bodleian MS. Don. d. 4, ff. 143, 145; d. 5, fol. 310b).

[148] C.L. 435; C.U.L. i. 294, 297; Chambers, 172-7. The main authorities for this chapter are L.C. ii. 226—iii. 200; S.L. i. 229—ii. 118; Robberds, i. 472—ii. 234; Rickman, 93-148.

[149] Chambers, 169, 180.

[150] *Registers of Crosthwaite Church* (Cumberland & Westmorland Antiquarian Society, 1928-31), iii. 209. Crosthwaite church was then the parish church of Keswick : St. John's was not built until 1838.

[151] He expressed strong disapproval of the treatment Keats received at the hands of the *Quarterly* (see p. 171 and Scott, *Letters*, viii. 377n).

[152] See, for instance, the letters of 10th February, 1805 (B.L. c. 23, fol. 171), 10th November, 1806 (S.L. i. 396), 14th March, 1807 (ibid., 419) and 4th April, 1807 (ibid., 428); also R.S. to Wynn, 11th March and 28th September, 1807 (N.L.W. MS. 4812, Nos. 190 and 202).

[153] R.S. to T.S., 17th December, 1803 (Boult MSS.).

[154] 1 W.L. 343, 401, 448-9, 485; N.L.W. MS. 4812, Nos. 146 and 150. Cuthbert Southey has again blundered in the dating of his father's letters at this point. That dated 11th February, 1804 (L.C. ii. 256) belongs, it is clear, to 11th February, 1805; while that of 3rd April (ibid., 321) is plainly dated 13th February in the original (N.L.W. MS. 4812, No. 145). There seems to be some doubt as to whether the news reached Southey on the 11th or the 13th.

[155] Scott, *Letters*, i. 277-8. See also Lockhart, ii. 277-80.

[156] See, for example, Scott's *Journal, 1827-28*, ed. J. G. Tait (1941), I, 23.

[157] Bodleian MS. Don. d. 3, ff. 58, 61; B.L. c. 24, fol. 7.

[158] B.L. c. 23, fol. 177.

[159] Bodleian MS. Don. d. 3, fol. 54.

[160] N.L.W. MS. 4811, No. 89. When he died in 1811, Thomas Southey left his property away from his family, "his last boast being (like that of John Southey before him), that no one of his own name should ever be a shilling the better for him" (S.L. ii. 222). Southey's one other expectation of money from his family was similarly disappointed. He thought he should have inherited property through an entail on the death of Lord Somerville, a distant cousin, in 1819. But on inquiry it proved that the sum he might have been entitled to would not have been sufficient to pay the legal expenses necessary for its recovery (S.L. iii. 152, 153, 157-8, 179; B.L. c. 26, fol. 34).

[161] Byron, *Letters and Journals*, ed. Prothero (1922), i. 336.

[162] In his introduction to the "Muses' Library" edition of Kirke White's poems [1908]. On Kirke White see also *Monthly Review*, n.s., xliii. 218, 335-6; *Transactions of the Thoroton Society*, x. 83-9; J. T. Godfrey and J. Ward, *The Homes and Haunts of Henry Kirke White* (1908).

[163] On the *History of Brazil* generally, see Senhor J. de Sousa-Leão's recent paper "Southey and Brazil" in the *Modern Language Review*, xxxviii. 181-91.

[164] R.S. to H.H.S., 23rd February, 1807 (Bodleian MS. Don. d. 3, fol. 63).

[165] R.S. to Danvers, 30th January, 1807 (Boult MSS.); C.U.L. i. 364-5; Chambers, 196-7, 199. Southey gave another striking account of Coleridge's condition at this time in a letter written to Miss Barker, printed in the *Atlantic Monthly*, lxxxix. 38.

[166] R.S. to Danvers, 26th June, 1806 (Boult MSS.); *Letters from the*

Lake Poets to Daniel Stuart (1889), 394-5; W. Jerdan, *Men I Have Known* (1866), 411; Haller, 316.

[167] It was praised by Coleridge (*Biographia Literaria*, ed. Shawcross, i. 42; *Fragmentary Remains of Sir Humphry Davy*, 103), by Leigh Hunt (*Autobiography*, "World's Classics" edition, 186-7) and by Shelley (*Letters*, ed. R. Ingpen, 1909, 320). A French critic, Philarète Chasles, described it as "une des œuvres de critique et d'histoire les plus remarquables de ces derniers temps" (*Revue contemporaine*, iii. 552).

[168] Lockhart, iii. 31, 35.

[169] De Quincey, ii. 311-2, 317-8.

[170] Lockhart, iii. 29-32; B.L. c. 24, fol. 61. Southey is explicit as to his income in a letter to Bedford of 25th March, 1807 (ibid., fol. 39): he speaks there of having "a certain income of only £160 a year, which my utmost exertions cannot double".

[171] Quoted in E. L. Griggs, "Robert Southey and the *Edinburgh Review*", *Modern Philology*, xxx. 100-3.

[172] Cottle, 306; Chambers, ch. xii, 350; *Letters from the Lake Poets to Daniel Stuart*, 415.

[173] It was Southey, too, who arranged for Coleridge's lectures of 1811-12 to be taken down in shorthand, with the result that of this course "we have more information than of any others given by Coleridge" (Chambers, 244: the reference should be to S.L. ii. 247).

[174] C.R.W. 51-2.

[175] B.L. c. 24, fol. 71.

[176] Southey told Daniel Stuart that if Wordsworth had not made up his mind to write about the Convention, he would have done so himself, "for no public event ever distressed me so greatly. He has more leisure than I have, and will do the thing better" (*Letters of the Lake Poets to Daniel Stuart*, 397).

[177] *Edinburgh Review*, xii. 443, xiii. 233 (my italics); Lockhart, iii. 126n.

[178] On the origin of the *Quarterly Review* see S. Smiles, *Memoir and Correspondence of the Late John Murray* (1891), i. 91-169; *Autobiographical Memoir of Sir John Barrow* (1847), 492-515; Lockhart, iii. 124-51, 163-9, 187-8.

[179] B.L. c. 24, fol. 99.

[180] Southey particularly disliked the hostile and patronising attitude the *Quarterly Review* took up towards the United States. Though this was natural enough in a Tory journal, he continually complained of it, but to no effect. He always went out of his way to show personal civility to Americans in England. (L.C. v. 119, 141; S.L. iii. 341; G. S. Hillard, *Life, Letters and Journals of George Ticknor* (1876), i. 135-6, 285-7, 434, ii. 166.)

[181] Scott, *Letters*, ii. 171n; B.L. c. 24, fol. 109.

[182] A. Lang, *Life and Letters of Lockhart* (1897), ii. 6.

[183] When Gifford's health broke up in 1822, Southey thought he

might be asked to become his successor. He made up his mind to refuse the offer if it came to him—but in fact it did not. Gifford was succeeded at the beginning of 1825 by J. T. Coleridge (S. T. Coleridge's nephew), largely on Southey's recommendation. This was, however, a temporary arrangement: Coleridge considered himself as only a stop-gap, and at the end of the year Murray appointed Lockhart permanent editor in his place. As the leading contributor to the *Review* Southey felt he had a right to be consulted, and he was very much annoyed by what he considered Murray's high-handed action. However, in time he grew reconciled to Lockhart, largely through the mediation of his father-in-law Scott. (L.C. v. 127-8, 194; S.L. iii. 346, 350, 514, iv. 2-3; Smiles, *A Publisher and his Friends*, ii. 160; Scott, *Letters*, ix. 297-9, 309-12; Scott, *Journal, 1825-26*, 18-19, 22-23; Lang, *Lockhart*, i. 359-83; T.L.S., 5th February, 1944, 72.)

[184] B.L. c. 25, ff. 5, 28; d. 47, fol. 96.

[185] Smiles, *A Publisher and his Friends*, i. 260.

[186] The dates of finishing *Kehama* and beginning *Roderick* are given in P.W. vol. viii, p. xvii, and vol. ix, p. ix. Canon FitzGerald, who has made a careful comparison of the texts of the two earliest editions of *Thalaba*, points out to me that the text of the second edition (1809) is "more heavily stopped than that of 1801, to the great improvement of the verse". The general authorities for this chapter are L.C. iii. 201—iv. 175; S.L. ii. 119—iii. 25; Rickman, 148-79; Robberds, ii. 261-463.

[187] 2 W.L. 333, 396, 416.

[188] M.T. 11, 16, 17; B.L. c. 24, fol. 147.

[189] I owe this information to Canon FitzGerald, who had it direct from Mr. E. H. Coleridge himself. Writing to Bedford on 29th May, 1814, Southey said that Mrs. Coleridge and her children "have only at this time an income of £67 10s., the whole of which as you may well suppose is required for the schooling and clothing of the two boys. If they are to be put forward in life, it must literally be by the charity of their father's friends, and the mother and daughter fall upon me for support" (B.L. c. 25, fol. 86).

[190] Hartley Coleridge, *Letters*, 186. Mr. Hartman (*Hartley Coleridge: Poet's Son and Poet*, 1931, 60n) is mistaken in stating that Southey gave £40 a year towards Hartley's Oxford expenses. In telling Thomas Poole of the various contributions that had been promised, Wordsworth referred to "his Uncle's £40" (2 W.L. 644). That this does not refer to his Uncle Southey but to one of his Coleridge uncles (or should the word be read "Uncles'"?) is made clear by Southey's statement to Bedford in a letter of 14th January, 1815: "Lady Beaumont gives an annual £30, Poole £10, Cottle £5, and his uncles at Ottery £40. Of his father we know nothing" (B.L. c. 25, fol. 149).

[191] C.B. 193-4; H.C.R. 40-41. Cf. *The Doctor* (1848 ed.), 473-6, where Southey speaks of Blake as "that painter of great but insane genius" and quotes "The wild winds weep" from the *Poetical Sketches*.

[192] J. Forster, *Walter Savage Landor* (1869), i. 326-9; Landor, *Poetical Works*, ed. S. Wheeler (1937), iii. 30-1.

[193] For Southey's letter to the Ladies of Llangollen, thanking them for "the hospitalities of their delightful retirement", see *The Hamwood Papers*, ed. Mrs. G. H. Bell (1930), 344-5.

[194] R. W. Armour and R. F. Howes, *Coleridge the Talker* (1940), 220.

[195] Shelley, *Letters*, ed. R. Ingpen (1909), 171, 197, 200. For these meetings between Southey and Shelley see also E. Dowden, *Life of Shelley* (1886), i. 210-6, and W. E. Peck, *Shelley: his Life and Work* (1927), i. 203-8.

[196] Even at this early age, Shelley was immeasurably his host's superior in dialectical skill. It is probable, as Dowden acutely suggests, that Southey was completely out-argued in these discussions.

[197] B.L. c. 24, fol. 184.

[198] On this point see Peck, i. 59, 306, 425-6; ii. 138, 221n.

[199] Shelley, *Letters*, 209, 224, 250.

[200] Southey was away from Keswick at the time of Shelley's second visit, in 1813. Peacock, in his *Memoirs of Shelley* (ed. H. F. B. Brett-Smith, 1909, 50), states that Shelley met Southey again in the autumn of 1814. But it is odd that no other reference to this meeting should have survived, since each man was in his own way so much interested in the other; and I agree with Dowden (C.B. xi) in thinking that Peacock, writing many years afterwards, was probably mistaken.

[201] Scott, *Letters*, ii. 202, 205. Southey also asked for Sir George Beaumont's good offices in this connexion: *Memorials of Coleorton*, ed. W. Knight (1887), ii. 76.

[202] Scott, *Letters*, iii. 123-6. Again Southey asked for Sir George Beaumont's help : *Memorials of Coleorton*, ii. 166.

[203] Scott, *Letters*, iii. 335-6.

[204] Lockhart, v. 45, vi. 208. The history of Southey's appointment to the Laureateship is not entirely clear. He himself was told in London at the time that it had all along been the Prince Regent's intention to appoint him, and that the post was offered to Scott by the Lord Chamberlain without the knowledge of the Regent, who was much annoyed when he learnt the truth and declared that Southey should have it in spite of everything. But there is no trace of this in the letters to Scott from the Regent's Librarian and from the Lord Chamberlain (Lockhart, iv. 107-8), except Clarke's cryptic remark that "you are the man to whom it ought first to have been offered"; and there is not the slightest evidence to suggest that it was offered to Southey *before* Scott. On the whole it seems that Lockhart's version of the story is substantially correct. The authorities for the episode are L.C. iv. 37-42; S.L. ii. 335-7; P.W. vol. iii, pp. xi-xiv; Scott, *Letters*, iii. 322, 324, 338-54; Lockhart, iv. 101, 103-20.

[205] *Letters from the Lake Poets to Daniel Stuart* (1889), 219.

[206] Scott had just made this point to Byron. In a letter written three weeks earlier he described Southey as "a real poet, such as we read of in former times, with every atom of his soul and every moment of his time devoted to literary pursuits" (Scott, *Letters*, iii. 373).

s.

Q

[207] Sir Henry Taylor, *Correspondence* (1888), 20-21; Byron, *Letters and Journals*, ed. Prothero (1922), ii. 266, 331.

[208] B.L. c. 24, fol. 134.

[209] See Sir Geoffrey Callender's useful edition of the *Life of Nelson* (1922), especially pp. xxix-xxxi.

[210] ibid., xxxviii.

[211] H.C.R. 133.

[212] M.T. 39.

[213] See his *Journal of a Tour in the Netherlands in the Autumn of 1815* (1903).

[214] P.W. x. 7.

[215] 2 W.L. 518, 592; De Quincey, ii. 330.

[216] R.S. to Cottle, 9th February, 1810 (Rawnsley MSS.). For other examples of this trait, see L.C. iii. 229; S.L. i. 241, ii. 68; Koster, 36.

[217] De Quincey, ii. 331-2; 2 W.L. 744-5; Bodleian MS. Don. d. 3, ff. 116, 123; M.T. 42-3.

[218] A list of the papers contributed by Southey to the *Quarterly Review* is given by his son in L.C. vi. 400-2. The general authorities for this chapter are L.C. iv. 161—v. 279; S.L. iii. 26—iv. 40; Rickman, 179-233; C.B. 1-109.

[219] All the miscellaneous papers mentioned above were later reprinted in his *Essays, Moral and Political* (1832). They take up the whole of vol. i of that collection, and pp. 35-180 of vol ii. That "On the Means of Improving the Poor" (1818) was written almost entirely by Rickman, who deeply influenced all Southey's work in this field: Rickman, 197-203, 236-7.

[220] *Essays, Moral and Political*, i. 14, 16.

[221] Scott, *Letters*, iii. 126; J. R. M. Butler, *The Passing of the Great Reform Bill* (1914), 34-5.

[222] B.L. c. 24, fol. 78. Cf. Scott's remark after passing through Lancashire in 1826: "God's justice is requiting, and will yet further requite those who have blown up the country into a state of unsubstantial opulence, at the expense of the health and morals of the lower classes" (*Journal, 1825-26*, 282).

[223] *Essays*, i. 114-5, 117.

[224] See for instance L.C. vi. 200-1; S.L. iv. 273-4, 328; and his letter to J. W. Warter of 23rd January, 1833 (Boult MSS.).

[225] E. Hodder, *Life and Work of the Seventh Earl of Shaftesbury* (1886), i. 113, 262.

[226] *Essays*, i. 116, 220-6, ii. 170; *The Doctor* (1848 ed.), 39; *Colloquies*, i. 94. For his earlier interest in the condition of the working classes, see pp. 71-2 above.

[227] L.C. iii. 296. Cf. *Essays*, i. 143.

[228] *Essays*, i. 10 (see also 17); S.L. iii. 110.

[229] *Essays*, i. 44, 142-9, 154-5; ii. 155. On the army, cf. L.C. iii.

335-6; on the colonies, cf. L.C. v. 267-8; S.L. iv. 28-9; *Colloquies*, ii. 183-4.

[230] Southey, who was a personal friend of Dr. Bell and steadily championed his system against his rival Joseph Lancaster, published an article on the controversy between them in the *Quarterly Review* for August, 1811. This appeared in book form (anonymously) in 1813. Dr. Bell left Southey £1000 in his will (1832), with the desire that he should write his life. Southey finished only one volume: the work was completed by his son Cuthbert. (L.C. vi. 179-80; S.L. ii. 298, iv. 222, 327-8, 339-41.)

[231] C. Whibley, *Lord John Manners and his Friends* (1925), i. 260-1; F. Maurice, *Life of F. D. Maurice* (ed. 3, 1884), i. 9, ii. 92-4; C. E. Raven, *Christian Socialism, 1848-1854* (1920), 47-51. Southey also took an interest in the Co-operative Movement (L.C. vi. 80-3, 86; S.L. iv. 146-9; Rickman, 246-8). For further discussion of Southey's political ideas, see Crane Brinton, *Political Ideas of the English Romanticists* (1926), and Alfred Cobban, *Edmund Burke and the Revolt against the Eighteenth Century* (1929).

[232] B.L. d. 53, ff. 64, 66, 71.

[233] H.C.R. 204-6; *The History of* The Times, i. (1935), 167-70. Cuthbert Southey's account of Walter's offer, which is questioned in *The Times* history, is proved correct from Crabb Robinson's diary. For Barnes, see D. Hudson and H. Child, *Thomas Barnes of* The Times (1943).

[234] It retained its popularity for many years, and was frequently reprinted without Southey's authority. An edition published after the accession of Queen Victoria was shown at the Southey centenary exhibition at Keswick in 1943.

[235] Bodleian MS. Don. d. 4, fol. 137; P.W. ii. 22.

[236] *Hansard*, xxxv. 1092-4.

[237] C.U.L. ii. 194. The *Letter to William Smith* is reprinted, with the relevant part of Smith's speech, in L.C. iv. 367-90.

[238] Scott, *Letters*, iv. 444-5; C.R.W. 92-3; Hazlitt, *Works*, ed. P. P. Howe (1930-4), vii. 193-4.

[239] Keats, *Letters*, ed. M. B. Forman (1935 ed.), 24-5. Keats never saw Southey. He was invited to a supper-party to meet him in June, 1820, but he was too unwell to risk going out at night (ibid., 493).

[240] Byron, *Letters and Journals*, iv. 117-8.

[241] H.C.R. 206; cf. 212.

[242] A manuscript journal of this tour is in the possession of Mrs. Rawnsley. While he was in Paris, Southey visited Wordsworth's French daughter: see his letter to his wife of 17th May, 1817, printed by Mr. Kenneth Curry in *Publications of the Modern Language Association of America*, lix. 599-602.

[243] *A Letter to Robert Southey, Esq. . . . on his Life of the late Mr. Wesley* [1820]. For a similar complaint by another Moravian, see G. Greever, *A Wiltshire Parson and his Friends* (1926), 37-8.

[244] The *Observations on Southey's Life of Wesley* were republished in Watson's *Works* (1834-7), v. 351-532.

[245] *Life of Wesley*, ed. M. H. FitzGerald (1925), vol. i., p. xxxi. The observations of Knox and Coleridge were printed by Cuthbert Southey in the third edition of the book (1846): they are reproduced in Canon FitzGerald's edition.

[246] H.C.R. 303.

[247] M.T. 93. His views on Catholic Emancipation are most fully developed in the three *Quarterly* papers reprinted in *Essays, Moral and Political*, ii. 277-443. See also his letter to Sir Robert Inglis of 22nd February, 1829, and his correspondence with the Rev. Richard Shannon (L.C. vi. 25-37).

[248] S.L. ii. 31; H.C.R. 336.

[249] Southey's correspondence with Shelley is printed in C.B. 356-66.

[250] Shelley, *Letters* (1909), 648. The review was written by John Taylor Coleridge: Lord Coleridge, *The Story of a Devonshire House* (1905), 271-2.

[251] Shelley, *Letters*, 734-5.

[252] E. Dowden, *Life of Shelley*, ii. 427.

[253] R.S. to an unknown correspondent, 26th November, 1822 (Boult MSS.). Cf. C.B. 27, 72, 76.

[254] E. C. Mayne, *The Life of Lady Byron* (1929), 135.

[255] P.W. x. 206.

[256] e.g. Hartley Coleridge, *Letters*, 65-6. On the spirit of Southey's poem, cf. H.C.R. 289.

[257] It should be noted that Southey had been parodied, in a stricter sense, several times before, e.g. in *The Anti-Jacobin* (see pp. 69-71, 74-5 above), by the brothers Smith in *Rejected Addresses* (1812: A. Boyle's edition, 1929, 59-65) and by James Hogg in *The Poetic Mirror* (1816), 231-56.

[258] *Blackwood's Magazine*, xvi. 711. The details of this controversy were exhaustively discussed by the late Lord Ernle in his edition of Byron's *Letters and Journals* (vi. 377-99). I have discovered no important documents to add from Southey's side. The incidental literature of pamphlets is said to have been enormous (W. Jerdan, *Men I have Known*, 1866, 416).

[259] *Quarterly Review*, xxviii. 524; L.C. vi. 288. For his private opinion of the book, expressed to Wynn, see S.L. iii. 374-5.

[260] *The Times*, 6th August, 1830; S.L. iv. 394; E. Blunden, *Charles Lamb and his Contemporaries* (1937 ed.), 134. For another charming tribute to Lamb, see C.B. 352.

[261] Koster, 56-7.

[262] R. A. Humphreys, *Latin America* (1941), 14. Herman Merivale made extensive use of the *History of Brazil* in his *Lectures on Colonization*

and Colonies, originally delivered in 1839-1841: see for example pp. 45, 49-50, 290-1 (1928 ed.).

[263] For the substance of this paragraph I am indebted to Senhor de Sousa-Leão: see also his article in the *Modern Language Review*, xxxviii. 181-91, especially pp. 186-7, 189. Southey was honoured in his life-time for his work on the history of Brazil by the Queen of Portugal, who created him a Knight of the Order of the Tower and Sword in February, 1839 (Bodleian MS. Eng. Letters d. 9, fol. 197).

[264] T.L.S., 30th October, 1937, 24th April, 8th and 15th May, 1943.

[265] Cf. Southey's own explicit statements, made at the time, with Gleig's in the preface to his book: *Memoirs of the Life of Warren Hastings* (1841), vol. i, p. iv.

[266] Southey's *History of the Peninsular War* caused great indignation among professional soldiers, especially his treatment of Moore. For Wellington's opinion, see *Recollections of the Table Talk of Samuel Rogers* (1856), 239; for Sir John Colborne's, G. C. Moore Smith, *The Life of Lord Seaton* (1903), 253, 393-6. Napier, admitting a mistake in his own book, remarked severely that it "was not drawn from Mr. Southey's history, though I readily acknowledge I could not go to a more copious source of error" (*History of the War in the Peninsula*, 1892 ed., vi. 357).

[267] Bodleian MS. Don. d. 4, fol. 131; B.L. d. 47, fol. 69.

[268] *Voyage historique et littéraire en Angleterre et en Écosse* (1825), ii. 422. For Pichot's life, see L. Bisson, *Amédée Pichot* (1942).

[269] Forster, *Walter Savage Landor*, i. 208; N.L.W. MS. 4812, No. 260. Cf. his tribute to Danvers in *Colloquies*, i. 240.

[270] The date is given in a letter from Mr. Hill to Southey, dated the same day, in a commonplace book of Bertha Hill (*née* Southey), now in the possession of Miss L. S. Awdry.

[271] H.C.R. 189.

[272] The best account of Caroline Bowles is given in Dowden's introduction to C.B. For a modern sketch, see Janet E. Courtney, *The Adventurous Thirties* (1933), 33-43; and for a favourable estimate of her poetry A. Symons, *The Romantic Movement in English Poetry* (1909), 233.

[273] *Journal of a Tour Made in Scotland in 1819*, ed. C. H. Herford (1929), 264. The visit to New Lanark is described on pp. 258-66. For further references to Owen, see S.L. iii. 45, 174, iv. 146; *Colloquies*, i. 132-45.

[274] The chief authority for Taylor's life is his own *Autobiography* (1885). See also his *Correspondence*, ed. E. Dowden (1888), and Una Taylor, *Guests and Memories* (1924). For Southey's view of Taylor's politics, see his letter to Sir Egerton Brydges of 8th April, 1830 (*Bentley's Miscellany*, xiii. 599).

[275] Taylor, *Autobiography*, i. 101.

[276] A manuscript journal of this tour is in the possession of Mrs. Rawnsley.

[277] Bodleian MS. Don. d. 4, fol. 234.

[278] R.S. to John King, 28th February, 1805 (Boult MSS.); W. J. Hardy, *Book Plates* (ed. 2, 1897), 109-10 (a reproduction of the plate itself is on p. 111). The general authorities for this chapter are L.C. v. 279—vi. 396; S.L. iv. 37-575; C.B. 111-356; Rickman, 233-320.

[279] R.S. to Lightfoot, 10th June, 1828 (Lightfoot MSS.); Bodleian MS. Don. d. 4, fol. 173.

[280] R.S. to his daughter Edith May, 8th November, 1831 (Boult MSS.).

[281] Cf. the case of Exeter, described in T. Shapter, *History of the Cholera in Exeter in 1832* (1849), and R. S. Lambert, *The Cobbett of the West* (1939), 55.

[282] *The Greville Memoirs*, ed. Lytton Strachey and Roger Fulford (1938), ii. 58.

[283] *Letters of John Stuart Mill*, ed. H. S. R. Elliot (1910), i. 13. The whole of Mill's analysis of Southey's mind and character, given in this letter, is extremely interesting.

[284] *Early Letters of Thomas Carlyle* (1886), i. 110, 305.

[285] Carlyle, *Reminiscences* (" Everyman " edition), 345-9. For his other descriptions of Southey at this time, see *Letters of Thomas Carlyle* (1888), ii. 284, 295-6, and *The Correspondence of Thomas Carlyle and Ralph Waldo Emerson* (1883), i. 72.

[286] Scott, *Journal, 1827-28*, 252; *Letters*, xi. 25.

[287] C.U.L. ii. 193-5, 448; M.T. 122, 142; Greever, *A Wiltshire Parson and his Friends*, 62. This last letter corrects Moore's statement that Southey said his brother-in-law died "lamented by few, and regretted by none" (*Memoirs, Journal and Correspondence of Thomas Moore*, 1853-6, vii. 72).

[288] S.L. iii. 135.

[289] R.S. to Wynn, 18th February, 1804 (N.L.W. MS. 4811, No. 121). The reference is to Moore's *Poetical Works of the Late Thomas Little* (1801). Cf. Southey's qualified liking for the poems of Crabbe (S.L. ii. 90-1; L.C. iv. 355).

[290] See, for example, L.C. ii. 278, iv. 91, 105; Robberds, i. 440, ii. 77; and p. 69 above.

[291] H.C.R. 87; 3 W.L. 1231. Cf. Coleridge's similar opinion (C.U.L. i. 70-1).

[292] C.R.W. 327, 329, 857-8 (cf. Landor's phrase in the second Imaginary Conversation between Southey and Porson : *Works* (1846), i. 72); 2 W.L. 633.

[293] 3 W.L. 680.

[294] C.B. 131; R.S. to J. W. Warter, 24th June, 1835 (Boult MSS.).

[295] C.R.W. 859; H.C.R. 565.

[296] *Letters of the Lake Poets to Daniel Stuart*, 428.

[297] *The Diaries of William Charles Macready*, ed. Toynbee (1912), i. 185.

[298] R.S. to his daughter Edith May, 18th August, 1832 and 4th October, 1834 (Boult MSS.); R.S. to Caroline Bowles, 27th September, 1834 (ibid.).

[299] For the assistance he gave his brothers, see pp. 100, 113, 200-1 above and note 136; for his generosity to Coleridge's family, pp. 110-11, 132-3 above. 2 W.L. 596; L.C. v. 102-3; B.L. c. 26, fol. 78.

[300] Cf. Henry Taylor, *Notes from Life* (1847), 158-61. On the other hand, it is fair to note that Southey was offered, or was asked to stand for, several public posts: the Librarianship of the Faculty of Advocates at Edinburgh in 1818, the chair of Humanity at Glasgow in 1831, that of History in the newly-created University of Durham in 1832. All these he declined, on the ground that to accept them would have taken him away from Keswick and would have brought no net addition to his income.

[301] Taylor, *Autobiography*, i. 226-7.

[302] R.S. to J. W. Warter, 18th April, 1835 (Boult MSS.).

[303] See for instance the account of the Lisbon expedition of 1589 in the life of Hawkins and Drake (iii. 204-21). There is a convenient reprint of eight of the lives under the title *English Seamen*, edited by David Hannay (2 vols. 1895, 1904).

[304] N.L.W. MS. 4812, No. 141; L.C. ii. 327, 335.

[305] L.C. vi. 227.

[306] In Canon FitzGerald's edition the chapters are differently numbered: those referred to above appear there respectively as Nos. 11, 13, 22, and 69.

[307] R.S. to Lightfoot, 11th May, 1836 (Lightfoot MSS.).

[308] C. and F. Brookfield, *Mrs. Brookfield and her Circle* (1905), 34.

[309] *Memories of Old Friends. Being Extracts from the Journals and Letters of Caroline Fox*, ed. H. N. Pym (ed. 2, 1882), i. 23.

[310] R.S. to Caroline Bowles, 23rd February, 1837 (Boult MSS.).

[311] Mrs. Gaskell, *Life of Charlotte Brontë* ("World's Classics" edition), 119, 124-8; *The Brontës: their Lives, Friendships and Correspondence*, ed. T. J. Wise and J. A. Symington (1932), i. 156; C.B. 348.

[312] Bodleian MS. Don. d. 3, fol. 93; d. 4, ff. 158, 186, 210; d. 5, ff. 263, 305, 311.

[313] Carlyle, *Reminiscences*, 351-2, 354; *New Letters of Thomas Carlyle* (1904), i. 118.

[314] Bodleian MS. Eng. letters d. 9, fol. 135.

[315] I owe the substance of this paragraph to Canon FitzGerald. It is based on notes he made in 1912 from a series of letters written by Southey to Caroline Bowles, then in the possession of the late Miss Warter (Southey's grand-daughter) and now destroyed.

[316] H.C.R. 552-6; Forster, *Walter Savage Landor*, ii. 400.

[317] C.R.W. 392; Taylor, *Autobiography*, i. 284-5.

[318] N.L.W. MS. 4813, No. 498.

[319] H.C.R. 579; Smiles, *A Publisher and his Friends*, ii. 502-5; 3 W.L. 1030; A. P. Stanley, *Life and Correspondence of Thomas Arnold* (1844), ii. 239; C.R.W. 434, 444; Forster, *Walter Savage Landor*, ii. 405.

[320] Again I owe this information mainly to Canon FitzGerald. Several letters among Mrs. Boult's MSS. bear on this disagreeable quarrel: the most important is that from J. W. Warter to R.S. of 7th November, 1839.

[321] Hartley Coleridge, *Letters*, 264; E. Quillinan, *Poems* (1853), 218.

[322] Pichot, *Arlésiennes* (1860), 329-30.

[323] Southey revised *Joan of Arc* very heavily several times in later years (it went through at least five more editions in his life-time). It is most interesting in its original form, for in his attempts to improve it he took away much of its character without making it at all a better poem. My quotations are from the first edition, numbered by book and line: ii. 280-1, v. 94-7, viii. 667-73. There is a Miltonic catalogue of proper names in ii. 64-75, and in ii. 133-205 a procession of allegorical characters (Ambition, Superstition, Hypocrisy, etc.) reminiscent of Spenser.

[324] *Biographia Literaria*, ed. Shawcross, i. 46, and note, p. 221.

[325] B.L. c. 23, fol. 105. This passage was omitted by Cuthbert Southey from the published version of the letter (L.C. ii. 160).

[326] References for the passages cited, in order: P.W. iv. 53, 426, 151, 180. For another good descriptive passage, see the voyage of the little boat in Book XI (P.W. iv. 406-7).

[327] P.W. viii. 14-15.

[328] P.W. viii. 164.

[329] *Biographia Literaria*, i. 46; L.L. ii. 163-4.

[330] *Collected Essays and Papers* (1923-4), i. 256-7. Cf. p. 70 above.

[331] P.W. ii. 191, 257.

[332] P.W. ii. 97.

[333] P.W. vi. 223. "Little Book, in Green and Gold" was first printed in *Oliver Newman* (1845), 105-7. It also appears in Canon FitzGerald's edition of Southey's *Poems* (1909), 356.

[334] P.W. x. 3-9, 213-4.

[335] Cf. the opinion of an acute French critic of Southey: "On trouve quelquefois que ses poèmes sont un peu lourds dans leur éclat; qu'il y a là trop de récitatif et pas assez de chant ni de charmes" (Philarète Chasles, *Revue contemporaine*, iii. (1852), 563-4). Mr. Wallace B. Nichols, who has studied Southey's poetry—and especially his versification—in detail, points out to me that the long poems are admirably suited for speaking aloud from the skill and care with which the pauses are disposed, particularly in the blank verse of Roderick. He also considers that the narrative power shown in Southey's poems has not received its full due.

[336] C.B. ix-x, 366-84; Davy, *Fragmentary Remains*, 43-4.

[337] Wordsworth, *Poetical Works*, ed. E. de Selincourt, ii. (1944). 383, 386.

[338] *Literary Remains*, ed. H. N. Coleridge (1836), i. 239.

[339] "The Story of the Three Bears" made its first appearance in volume iv. of *The Doctor* (published in 1837).

[340] *Table Talk and Omniana of Samuel Taylor Coleridge* (1917), 255-6; Oliver Elton, *Survey of English Literature 1780-1830* (1912), ii. 8.

[341] For a specimen of his pompous and stilted early manner, see the extract from his review of the *Lyrical Ballads* quoted above, pp. 76-7.

[342] L.C. vi. 302; S.L. iv. 404.

[343] S.L. iv. 330-1. Cf. L.C. iii. 2, vi. 6.

[344] R.S. to his daughter Edith May, 3rd April, 1834 (Boult MSS.).

[345] R.S. to Bedford, 3rd June, 1821: B.L. c. 26, fol. 48.

[346] Bodleian MS. Eng. Letters d. 7, fol. 78.

[347] See p. 176 above, and cf. *Poems by Hartley Coleridge* (1851), vol. i, pp. xliii-xlvi.

[348] See pp. 24, 88 above, and for other examples of his humour P.W. vol. v, pp. xiv-xv (his visit to Anna Seward at Lichfield in 1807), and S.L. iv. 74-6 (his remarkable account of the Netherhall privy).

[349] See p. 117 above; L.C. iv. 316-7.

[350] See pp. 88-90, 111, 135, 145 above.

[351] *Life of Nelson* (ed. 1, 1813), i. 233-4. This is the perfect form of the episode. As it originally appeared in the *Quarterly Review* (iii. 251) it was shorter and less interesting; but in the second edition the paragraph was expanded with some additional details that mar the clarity and simplicity of the picture: ed. 2 (1814), i. 236-7.

[352] See for instance the account of the capture of Olinda in the *History of Brazil*, i. 469-71, and that of the battle of Talavera in the *History of the Peninsular War* (quarto ed.), ii. 408-19.

[353] *Colloquies*, i. 116-9.

[354] See for instance the moving letter he wrote to Cottle on 20th April, 1808 (L.C. iii. 135-7), and the perorations to the *History of Brazil* (iii. 879) and the *History of the Peninsular War* (quarto ed., iii. 921-9).

[355] Canon FitzGerald has made two notable contributions to this work with his charming selection from Southey's letters, which appears in the "World's Classics", and with his abridged edition of *The Doctor*.

[356] H. Read, *English Prose Style* (1937 ed.), xiii-xiv, 123.

[357] See p. 141 above.

[358] Hazlitt, *Works*, ed. Howe, xi. 84 (cf. also xii. 16); P. G. Patmore, *My Friends and Acquaintance* (1854), iii. 147.

[359] *Life and Letters of R. H. Barham* (1870), i. 251.

[360] Newman, *Essays Critical and Historical* (1872), i. 16; F. A. Gasquet,

Lord Acton and his Circle [1906], xix; Newman, *Apologia pro Vita Sua* (1864), 98.

[361] Sir G. O. Trevelyan, *Life and Letters of Lord Macaulay* ("World's Classics" edition), ii. 381-2; Bagehot, *Literary Studies* ("Everyman" edition), i. 122-3. But Macaulay's own essays owed much to Southey's example, and both he and Bagehot appreciated the merits of his prose: Macaulay, *Essays* ("Everyman" edition), ii. 189-90; Bagehot, *Literary Studies*, ii. 292.

[362] *English Notebooks*, ed. R. Stewart (1941), 179.

[363] *The English Humourists and The Four Georges* ("Everyman" edition), 415.

[364] *Letters to Robert Bridges* (1935), 19; *Letters to R. W. Dixon* (1935), 17.

[365] *Father and Son* (1941 edition), 226.

[366] *The Romantic Movement in English Poetry* (1909), 148-60.

[367] *Letters of Matthew Arnold to Arthur Hugh Clough* (1932), 145; *Personal Papers of Lord Rendel* (1931), 207; Leslie Stephen, *Studies of a Biographer* (1898-1902), iv. 45-85; *Cambridge History of English Literature*, xi. 152-71; Saintsbury, *Collected Essays and Papers*, i. 239-68.

ABBREVIATIONS USED IN THE NOTES

B.L.	Bodleian MSS. Eng. Letters c. 22-27, d. 47-57. (Southey's correspondence with Grosvenor Bedford.)
Boult MSS.	MSS. in the possession of Mrs. F. F. Boult, Southey's great-granddaughter.
C.B.	*The Correspondence of Robert Southey with Caroline Bowles*, ed. E. Dowden (1881).
Chambers.	Sir E. K. Chambers, *Samuel Taylor Coleridge* (1938).
C.L.	*Letters of Samuel Taylor Coleridge*, ed. E. H. Coleridge (2 vols. 1895).
Colloquies.	Southey's *Sir Thomas More : or, Colloquies on the Progress and Prospects of Society* (2 vols. 1829).
Cottle.	J. Cottle, *Reminiscences of Samuel Taylor Coleridge . . . and Robert Southey* (1847).
Cowper.	Southey's edition of the *Works of William Cowper* (8 vols. 1853-4).
C.R.W.	*The Correspondence of Henry Crabb Robinson with the Wordsworth Circle*, ed. E. J. Morley (2 vols. 1927).
C.U.L.	*Unpublished Letters of Samuel Taylor Coleridge*, ed. E. L. Griggs (2 vols. 1932).
De Quincey.	*The Collected Writings of Thomas de Quincey*, ed. D. Masson (14 vols. 1889-90).
Espriella.	Southey's *Letters from England: by Don Manuel Alvarez Espriella* (3 vols. 1807).
Haller.	W. Haller, *The Early Life of Robert Southey* (1917).
Hanson.	L. Hanson, *The Life of S. T. Coleridge: the Early Years* (1938).
H.C.R.	*Henry Crabb Robinson on Books and their Writers*, ed. E. J. Morley (3 vols. 1938).
H.H.S.	Henry Herbert Southey, the poet's brother.
Koster.	Southey's letters to J. T. and H. Koster, printed in the *Revista do Instituto Histórico e Geográfico Brasiliero*, vol. 178, pp. 33-60.
L.C.	*The Life and Correspondence of Robert Southey*, ed. C. C. Southey (6 vols. 1849-50).
Lightfoot MSS.	MSS. in the possession of Professor R. H. Lightfoot.
L.L.	*The Letters of Charles Lamb*, ed. E. V. Lucas (3 vols. 1935).
Lockhart.	[J. G. Lockhart], *Memoirs of the Life of Sir Walter Scott* (1839 ed., 10 vols).
M.T.	*Minnow among Tritons: Mrs. S. T. Coleridge's Letters to Thomas Poole*, ed. S. Potter (1934).
N.L.W. MSS.	National Library of Wales MSS. 4811-15. (Southey's correspondence with C.W.W. Wynn.)

P.W.	*The Poetical Works of Robert Southey* (10 vols. 1837-8).
Rawnsley MSS.	MSS. in the possession of Mrs. H. D. Rawnsley.
Rickman.	O. Williams, *Lamb's Friend the Census-Taker: Life and Letters of John Rickman* (1911).
Robberds.	J. W. Robberds, *Life and Writings of William Taylor of Norwich* (2 vols. 1843).
R.S.	Robert Southey.
Scott, *Letters.*	*The Letters of Sir Walter Scott,* ed. Sir H. J. C. Grierson (12 vols. 1932-7).
S.L.	*Selections from the Letters of Robert Southey,* ed. J. W. Warter (4 vols. 1856).
T.L.S.	*The Times Literary Supplement.*
T.S.	Thomas Southey, the poet's brother.
1 W.L.	*The Early Letters of William and Dorothy Wordsworth,* ed. E. de Selincourt (1935).
2 W.L.	*The Letters of William and Dorothy Wordsworth: the Middle Years* (2 vols. 1937).
3 W.L.	*The Letters of William and Dorothy Wordsworth: the Later Years* (3 vols. 1938).

INDEX